The Twentieth-Century Spanish American Novel

Raymond
Leslie
Williams

The Twentieth-Century Spanish American Novel

University of Texas Press
Austin

First edition, 2003

Requests for permission to reproduce material from this
work should be sent to Permissions, University of Texas
Press, Box 7819, Austin, TX 78713-7819.

⊗ The paper used in this book meets the minimum
requirements of ANSI/NISO Z39.48-1992 (R1997)
(Permanence of Paper).

Library of Congress Cataloging-in-Publication Data

Williams, Raymond L.
The twentieth-century Spanish American novel /
Raymond Leslie Williams.
        p.   cm.
Includes bibliographical references and index.
ISBN 0-292-79161-5 (cloth : alk. paper)
    1. Spanish American fiction—20th century—History
and criticism.   I. Title: 20th century Spanish American
novel.   II. Title.
PQ7082.N7 W56   2003
863'.609868—dc21
                                                    2002013110

Contents

vi The Twentieth-Century Spanish American Novel

Preface

In 1966, Octavio Paz wrote that since the nineteenth century, the Latin American writer desired to be modern: "Modernity has been our style for a century. It's the universal style. To want to be modern seems crazy: we are condemned to be modern, since we are prohibited from the past and the future."[1] Indeed, several generations of Latin American writers since the late nineteenth century have exhibited their urgent desire to be modern, to participate in modernity. This postromantic desire assumed numerous guises and variations for Latin American writers over the twentieth century.

From the work of Nicaraguan poet Rubén Darío at the turn of the century to that of Argentine writer Jorge Luis Borges and Mexican novelist Carlos Fuentes, as well as among the younger writers of today, the idea of being modern often has taken some form of cosmopolitanism. For the poet Darío and his cohorts, this cosmopolitanism meant being simultaneously very Latin American and very French. For Borges, it meant trips to Madrid and Paris in the 1920s, bringing the innovations of *ultraísmo* to Argentina and a transatlantic dialogue with writers across the continents and across the centuries. For Fuentes, being modern and cosmopolitan has meant not only residing in the major cities of Latin America, Europe, and the United States most of his adult life but also assuming the innovations of European modernism and fully accepting his multicultural heritage from Latin America, Spain, and France. For postmodern writers such as the Chilean Diamela Eltit and the Argentine Ricardo Piglia, being modern has meant participating in a transnational cultural life and literary dialogue with Latin American and European writers as well as with theorists of literature and politics.

But the cosmopolitan postures and intellectual urbanity of the Latin American writer, as constant as they might have been in the twentieth century, were only the external trappings and sometimes necessary masks of a far more significant and profound series of cultural interventions in Latin America. In most of the first half of the century, relatively few Latin American writers found success in their search for a way to be both authentically Latin American (or Mexican, or Argentine, etc.) and participants in the fin-de-siecle and later modernist projects of their European and North American counterparts. Their appropriation of modernist aesthetic practices from the 1940s to the end of the century, however, met huge success in both Latin America and abroad, highlighted by the "Boom" of the Spanish American novel written in the 1960s.

For some critics, postmodern culture present in Western societies since approximately the late 1960s has been lacking in political substance. Nevertheless, since 1968, the variant of modernist fiction writing described in Latin America as "postmodern" had its own innovative technical features, critical stances, and politically significant (or thematically substantive) approaches to being modern.[2]

Despite the occasional outdated admonitions about the traditionalism of the Latin American novelist and despite the consistent resistance by more traditional writers and critics alike to these ongoing attempts at being "modern," the Latin American writer has often been, in fact, condemned to being hypermodern—from the hypermodern Darío and Borges to the hypermodern Fuentes and Eltit. The cultural environment in which the search for the modern has taken place has been polemical, from early debates about the new republics to recent controversies about postmodern culture. Rubén Darío, Jorge Luis Borges, Carlos Fuentes, and many other Latin American writers were accused by some of their compatriots of being too modern (i.e., too European) and somehow not authentically "national" enough.

In this study of the Spanish American novel, I have organized my readings and critical history of the novel around five moments when the desire to be modern took different (but not entirely contradictory) directions. The first moment (Part I of this book) is associated in Spanish America with *modernismo*, but throughout Latin America, modernism ostensibly involved oppositional forces centered, on the one hand, on fin-de-siècle symbolist and Parnassian aesthetics and, on the other, positivism and more scientific approaches to culture and society. This was the moment captured in the work of Rubén Darío. The second moment (Part II) was the period when the desire to be modern led some writers to the European avant-garde movements, while others maintained that the new (modern) nation-state needed to be supported by a more autochthonous writing. This was the moment of Ricardo Guiraldes, Rómulo Gallegos, Teresa de la Parra, Jaime Torres Bodet, and many others. Part III involves the third moment of desiring to be modern, a moment that produced the modernist novel throughout Spanish America in the 1940s and 1950s. This was the modernist novel of Miguel Angel Asturias, Alejo Carpentier, Agustín Yáñez, and others. The fourth moment (Part IV) was in the 1960s, when the modernity and accomplishment of Spanish American writing was internationally recognized as never before. A select group of the most modern, cosmopolitan, and accomplished of these writers (García Márquez, Fuentes, Vargas Llosa) came to be associated with the Boom of the Spanish American novel. Part V deals with the moment from the 1970s to the 1990s that some critics called the "Postboom" at the outset but which to some extent was a refining, a hypermodernist writing more appropriately identified as postmodern. In reality, both modernist and postmodern aesthetic practices were important in the last decades of the century, and the presence of women writers was remarkable.

This book is a study of the twentieth-century Spanish American novel; I offer brief analyses of specific novels and a critical overview of the Spanish American novel published from 1900 to 1999. In developing this analysis and overview of the Spanish American novel, I have kept a broader Latin American context in view, and I occasionally mention Latin American novels not published in Spanish. I offer these comments to deepen the understanding of the Spanish American novel and not as a review of the Latin American novel published in Brazilian Portuguese or Caribbean French and English. Such a study would be considerably more ambitious than space allows in this book.

I have organized each of the book's five parts into two sets of chapters. In the first chapter of each part, I introduce the novels, literary contexts, some cultural debates, and references to the Brazilian, Caribbean, and U.S. Chicano novel. In the following chapter (or chapters) of each of the five parts, I analyze a more limited number of Spanish American novels.

Several well-informed and well-conceived studies of the Spanish American novel are predecessors to this study. John S. Brushwood's *The Spanish American Novel: A Twentieth-Century Survey* (1975) is also a partial model, as is Jean Franco's *An Introduction to Spanish-American Literature* (third edition, 1994). Gerald Martin's *Journeys through the Labyrinth: Latin American Fiction in the Twentieth Century* (1989) offers incisive commentary on a broad range of twentieth-century fictional texts. Giuseppe Bellini's *Historia de la literatura hispanoamericana* (1985) is impressive for its thoroughness and detailed scholarship. Naomi Lindstrom's *Twentieth-Century Spanish American Fiction* (1994) offers much of the breadth and rigor found in the surveys of Brushwood and Bellini. The present study differs from these predecessors in two fundamental ways: it covers the entire twentieth century (1900–1999), and it is different in structure, focus, and emphasis.

Of course, the term "Latin America" has been amply debated for several decades now, and Carlos Fuentes has pointed out that the term was coined by the French in the nineteenth century to justify their own colonial interests in the region. Fuentes proposes that the most appropriate and accurate term for the region is "Indo-Afro-Iberoamerica." I concur and occasionally use Fuentes's term to refer to this region. The main problem with Fuentes's term, however, is its stylistic clumsiness. For the sake of style, I use the term "Latin America" most frequently. Of course, when I refer to the "Spanish American" novel, I am using a term limited specifically to novels written in the Spanish language.

Much has happened to the Spanish American novel and literary criticism since Brushwood published his survey in 1975. Both the theory revolution and the critical work of the next generation of prominent scholars of the Latin American novel—notably Carlos Alonso, Debra Castillo, Sara Castro-Klarén, David William Foster, Aníbal González, Roberto González-Echevarría, Lucía Guerra-Cunningham, Cathy Jrade, Naomi Lindstrom, Sharon Magnarelli, Francine Masiello, Gustavo Pérez Firmat, Nelly Richard, Beatriz Sarlo, Elzbieta Sklodowska, Doris Sommer, and Cynthia Steele—have changed much of the way we read Spanish American fiction of the twentieth century. Since the mid-1970s, women's writing has become much more prominent throughout Latin America. I take particular account of Carlos Alonso's *The Burden of Modernity: The Rhetoric of Cultural Discourse in Spanish America* (1998), Debra Castillo's *Talking Back: Toward a Latin American Feminist Literary Criticism* (1992), Naomi Lindstrom's *The Social Conscience of Latin American Writing* (1998), Gustavo Pérez Firmat's *Idle Fictions: The Hispanic Vanguard Novel, 1926–1934* (1982), Cathy L. Jrade's *Modernismo, Modernity, and the Development of Spanish American Literature* (1998), and Doris Sommer's *Foundational Fictions: The National Romances of Latin America* (1991).

I am indebted to numerous colleagues, students, and writers for their goodwill and collaboration over the years. A complete list of all of them would be difficult to compile and include in this brief preface. Most recently, I have appreciated the dialogue and information offered by speakers on the campus of the University of California, among them Alicia Borinsky, Debra Castillo, David William Foster, John Kronik, Elzbieta Sklodowska, and Randolph Pope. Directly or indirectly, they have contributed to this book. Graduate research assistants Martín Camps, Traci Roberts, Kevin Guerrieri, and Mark Anderson were exceptionally efficient and helpful. I am particularly indebted to those colleagues who read part or all of this manuscript at its various stages or who provided valuable information: John S. Brushwood, Debra Castillo, Diamela Eltit, Isabelle Favre, Michael Handelsman, George McMurray, Seymour Menton, Otto Morales Benítez, John Ochoa, José Miguel Oviedo, Federico Patán, Lizabeth Paravisini-Gebert, David Toscana, Catharine Wall, and William Wiley. Certainly I do not wish to hold them accountable for any shortcomings the book may have; rather, I hope they may find some satisfaction that rewards their cooperation.

I dedicate this book to my earliest mentors: my sister Judith Williams and my high school teachers of Spanish and French, Ms. Grace Swan and Mrs. Sharon Erickson. Their early teachings were extremely important, and without them, this book would not have been possible.

The Twentieth-Century Spanish American Novel

Part I **The Literary Tradition and Modern Science, 1900–1921**

One Novelistic and Cultural Contexts at the Turn of the Century

In Latin America, the early twentieth century really belonged culturally to the nineteenth in many ways, particularly at the immediate turn of the century, when Spanish American *modernismo* was, among other things, the Spanish-language version of the Parnassian and symbolist writing recently in vogue in France and elsewhere in Europe. The most "modern" (in the general sense of contemporary) writing of the period was generally perceived to be the poetry of *modernismo*. In this first moment of desiring to be modern, the first two decades of the century, the *modernistas* of Spanish America predominated only in poetry, for the production of *modernista* novels was scarce. The *modernista* poets of Latin America thought of themselves as the most cosmopolitan and modern intellectuals of their time and, in many ways, they were.

The subjects of novels written in the early part of the century frequently faced problems and conflicts related to the old aristocracies and patriarchal order that still lingered in most regions of Latin America. Many of the writers of this period, such as Colombian Tomás Carrasquilla, made statements or literary manifestos expressing their desire to be modern. Nevertheless, they were not uniformly consistent in their ability to reject the past and embrace modernity. Several women were actively writing fiction, but they were clearly a minority voice in the totality of Latin American fiction of this period.[1]

Often misinterpreted as aloof from society at large and disinterested in social and political concerns, the *modernistas*, in reality, were fundamentally horrified by the new bourgeois values taking hold in the nascent middle-class society appearing in Latin America. For these turn-of-the-century intellectuals, many of the cultural values of the new middle classes were materialistic to the point of being vulgar and consequently were unacceptable and to be rejected. They preferred to cultivate only the more refined elements of cultural modernity and in so doing protested against bourgeois society and its values.[2]

As Jrade has pointed out, the *modernistas* proposed a worldview that imagined the universe as a system of correspondences in which language was capable of revealing profound truths regarding the order of the cosmos.[3] They sought to invent a new discourse that might reveal hidden realities as well as address matters related to the empirical reality of Latin America. Novels such as the Venezuelan Manuel Díaz Rodríguez's *Sangre patricia* (1902) reveal both the search for profound truths and the concern for the political reality of Venezuela.

A competing early-twentieth-century perception of being modern embraced a more scientific model, even though many aspects of this late-nineteenth-century "science" are considered pseudoscience today. Of science that endured, Darwin's theses about the respective roles of heredity and environment had enormous impact on what was the naturalist novel that appeared in Latin America in a variety of permutations in the late nineteenth and early twentieth centuries.

Numerous forms of rationalist intellectual rigor were in vogue throughout Latin America at the turn of the century, particularly positivism, which promoted the idea of progress with empirical science and free enterprise as its vehicle. A positivistic, materialistic, and pragmatic discourse predominated in literary expression. In Latin America, the novelistic outcome of this more scientific worldview was the realist and naturalist novel. In addition, turn-of-the-century intellectuals published a broad spectrum of pseudoscientific texts, some of which were novels. In fact, the Argentine doctor Francisco Sicardi wrote a lengthy and digressive novel, *Libro extraño* (1894–1902), a pseudoscientific narrative in which a prostitute circulates, contaminating the other characters in the novel. In this 1,200-page pastiche, Sicardi the scientist suggests the difficulties inherent in finding order (in a text and in a nation) when cultural heterogeneity and social disorder were on the rise.[4]

One legacy of positivism, as Masiello has explained, involved a strong interest in the position of women in Argentina.[5] In nineteenth-century and early-twentieth-century texts, women often served as mediators between civilization and barbarism, between Europe and America, and also as an intermediary element against what was perceived as the savagery of the natives. During this period, women were increasingly present in the public sphere, particularly in Chile, Argentina, and Colombia. In Argentina, the desire to be modern was manifested by some women as a desire to integrate art and personal experience, mixing the previously fixed categories of the public and the private spheres. In Brazil, the end of the nineteenth century had witnessed the publication of what can be viewed as the first gay novel in Latin America, *Bom-Crioulo* (1895) by Adolfo Caminha.[6]

In the fiction produced in Latin America during the early part of the century, realist and naturalist models predominated to such a degree that it is appropriate to speak of a "realist-naturalist" novelistic production.[7] The hyphen is an indicator of the consistent blending of the two novelistic traditions that in Europe remained more distinctive. This realist-naturalist fiction, as traditional as it may seem for many readers a century later, was quite modern for the intellectuals of the time, for this writing was a dialogue with many of the latest scientific ideas. This was the case of one of the masters of the traditional art of fiction, the short-story writer Horacio Quiroga. The publication of Quiroga's stories during the second decade of the century was a clear indicator that the art of fiction in Latin America had was becoming sophisticated in its use of the modalities of the realist-naturalist tradition. For Beatriz Sarlo, Quiroga is typical of the paradigmatic figure of modernity that arose in the early twentieth century: the amateur technologist and inventor.[8]

The Latin American novel written by the *modernistas* has often been rejected and disregarded except by literary historians; the realist-naturalist tradition of the nineteenth century, on the other hand, has maintained a more viable literary space throughout the Americas. Even the most accomplished *modernista* novels, for example, such as Manuel Díaz Rodríguez's *Idolos rotos* (1901) and *Sangre patricia* (1902), as well as Enrique Larreta's *La gloria de don Ramiro* (1908) are books remembered primarily as artifacts of literary history rather than as literature broadly read over the decades. As Aníbal González has pointed out, the prestige of certain novelists and poets of the 1920s overshadowed the *modernista* novelists.[9]

La gloria de don Ramiro has been described appropriately as a sumptuous novel which hints that Spanish American civilization arose from Spain's decadent features.[10] Set in Spain during the period of Phillip II, it is an historical reconstruction focused on the city of Avila. Written in a style that imitates the Spanish language of the time in Spain, it seems to fit the cliché about *modernista* works that were an escape from the everyday reality of early-twentieth-century Argentina. Reviewed carefully, however, it is a novel that deals with both the archaic and the modern. Aníbal González has demonstrated how *La gloria de don Ramiro* is a multilayered text and is very much concerned with the sociohistoric origins of Spanish America.[11]

Many novelists throughout Latin America responded to the political scenario with moral indignation. Díaz Rodríguez's *Idolos rotos* relates the story of a Venezuelan artist using the backdrop of Venezuelan politics. The artist, Alberto Soria, is a sculptor who, after returning home from a stay in Paris, finds it enormously difficult to withstand the lack of cultural sensitivity, poor manners, and vulgar values of the local bourgeoisie. He finds a personal relationship with María Almeida but leaves her in favor of a more intriguing married woman. Working out of a studio near Caracas, he becomes involved in both the cultural and political scene in Venezuela. A military coup results in the rise of a brutal regime that respects Alberto's art and artistic sensitivity even less than did the bourgeoisie, resulting in his deciding to leave Venezuela and denounce his *patria*. As Aníbal González has explained, Alberto's ideology is an elitist vision that seeks to move artists and intellectuals to political action.[12] Like some prominent intellectuals in Colombia at the turn of the century, Díaz Rodríguez hoped for a type of moral "regeneration"—led by intellectuals—that would place Venezuela on the right course.

Venezuelan Rufino Blanco Fombona was a moralist whose novels were a response to the dictatorships of Cipriano Castro and Juan Vicente Gómez. His novels *El hombre de hierro* (1907) and *El hombre de oro* (1916) were important contributions to the process of nation building even though Blanco Fombona did not write fiction with the stylistic nuances of Díaz Rodríguez or the technical sophistication of Azuela. Rather, like Carlos Reyles, Pío Gil, and many other fiction writers of this period, Blanco Fombona was far more interested in his nation's immediate political circumstance than in writing compelling fiction.

In Brazil, early-twentieth-century fiction was as much a dialogue with nineteenth-century ideas and writing as it was elsewhere in Latin America and the Caribbean. Brazilian novelists wrote predominantly in the realist-naturalist mode and somewhat under the shadow of a master of fiction in Brazil and Latin America: Machado de Assis. In Brazil, the novelists and intellectuals were intensely engaged in a self-examination on issues of national identity that were also present among their counterparts in Spanish America.

These Brazilian reflections on national identity appeared in essays as well as novels with strong essayistic components. The result was books such as Alfonso Celso's *Por que me ufano do meu país* (1900) and Euclides da Cunha's *Os sertões* (1902). These two writers explored what they considered the "national character" in works that were not easy to classify in terms of genre. Much of the fiction of the time, in fact, represented a viable dialogue on national identity when read in the context of these debates. The predominance of ideas and the essay form over story and character development was a general trend in the Brazilian novel and much Latin American fiction of the period.

Os sertões is most appropriately read not as a novel, but as a multi-layered text comparable to Sicardi's *Libro extraño*. The Brazilian text consists of fiction, history, sociology, scientific treatises, and other quasi-scientific discourses. After having worked for several years as a journalist, da Cunha was sent to Canudos, Brazil, in 1896 to cover an uprising of a group of religious fanatics, material that would later become the basic plot for Vargas Llosa's *La guerra del fin del mundo* (1981; see chapter 13). Five years after the fall of Canudos to government troops, da Cunha's magnum opus of more than five hundred pages appeared, in 1902.

These trends and the issues of national cultural autonomy debated throughout Latin America were developed in *Canaã* (1902) by José Pereira da Graça Aranha. Along with *Os sertões*, *Canaã* was one of the most widely read and discussed books in Brazil in the early part of the century. *Canaã* is a work of ideas rather than actions, and one of the central ideas that Graça Aranha promotes is that culture in the broadest sense *(cultura)* is the ultimate answer to society's ills.

The advent of the republic in 1889 was an important factor in the dialogue about national identity in Brazil. National identity and cultural autonomy were also the foci of discussions among intellectuals of the Caribbean. Cuba had just received its independence from Spain in 1898, and the colonies of the French and British secured their independence at different times during the nineteenth century. Haiti was among the first, liberating itself from France in 1804 and immediately entering into a series of failed attempts at agrarian reform.

By the late nineteenth century, some groups in Puerto Rico had organized strong independence movements in order to gain political autonomy from Spain, and the movements enjoyed considerable success. Landowners and middle-class Puerto Ricans were given the power to rule Puerto Rico with some political autonomy from Spain when the invasion of American troops in 1898 resulted in U.S. control of the island. Diverse economic and political sectors reacted in a variety of ways to this situation, with most groups finding a way to adapt to the change from Spanish to U.S. rule on the island.

At the end of the nineteenth century, a series of novels was published in Puerto Rico by Manuel Zeno Gandía, a writer typical of his time who, as a journalist and physician interested in politics, was comparable to the Mexican Mariano Azuela. His realist-naturalist works of that time still are considered canonical works in Puerto Rico and served as a model for early-twentieth-century novelists writing in the realist-naturalist mode, such as Matías González García, Ramón Juliá Marín, and José Elías Levis. These novelists wrote with an acute awareness of their immediate social and political circumstance, offering detailed descriptions of social, political, and cultural life in Puerto Rico during and after the U.S. invasion of the island. These realist-naturalist novels included González García's *Gestación* (1904), Juliá Marín's *Tierra adentro* (1911), and Levis's *Mancha de lodo* (1903).

Cuban and Haitian novelists of the early part of the century were as imbued with the realist-naturalist tradition as were their contemporaries elsewhere, and the Cuban writers tended to view the social and political realities of their recently independent nation through the same lens of nineteenth-century positivism that was the case throughout Latin America. Understandably enough, given Cuba's longstanding subservient role under colonial powers, they were also markedly nationalistic. These novelists, such as José Antonio Ramos, Miguel Carrión, and Jesús Castellanos, tended to portray a black and white world of binary oppositions. Ramos was an essentially nineteenth-century writer who published *Humberto Fabra* (1909) and later novels that attempted to surpass the clichés of nationalism. *Humberto Fabra*, however, was his attempt to portray Cuba's social and economic injustice. Carrión's novels *Las honradas* (1918) and *Las impuras* (1919) were the writer's playing out of naturalist schemes in a Cuban setting. Jesús Castellanos set forth the conflict between idealism and materialism, as has been seen in *modernista* novels, in *La conjura* (1909).

Haitian novelists of the early twentieth century wrote within the established models of the nineteenth-century French novel. These novelists wrote in proper French and imitated the realist mode established in France. Nevertheless, Frédéric Marcelin, Fernand Hibbert, Antoine Inanocent, and Justin Lhérisson were the founders of the national novel in Haiti, primarily because they were the first generation in Haiti to write fiction based on Haitian customs, family traditions, and political issues. Marcelin wrote accounts of his experience working in the government, culminating in his autobiographical novel *Au gré du Souvenir* (1913).

At the turn of the century, Chicano intellectuals were facing issues of national identity, but of a different sort. According to the Treaty of Guadalupe Hidalgo, Mexicans living in Texas could choose either to remain in Texas and become American citizens or go to Mexico. Those who chose to remain became the ethnic group that has been the historical root of Chicano literature, the first of which was published in the nineteenth century. In the first two decades of the twentieth century, massive Mexican immigration came into Texas as Mexican workers filled the need for an increased labor force caused by World War I; at the same time, many fled Mexico as a result of the Mexican Revolution. A set of renowned Mexican intellectuals—including Mariano Azuela, José Vasconcelos, and Martín Luis Guzmán—also went into exile.

In the early part of the twentieth century, most of the Spanish American republics were suffering from a variety of crises and forms of political instability. Over a thin glaze of progressive reforms intended to rapidly modernize these republics into replicas of modern European states were a generalized chaos and growing desire for a heterogeneity that did not easily fit with the dominant values of positivism and the new bourgeoisie. The most renowned of these modernization efforts was that of Mexico's Porfirio Díaz, whose dictatorship resulted in the construction of railroads, wide avenues, and monuments in Mexico City and the like. Colombia was in the grips of the "Regeneration" at the turn of the century; this was a conservative reaction against liberal reforms in the latter half of the nineteenth century. In Argentina, Leandro N. Alem headed a middle-class revolution against ex-President Julio Roca and the oligarchs at the end of the nineteenth century. This revolution forced Roca's right-hand man, Juárez Celman, out of power and replaced him with Carlos Pellegrini and bolstered the Radical party, which elected Hipólito Irigoyen in 1916. Venezuela was still recovering from the dictatorship of Guzmán Blanco when Cipriano Castro took power in 1899; Castro, in turn, maintained his own dictatorship until 1908, when he handed the power over to Juan Vicente Gómez.

In both the politics and culture of much of Latin America, competing views pitted the modern and progressive ideas of science and positivism against ideas that related to traditionalism. Many of the writers expressed a desire to be modern, yet they embraced seemingly conflicting views of what that might mean. For the new middle classes, being modern meant assuming ideas of positivism and pragmatism; for some of the writers, being modern meant rejecting these ideas and embracing a combination of new European aesthetics and certain ideals of romanticism. Aesthetic programs were effected in a manner similar to the way politics were practiced, that is, in a contradictory and chaotic fashion. Many of these writers, such as Carlos Reyles and Pío Gil, wrote in the mold of their nineteenth-century predecessors: they were much more concerned about immediate political circumstances than the aesthetics of fiction. An exception to this generalization was Mariano Azuela, who was both politically motivated and a master in the art of fiction. For Reyles and Pío Gil, being modern meant associating with a pragmatic vision of the world ushered in by the scientists. Consequently, they thought of themselves as modern even though they are not generally read today as progressive writers.

The fiction of the Uruguayan novelist Carlos Reyles embodied some of these contradictions, for quite unlike the *modernista* writers and many of the intellectuals of the period, Reyles supported positivism and pragmatism of fin-de-siecle progress. His novel *Raza de Caín* (1900)—written in the realist-naturalist mode—tells the story of a pragmatic character who dominates an idealist. Reyles wrote in favor of the accumulation of material wealth, a position rarely found among intellectuals of the period, although, of course, many other intellectuals welcomed positivism, nineteenth-century science, and material progress as priorities for Latin America. In Reyles's novel *El terruño* (1916) about doña Angela, who owns a *pulpería*, he exhibits a preference for the practical-minded and common-sensical as opposed to the dreamy ideals of the romantics and the *modernistas*.

Los caranchos de La Florida (1916) was Benito Lynch's major contribution in the ongoing cultural dialogue that included Ricardo Guiraldes in Argentina. Like Reyles and Guiraldes, he set his novels in rural areas and wrote in the conventional (realist-naturalist) mode. In the process of providing descriptions of gaucho life in specific and social customs in general, Lynch constructed a plot built around a conflict between a father and his son. In addition to interpreting the gaucho tradition, Lynch was interested in exploring psychological traits of human beings. Lynch was not sophisticated enough with narrative technique to actually use interiorizations in this novel, although he demonstrated the ability to handle both literary language and the standard narrative techniques of the realist-naturalist tradition.

Many novelists of this period, such as Rufino Blanco Fombona, wanted to denounce the dictators and strongmen who were forcing economic progress onto some sectors of Latin American society at the cost of individual freedom and human rights. The Venezuelan Pío Gil wrote a denunciation of the dictatorship of Cipriano Castro titled *El Cabito* (1909). Like Reyles, Pío Gil is far more interested in politics than in aesthetics. *El Cabito* is a political novel whose protagonist misses an opportunity to assassinate the tyrant and whose heroine who dies in a convent. Pío Gil's critique is directed against a particular group: political opportunists who operate between the people and the president. The narrative focus alternates between groups and individuals. Unlike Reyles, who was convinced that accumulating wealth was a noble goal in itself, Pío Gil communicates a sense of futility in individuals' attempts to rise in social status or function at all in society at large.

Pedro Prado and Rafael Arévalo Martínez wrote with a keen awareness of both realist and *modernista* aesthetics. Prado published two novels during this period, *La reina de Rapa Nui* (1914) and *Alsino* (1920). The first is about characters who belong to an ancient civilization, seen with the critical distance of the twentieth-century reader and writer. Prado creates a variety of highly inventive situations to allow the reader to judge morality in social contexts. Written in the form of a journalist's diary, Prado questions traditional beliefs of contemporary Chilean society. Prado uses a similar technique in *Alsino*, a novel in which a young boy tests the social order in Chile. Written in the tone of a children's story, this novel's protagonist is a country boy capable of flying. Brushwood points out that the allegorical implications of *Alsino* deepen the experience for the reader.[13] Arévalo Martínez wrote fiction in something of the allegorical mode, in some ways comparable to the work of Prado. His short novel *El hombre que parecía un caballo* (1916) functions in this manner. It deals with a human relationship that develops in both a positive and negative fashion; Arévalo Martínez's technique can be associated with those of symbolists, placing his work in the sphere of the *modernistas.*

The role of women as citizens and as intellectuals was in transition in much of Latin America. Government policy toward education, as well as laws concerning marriage and voting, were debated throughout Latin America. In Argentina, for example, Ernesto Quesada published a book in 1899, *La cuestión femenina*, arguing in favor of laws ending discrimination against women and of recognizing women's contributions to labor.

The Mexican Revolution had been the result of an increasing need for social justice in Mexico, where an elite had been ruling in tandem with the dictatorship of Porfirio Díaz for several decades. The revolution began in 1910 under the leadership of the idealist Francisco Madero. The chaotic struggle that ensued brought to the forefront other leaders—Villa, Zapata, Orozco, Carranza—and it embodied numerous ideologies as well as interests of both middle-class and proletarian sectors of Mexican society. In 1917 a constitution was written and promulgated, making radical revisions to a constitution ratified in 1857. Mariano Azuela witnessed this entire process up close. Trained as a physician, like Sicardi and several other of these early-twentieth-century writers, Azuela came out of the educated middle class. He was a medic in the Mexican Revolution in its early stages, thus allowing him to experience the process as a participant, and he published the first novel of the revolution, *Andrés Pérez, maderista* (1911). With no pretense of being a revolutionary novel in itself, *Andrés Pérez, maderista* takes the perspective of a journalist who travels from Mexico City to the north to write about the Madero uprising. Consequently, the journalist becomes involved with the revolution. He observes multiple forms of opportunism and political expediency among individuals representing various sectors of Mexican society, from institutional authorities to wealthy landowners. Generally considered an aesthetic failure despite Azuela's already proven competence as a writer, this novel's weaknesses can be explained as Azuela's overly intense reaction to his theme.[14]

The opportunism of some participants in the Mexican Revolution is also evident in Azuela's *Los de abajo* (1916), but this is one of the more accomplished novels of the period; indeed, it is one of the masterpieces of the traditional art of storytelling (see chapter 2). Azuela had established his credentials as a traditional storyteller in

Mala yerba (1909), a novel about a conflict between the ruthless son of a wealthy landowner (Julián) and an attractive young woman who is the daughter of peons (Marcela). Julián abuses his power with Marcela, but Azuela does not present the typical good/bad dichotomy found in many nineteenth-century novels. Rather, he suggests that all individuals and institutions suffer from corruption. Before *Mala yerba* and *Andrés Pérez, maderista,* Azuela had published his first two novels—*María Luisa* (1907) and *Los fracasados* (1908). *María Luisa* is the story of a medical student's mistress who suffers from a disease and eventually dies; its stylistic and thematic innocence make it noteworthy only as the first novel of a prominent writer. *Los fracasados* is set in the Porfirio Díaz period in Mexico and satirizes attitudes common in a small town populated by individuals of obvious foolishness and selfishness. With respect to narrative strategies, Azuela's novels are the work of an essentially nineteenth-century novelist writing from the realist-naturalist tradition.

Colombian novelists at the beginning of the twentieth century were as entrenched in the previous century as Reyles, Azuela, and Blanco Fombona. The most recognized Colombian novelists at the turn of the century were Eustaquio Palacios, Soledad Acosta de Samper, José Manuel Marroquín, Tomás Carrasquilla, and José María Vargas Vila. Palacios, Acosta de Samper, and Marroquín were committed to a conservative political and cultural project identified in Colombia as the Regeneration, which, in many ways, operated like the political and ideological machinery of the *porfiriato* in Mexico. Most of the intellectuals associated with the Regeneration were gentlemen-scholars dedicated to the writing of poetry and political essays, although they did produce some fiction. One prominent exception to this generalization was José Asunción Silva's one novel of *modernista* aesthetic, *De sobremesa* (1896). Palacios, Soledad Acosta de Samper, and Marroquín published most of their novels in the nineteenth century.

The early fiction of Tomás Carrasquilla and José María Vargas Vila was not supportive of Colombia's Regeneration. Vargas Vila, in fact, was a strong liberal voice in numerous writings, and much of his work was in direct opposition to the Regeneration. Carrasquilla's *Frutos de mi tierra* (1896), like the fiction of Marroquín, communicates an awareness of signs of modernity in Colombia and expresses nostalgic attitudes toward a disappearing rural past. Vargas Vila was a critic of the status quo: his irreverent and anti-Regeneration attitudes constantly offended the upper class and the Catholic Church. If Marroquín embodied the Colombian Regeneration ideal of the gentleman-scholar who wrote well (exercising the craft of fiction adroitly in the realist-naturalist mode), Vargas Vila was his antithesis. Much of Vargas Vila's craft consisted of an amalgam of romantic clichés and the discourse of *modernismo* in vogue among Bogotá's cosmopolitan intellectuals.

Tomás Carrasquilla also was an independent intellectual who wrote in opposition to the values of Colombia's Regeneration, but without taking stances as irreverent as those of Vargas Vila. In 1906 Carrasquilla proclaimed a national literary independence, calling for a modern, national novel not based on foreign models. Despite the allusions to modernity and newness, Carrasquilla's fiction itself was, paradoxically, quite traditional—a reproduction of the nineteenth-century rural values and oral and popular culture of the Antioquia region. His novel *Grandeza* (1910) depicts Medellín's turn-of-the-century nouveaux riches and relates the eventual financial ruin of the woman protagonist, who becomes obsessed with taking care of her daughters. Criticizing the elitist aesthetics of the intellectuals in Bogotá, Carrasquilla states in his preface (in good nineteenth-century fashion) that *Grandeza* is a book of few aesthetic concerns—only some notes on his milieu. Much of Carrasquilla's fiction communicated a nostalgic feeling for the rural past of the region of Antioquia. In the case of Carrasquilla and Larreta, their stated desire to be modern is contradicted by a desire to return to a past they imagine as superior to the everyday reality of turn-of-the-century Latin America. Venezuelan novelist José Rafael Pocaterra shared Carrasquilla's paradoxically nostalgic attitude.

Colombian Clímaco Soto Borda never aspired to write the national novel. Soto Borda was a critic of the Regeneration, which was in power when he was writing his first novel, *Diana cazadora* (1915). Set in Bogotá during the Regeneration, *Diana cazadora* is an account of a young man's disillusionment, failures, and ultimate death. It is a novel of personal and national crisis. The characters suffer under the policies that the narrator calls the *ratonera regeneradora* (Regeneration thievery). The narrator also reveals a specific, critical attitude toward the Regeneration throughout the text.

At the turn of the century, writers like Azuela and Soto Borda were looking carefully at the traditional past and the modern future of their respective nations, attempting to make sense of the societal conflicts over the old ways and the new ways in the economic and political order. In Soto Borda's *Diana cazadora*, the protagonist's suffering is, in part, a crisis of modernity, the initial signs of which began to appear in conservative Bogotá at the turn of the century. Soto Borda was among the first writers to utilize these indicators in the setting of a novel. Having returned from Europe, one character notes the "progress" of Bogotá, including the new gas lights, the new water system, the foreign communities, the sicknesses, the secret police, the sudden deaths, the sermons, and other changes. The narrator places in doubt the very idea of modernity, speaking with obvious ironic overtones about the "heights of civilization" that Bogotá had reached. Just as modernity was arriving in Bogotá at a snail's pace, its objects fit uncomfortably into the Bogotá of Soto Borda.

The suffering of protagonist Fernando in *Diana cazadora*, in fact, represents a crisis of nascent modernity in Bogotá. An excessive participant in a newly decadent world, he ruins the family finances in his attempts to impress Diana—the modern woman par excellence. Fernando becomes an escapist consumer upon his return from Europe; increasingly he needs to flee from a harsh reality into alcohol. Near the end of the novel, when Fernando is alcoholic, the narrator describes him as desperate and violent. In the end, Fernando dies of his excesses, perhaps as a metaphor for modernity that fatally exceeded the conventions of Bogotá society. Fernando does not fit, and neither do the signs of Western modernity that he and others have brought to Colombia from abroad.

Like Vargas Vila and Soto Borda in Colombia, Argentine Manuel Gálvez was a controversial (and slightly oppositional) writer when he published his novels, even though he became associated with conservative values later in his life. In *La maestra normal* (1914), he relates the story of a young schoolteacher in a provincial town where she is eventually seduced. Typical of the period, many Argentines were offended by the novel's apparent questioning of conventional morals, and the residents of the town described were particularly offended by what they considered Gálvez's misrepresentation of their lives and values. The title character of Gálvez's next novel, *Nacha Regules* (1917), is led into prostitution by one man and then helped out of her situation by a social reformer. Set in Buenos Aires, this novel obviously emanates from the nineteenth-century naturalist tradition. More important, Gálvez relied on the pseudoscience of the period to foster a sentimental interest in the prostitute as a literary object.[15]

One of the best-selling novels of this period in Argentina was written by a woman, Emma de la Barra. Her novel *Stella* (1905) is the story of a young woman's maturation, in the context of the arrival in Argentina of the young woman, Alejandra, and her sister Stella, who is limited by a disability. Alejandra (called Alex in the text) assumes multiple roles including intellectual father figure and caring mother figure. For Masiello, de la Barra formulates a radical self-consciousness for her female characters, and *Stella* is really about self-constitution of women in fiction.[16]

Colombian Soledad Acosta de Samper was not as progressive as de la Barra. A prolific nineteenth-century novelist, Acosta de Samper published numerous books of fiction in the second half of the nineteenth century. She continued her realist-naturalist writing as one of Colombia's most prolific novelists in her time by publishing her last novels, *Aventuras de un español entre los indios de las Antillas* (1906) and *Un hidalgo conquistador* (1907), at the beginning of the twentieth. In an 1895 essay on the mission of the woman writer in Spanish America, Acosta de Samper explained her ideological project: "What is the woman's mission in the world? Undoubtedly to soften the customs, to moralize and to *Christianize* societies."[17] She believed that Colombian women should be educated in these principles and that society should treat these "correctly" educated women as men's equals. Although she was behind the times compared to many early-twentieth-century feminists, her positions on customs, morality, and women made Acosta de Samper an exceptional intellectual and a progressive among Colombians of her day.

While this early Colombian feminist was concerned with gender equality, Bolivia's Alcides Arguedas posed in her work another question of equality—that of justice toward indigenous peoples. Indeed, Arguedas was as concerned about failings of the political status quo as were the writers of Puerto Rico's Generation of 1930, the irreverent Vargas Vila, and the early Gálvez. In *Raza de bronce* (1919) Arguedas portrays the exploitation of the Bolivian Indian by the oligarchy. Using the Bolivian landscape as a backdrop, Arguedas also describes Indian rites and customs.

Among intellectuals in Latin America at the turn of the century, there were multiple and contradictory ideas about what it meant to be modern, what it meant to belong to a particular Latin

American nation, and what it meant to be a novelist in one of those nascent nations. For Díaz Rodríguez and the conservative intellectuals in Colombia, being modern meant a "regeneration"—a reactionary move. The scientific view was that of the naturalists and positivists, who were obviously unaware of how simplistically their Manichean schemes with their binary oppositions operated. Of course, some writers blurred the boundaries between this very binary opposition itself of *modernismo* versus realist-naturalist. However modern these writers liked to consider themselves, many of the social and political debates implied in their novels were intellectual outgrowths of the nineteenth century. And as one critic has pointed out near the end of the twentieth century, in retrospect, these "modern" authors employed a basically "masculinist aesthetic."[18]

Writers such as Federico Gamboa and Manuel Gálvez were seduced by the exuberance of women as a way to fictionalize the contradictions of artistic experience and modernity. The generation of 1880 in Argentina was typical of groups in different parts of Latin America at the turn of the century: it attempted to curb female excess through technology, even though some of its writers were seduced by the potential of women as sex objects in their fictions.

As Jrade convincingly argues, *modernismo* represents Spanish America's full-fledged intellectual response and challenge to modernity.[19] The resulting novelistic dialogue with the new modern values and ideas was complex because it was shaped by numerous conditions. In this period, novels such as Sicardi's *Libro extraño* and Gálvez's *El mal metafísico* were among those that set forth these complexities. Above all, the contradictions of these writers were evident, for neither their aesthetic nor ideological programs were consistent and coherent.

Discussions about the nation involved debates on the national novel and analyses of national character, and discourse on civilization versus barbarism remained strong at the turn of the century. Intellectuals of the generation of 1880 in Argentina, for example, began to analyze the national character as a case study for psychopathology; hygiene, public medicine, and sanitation were conceived to produce citizens both "clean of mind and body" and free of all traces of barbarism.[20] The Peruvian Clorinda Matto de Turner was dismayed with the social unrest of her time, and she believed that the proper solution to most problems behind this chaos was a retreat to science and ethics.

In many regions of Indo-Afro-Iberoamerica, the debate that had begun about the "national" novel was an important prelude to the publication and acclaim of now-canonical novels in the 1920s and 1930s throughout Latin America. In the early part of the century, the literary conventions and thematic interests tended to be limited to the concerns of middle-class and upper- and middle-class male novelists who predominated in the literary scene. This was the case for both the *modernistas* and the realist-naturalist novelists. Consequently, it is not difficult to support the proposition that these novels were the product of a masculinist aesthetic.[21]

The early-twentieth-century novel published in Latin America was ostensibly a hegemonic product of the upper middle class and dominated by males. Gálvez and Azuela were typical of the middle-class, well-educated writer who in some ways represented this hegemony, even though both writers occasionally questioned conventional bourgeois values. Nevertheless, there was a small and virtually invisible undercurrent of implicitly oppositional narratives authored by women writers who were marginalized by the literary establishment. The more successfully they appropriated male discourse and held the proper class credentials—as did Soledad Acosta de Samper—the less likely they were to be marginalized. Beneath the thin veneer of homogeneity among male writers, turn-of-the-century culture was strained by a minimally visible new heterogeneity. Both *modernistas* and realists, male and female, tended to question the values (and poor manners) of the new middle class. For this reason and other factors, the novel was a problematic genre at the beginning of the twentieth century.

Two **Rereading Spanish American Classics**

Novels published by Manuel Díaz Rodríguez, Federico Gamboa, Mariano Azuela, José Rafael Pocaterra, and Manuel Gálvez suggest the major directions for the Spanish American novel during this period, including the *modernistas* and the positivists. Díaz Rodríguez's *Sangre patricia* (1902) was one of the most outstanding examples of *modernista* fiction; Gamboa's *Santa* (1903) and José Rafael Pocaterra's *Política feminista* (1913) were remnants of nineteenth-century realism-naturalism; Azuela's *Los de abajo* (1916) represented realism in the most classic novel of the Mexican Revolution; Gálvez's *El mal metafísico* (1916) is also of the realist-naturalist mode but was an example of the interior, psychological type of fiction being written in this period. All five novelists participated in the ongoing struggle of the Latin American writer to establish an identity for the novel and, just as important, as novelists of their respective nations.[1] At the same time, it has been argued that these writers were representative of a masculinist aesthetic that was typical of the period.[2]

The *modernistas'* desire to be modern meant rejecting what they viewed as a traditional society populated by individuals interested in crude materialism devoid of any appreciation for the spiritual and the philosophical. For these writers, the novels of the realist-naturalist tradition were in part designed to set forth this assessment of the status quo. Consequently, for Díaz Rodríguez, the novels of writers such as Gamboa did not represent an acceptable approach to artistic creation. The reaction of these *modernistas*, then, was a hyper-aestheticism. Four of the five novelists discussed in this chapter offer a similar conclusion—that life is marked by futility—even though they differ considerably among themselves in most other aspects of worldview. The *modernistas* tended to reject many of the excesses of romanticism, yet they remained most committed to the romantics' yearning for the unattainable.

The protagonist of Díaz Rodríguez's *Sangre patricia*, twenty-five-year-old Tulio Arcos of Venezuela, is a fictionalized manifestation of this yearning as he constantly attempts to transcend everyday reality in search of something beyond his reach. *Sangre patricia* is not a novel of action in the traditional sense; instead it portrays Tulio in Paris waiting for the arrival of the exotic female other (Belén), whom he has married by proxy. She dies en route from Venezuela, however, and is buried at sea. After lengthy philosophical discussions at sea about life, society, and his sorrow over the absence of Belén, he commits suicide during his voyage home from Paris by leaping off the ship and into the sea.

Although Díaz Rodríguez is interested in the psychological development of characters, Brushwood points out that Tulio's problem of adjustment is more philosophical than psychological.[3] Two different philosophical outlooks on life are personified by Tulio's friends: Borja the idealist and Ocampo the pragmatist. The embodiment of the middle ground between these two is a musician, Martí, who stands out as both a creator and an individual capable of dealing with social institutions.

The first chapter of *Sangre patricia* introduces Tulio and reveals that Belén has died. The opening pages focus on one topic: exotic feminine beauty in its ideal form as embodied by Belén. She is described in the opening line as a *presencia milagrosa*, and her physical beauty is such that, in good *modernista* fashion, it even affects the passengers on the ship: "la admiración por la belleza de Belén cambió de carácter en casi todos los viajeros" (admiration for Belén's beauty changed the nature of nearly all the passengers).[4] In accordance with the *modernista* search for the unattainable and transcendent, her characterization emphasizes "algo sobrenatural y misterioso" (something supernatural and mysterious) (*Sangre patricia*, 11). In the passengers' lament of her death, their grief seems to stem as much from the loss of this beauty as from the loss of a human life. Her burial at sea is portrayed not as a religious ceremony but as a *modernista* aesthetic act in which the urn is lowered into a blue sea under blue skies. This aesthetic act, which is described in three paragraphs, culminates with this "fruit of beauty" descending miraculously into the depths of the sea: "Ya por milagro, como pensaron unos, ya por mala dispocisión del peso, como creyeron los más, la caja, descendida hasta el agua, quedó algún tiempo a flote: al fin se inclinó de un lado, luego del otro, y la mar cerró su boca insaciable y azul sobre aquel fruto de belleza" (Whether by a miracle, as some thought, or by poor weight distribution, as the others believed, the coffin as it descended into the water floated for some time: finally it leaned to one side, then the other, and the sea closed its insatiable blue mouth over that fruit of beauty; *Sangre patricia,* 14). In this passage, the narrator recognizes implicitly the existence of the two worldviews in constant play in the novel: on the one hand, the idealists and aesthetes who observe a *milagro;* on the other hand, the pragmatists of scientific worldview who notice the distribution of the physical weight in the coffin as it wobbles on the water before sinking. The omniscient narrator of this passage thus recognizes both worldviews yet seems to associate more closely with the aesthetic position: he describes the act *first* as a *milagro* and chooses to describe the descending corpse as a *fruto de belleza* disappearing into the blue sea. Debicki has pointed to two positions of the omniscient narrator that correspond to these two worldviews.[5] Nevertheless, the narrator does seem to identify more closely with the aesthetic and *modernista* view of the world. The reader associates with Tulio for a technical reason: he frequently functions as the focalizer through whom the fictional world is seen. Throughout the novel, in accordance with its masculinist aesthetics, the reader sees the people and objects that Tulio notices and contemplates.

In accordance with symbolist techniques inherited by the *modernistas,* Díaz Rodríguez uses images from the empirical world to convey the emotional state of the characters. As Tulio contemplates the Loire River, for example, the objects that he observes reflect his emotional state in suffering the loss of Belén; the river waters seem to reflect his soul as they enter the sea, which sings and smiles indifferently. Díaz Rodríguez's symbolist agenda is explicitly evident in later passages, particularly in one passage describing the objects surrounding Tulio and how the objects' *almas* (souls) begin to weep (*Sangre patricia,* 49).

It has been a simplistic commonplace among some readers to see *modernista* literature as an escape from social and political realities and a flight into "art for art's sake." A superficial reading of *Sangre patricia* could lead one to such a conclusion. Indeed, Tulio often does seek escape from his circumstance, using drugs, dreaming, and sleep as his escape before finding his final solution. Nevertheless, his actions should be understood as a protest against what Tulio (and Díaz Rodríguez) viewed as a society too vulgar to be tolerable. Along the same lines, the idealistic Borja suffers from the behavior of an adultress wife, and the narrator describes the affair and her lover as *vulgar*. In general, the traditional morés of bourgeois society are seen as signs of mediocrity.

Despite the negative attitude toward American capitalism, the characters in *Sangre patricia* are fascinated with the signs and objects that they associate with modernity. These objects also appear in *Los de abajo, Santa, Política feminista,* and *El mal metafísico.* In *Sangre patricia,* the characters make frequent reference to new "science"— such as telegraphy—as well as new ideas in the realm of spirituality and religion (such as telepathy), as the "miracles" of the times. Only by embracing this modernity can they escape the vulgarity, then, of the status quo. This generalized pattern is underscored by Gálvez's Carlos Riga, who vehemently rejects vulgar middle-class values.

More than a crisis of modernity, however, the characters suffer from a crisis in belief systems in this new modern age. Through much of the novel they discuss exactly what is worthy of belief. For example, Tulio and Borja ponder the validity of Tulio's belief in *sirenas,* typifying the crisis over the ancient beliefs they still find attractive even in the early twentieth century. Both of these belief systems merely reaffirm the patriarchal order that predominates in the fiction of this period.

The main characters in Azuela's *Los de abajo* also suffer a crisis in belief systems, although none of them are nearly as prone to introspection as either Tulio Arcos and his friends in *Sangre patricia* or as Carlos Riga and others in *El mal metafísico.* Tulio seems to focus increasingly on himself; the protagonist of *Los de abajo,* Demetrio Macías, as well as his cohorts, are progressively subsumed by pure movement, void of thought. They are notably incapable of articulating any coherent ideological basis for their actions as players in a revolution for social justice. The one exception is Luis Cervantes, an intellectual who joins the forces with Demetrio Macías and eloquently, though hypocritically, espouses the social and political ideals of the Mexican Revolution.

Díaz Rodríguez paints a visual picture of the physical beauty of the setting, emphasizing the color blue (blue skies, blue sea, etc.) that the *modernistas* associated with art. Azuela, on the other hand, uses more conventional imagery to suggest character and settings rather than to explain them directly. Just as frequently as Díaz Rodríguez employs images of artistic beauty, Azuela uses animal imagery to characterize Demetrio and his men as humans who have been reduced to animal-like reactions to their immediate circumstance. In using this type of imagery, Azuela assumes the implicit role of the writer as nineteenth-century scientist who recognized the place of humans in the animal kingdom.[6]

Los de abajo is a novel of three parts, each of which corresponds to a specific moment of the Mexican Revolution.[7] The first part consists of twenty-one chapters that tell of the initial organization of the revolutionaries under the leadership of protagonist Demetrio Macías. In Mexican history, this is the period in which the revolution consists of fighting against Victoriano Huerta, who had assassinated the idealist Francisco Madero, hero of the peasants and working class. Huerta, on the other hand, represented a return to the forces of Porfirio Díaz. The first part ends with the battle in Zacatecas, which took place in June 1914 and signaled the downfall of Huerta. The second part, which contains fourteen chapters, emphasizes movement and consists of one battle after another. This part of the novel suggests the historical divisions among the groups under the leadership of Zapata, Villa, and Carranza. This process led to the Convention of Aguascalientes and the separation between Villa and Carranza. The third part of *Los de abajo*, consisting of seven chapters, relates the defeat of Demetrio's men as a kind of counterpart of their victories in the first part. Carranza's army ambushes them and, at the very end, Demetrio seems isolated, disoriented, and hopeless. The novel has a rather circular structure in which Demetrio is in the same place at the end that he was in the beginning. Given all that he has experienced, however, it is not really as much a figural circle as a figural spiral.

Azuela was a liberal humanist as well as a fervent follower of Madero, the idealist who took power after Porfirio Díaz. Azuela was an ally of Pancho Villa and bitter enemy of Carranza. In 1914, Azuela joined the revolutionary troops of Julián Medina as a medic. The experience of what he saw with these troops and what they related to him was the source of his disillusionment with the Mexican Revolution as well as the basis for his writing *Los de abajo*.

Azuela completed and published *Los de abajo* in El Paso, Texas; it appeared in serial form in the newspaper *El Paso del Norte* in 1915, an important year in Mexican history.[8] Carranza had come into power with a new ruling class and a new spirit of nationalism in Mexico. The leading intellectuals were figures such as Antonio Caso and Martín Luis Guzmán; Azuela, on the other hand, was marginal at best. Nevertheless, within a decade *Los de abajo* had a broad readership in Mexico and was considered the quintessential national novel of the Mexican Revolution.

In addition to his skill in suggesting and showing, rather than telling, Azuela uses a systematic set of images and symbols to communicate his idea of the essence of the Mexican Revolution. The first of these images is the *hoja seca* (dry leaf) that Camila observes fall dead at her feet in the fourteenth chapter of the first part of the novel.[9] Later in the first part, Solís explains how the revolution is a hurricane and, once again, an *hoja seca* (*Los de abajo*, 63). Near the very end of the first part, a third image of the revolution appears in the form of Luis Cervantes's observation of smoky clouds (*Los de abajo*, 73). In the third part, Valderrama describes the revolution as a volcano: "¡Amo la Revolución como amo al volcán que irrumpe! Al volcán porque es volcán; a la Revolución porque es Revolución!" (I love the Revolution like I love the volcano that erupts! The volcano because it's a volcano; the Revolution because it's Revolution; *Los de abajo*, 128). In the third chapter of the third part, Demetrio's men return to the town of Juchipila, the "cradle" of the revolution. As they enter Juchipila, Azuela employs images of burned, black crosses, images of destruction and death. Near the end of the novel, when Demetrio's wife asks him why he continues fighting, Demetrio responds: "Mira esa piedra cómo no se pára" (Look how that stone doesn't stop; *Los de abajo*, 137). Thus, the novel ends with an image of the revolution as the rolling rock that cannot stop, as movement with no content.

Azuela's journalistic style (which was innovative for the times) involved only brief descriptions of characters and settings, generally free of romantic exuberance and *modernista* adornment. His use of imagery to suggest emotional states is occasionally comparable to that of Díaz Rodríguez. In one passage that is not typical of the style of *Los de abajo* he uses the symbolist technique (of Díaz Rodríguez) to suggest an emotional state. In this passage, Camila finds objects expressing the emotion of sadness, which, of course, is an expression of her own sadness: "Todo era igual; pero en las piedras, en las ramas secas, en el aire embalsamado y en la hojarasca, Camila encontraba ahora algo muy extraño: como si todas aquellas cosas tuvieran mucha tristeza" (*Los de abajo,* 47).

The narrator in *Los de abajo* maintains a position of neutrality, attaining the Flaubertian ideal of "transparence" throughout virtually every page of the text. In only three passages does the narrator editorialize briefly. Azuela was well aware of his craft, having published an article in criticism of Federico Gamboa's lack of novelistic sophistication by including editorial comments in his later fiction.

In terms of style and characterization, Federico Gamboa and Manuel Gálvez proceeded as nineteenth-century novelists. In *Santa,* Gamboa writes in the mode of the most refined of the novelists of the previous century, using a self-consciously "correct" style that imitated the Spanish masters of realist fiction. It is also obvious that he was aware of the stylistic tours de force of the *modernistas.* In the early chapters, he introduces characters and settings painstakingly, with detailed descriptions of the characters' physical appearance and background as well as room-by-room descriptions of dwellings. Like Díaz Rodríguez, Gamboa begins in the present situation and then goes into the main character's background in the second chapter that functions as a flashback.

Santa is a two-part novel with five chapters in each part. With the exception of the second chapter, the novel develops in a basically chronological manner, telling the story of the transgressive young rural woman, Santa, who becomes corrupted in the city. In her rural setting, she is described as pure and innocent. "Dishonored" by a soldier, Santa is rejected by her family and must go to the city to make a living as a prostitute. Eventually she falls in love with a bullfighter who provides a stable economic life for her, but she abandons him to return to her former profession. From there, she fails in her attempts to reform herself, and her life degenerates: she fails in her relationship with another man and is no longer allowed to work in any of the houses of prostitution. At the end, shortly before dying, she joins with Hipólito, a blind man who had loved her from the beginning and who rescues her. Hipólito is a physically unattractive character who had fallen in love with Santa because she had been kind to him and because he recognized a certain human decency in her that few others were able to perceive.

In *Santa,* as in *Sangre patricia,* there is a sense of unrest and uneasiness. In both novels, a revision of values is suggested, as the main characters seem unable to tolerate the established values of the status quo—a patriarchal, heterosexist, and bourgeois society. The values in *Santa*, of course, are those of the *porfiriato*; Porfirio Díaz's regime of "peace and order" was becoming increasingly illegitimate and in fact having less and less to do with either peace or order. The overall vision that Gamboa offers is pessimistic. As Pacheco has observed, there is a certain symmetry between Santa's destiny as part of the machinery exploited in the house of prostitution and the destiny of her brothers, who work as part of the machinery exploited in a factory.[10] Similarly, Debra Castillo points to the mechanized nature of human activity and, more specifically, the equation established between human beings and meat for consumption.[11]

Gamboa's language—closer to Galdós's than to Azuela's—demonstrates the style of a writer who self-consciously wanted to communicate to the reader that he was a literary stylist and a modern novelist in a nation where the genre of the novel still suffered a shaky identity. Gamboa's modernity was primarily that of being in tune with certain naturalist precepts of the time, carrying out his "scientific" experiment of observing the pure and innocent young girl in both a rural and an urban setting. As such, this story is introduced by Gamboa at the beginning of the second chapter as "La historia vulgar de las muchachas pobres que nacen en el campo y en el campo se crían al aire libre, entre brisas y flores; ignorantes, castas y fuertes; al cuidado de la tierra, nuestra eterna madre cariño; con amistades aladas, de pájaros libres de verdad, y con ilusiones tan puras" (The vulgar story of poor girls born in the country and in the country reared in fresh air, among breezes and flowers; ignorant, chaste, and strong; under the care of the earth, our eternal mother of affection, of winged friends, of free birds of truth, and with such pure illusions).[12]

Like Azuela, Gamboa thought of himself as a modern scientist whose characters, like animals, responded to instincts, as he reveals in one of his early descriptions of Santa as "guiada por un deseo meramente animal" (guided by mere animal desire; *Santa*, 731). Gamboa was also interested enough in the objective world of modernity around him to note the modern *tranvías*, the modern *focos eléctricos*, the movement in the modern city, and the like. For Gamboa, they are the objects of a corrupt modernity, a corruption that he had observed literarily in his European models of naturalism and a corruption that he was noting in the modern Mexican society of the Díaz regime. These attitudes make Gamboa an interesting case study of the

Spanish American novelist at the turn of the century. He was obviously aware of modern society, modern science, and the basic precepts of naturalism. Nevertheless, he does not communicate a strong commitment to the values of any of the three. Rather, he resists modernity. The end of *Santa* suggests why, for Gamboa's underlying world vision was marked considerably by Christianity. As Brushwood has pointed out, neither his naturalism nor his Christianity was strictly orthodox.[13]

For Castillo, *Santa* was clearly and unmistakably the product of a turn-of-the-century masculinist aesthetic.[14] In her reading of this novel, she argues that the workings of the Porfirian gestural economy define and displace sexuality onto an aesthetic representation that later in the century takes on its own afterlife. She also establishes important links between poverty and the fantasized erotic object.[15]

Gamboa was a novelist with neither the situation nor the inclination to be deeply critical of Mexican society and the Porfirio Díaz regime. On the contrary, he served in the diplomatic corps under Díaz and reconverted to Catholicism before writing *Santa;* near the end of *Santa,* Gamboa's Christian interests are evident. His description of the situation of Santa and Hipólito is as follows: "Sólo les quedaba Dios. ¡Dios queda siempre!" (All they had left was God. God always remains!; *Santa,* 918). In *Santa,* as in Gamboa's other novels, Christian concern and hope seem to offer a solution for the characters, but they are not strong enough elements to allow for a positive outcome. This quote also reveals one of the weaknesses of Gamboa as a stylist: his generally omniscient and neutral narrator begins to editorialize to the reader about these Christian principles. As a diplomat for the Díaz regime and as a practicing Catholic, then, Gamboa was not positioned as an independent novelist to be critical of the Mexican government, the Catholic Church, or a bourgeois and patriarchal society in general.

José Rafael Pocaterra, on the other hand, is openly satirical of the status quo in *Política feminista.* Set in a small town in Venezuela, this novel intends to function as a national novel: the omniscient narrator explains from the outset that, even though the novel is set in the provinces—the town of Valencia—the story could be the same in Caracas or anywhere else in Venezuela. It is basically an account of middle-class life in this small town, with the main plot line centered upon the desire that Bebé, a local politico, has for a young woman, Josefina, who belongs to one of the town's respectable families of *gente decente.* In the end, the novel is a self-conscious antiromantic work in which the couple does not fall in love and is never joined, and no one suffers death at the end.[16] The young and "decent" Josefina rejects the "vulgar" Bebé. Despite the explicitly antiromantic elements of the novel, Pocaterra does share Isaacs's interest in the material world of the couple's erotic lives (such as a fascination with the details of their clothing), and he does engage the reader in the observation of the characters' furtive *miradas.*[17] Consequently, the issue of materialism is as evident in *Política feminista* as it was in *Santa.*[18]

Pocaterra is known as a satirist and *costumbrista,* and he does, indeed, provide a detailed account of local customs. In the end, in fact, the reader reaches the conclusion that from Pocaterra's perspective, there is no real questioning of patriarchal heterosexist values: life in Venezuela would be acceptable if only manners could be improved. The politicians, for example, exhibit the worst manners, and Pocaterra implies that if the politicians could improve their manners and *mala conducta,* government would also improve. His satire, however, is directed against all, and he exhibits equal disdain for new bourgeois values and conservative Catholic beliefs.

To a large extent, as seen in *Sangre patricia* and *El mal metafísico,* the conflicts of *Política feminista* are based on differences in values and belief systems. On the one hand, the women in the novel represent the traditional values of Catholicism and the old aristocracy of Venezuela. Several of the men represent the new values of modernity and the bourgeoisie. Interestingly, Pocaterra associates good manners and values with reading. Josefina and her sisters are readers of literature, and they are portrayed as educated, well-mannered characters. Bebé, on the other hand, is not a reader of literature and is characterized as vulgar. Again, it appears that if only the politicians could read and write better, both government and national life would improve.

A more subtle dichotomy can be observed in the function of interior and exterior space in *Política feminista.* Near the beginning and near the end of the novel, the interior space inside the home of Josefina and her sisters is the space of reading, traditional values, and good manners. This is the feminine space. The exterior space which they observe through their window is the masculine space of modern values, lack of religion, poor government, and bad manners.

Política feminista is the only one of these five novels with a humorous tone. But Pocaterra uses a variety of methods to establish complicity with the reader, often evoking a nostalgic tone similar to the tone in the fiction of Tomás Carrasquilla. Like Carrasquilla, Pocaterra regularly uses demonstrative adjectives that lure the reader into assuming a role of experience shared with the narrator. For example, early in the novel he refers to "*esa* mezcla de vagabundería y sentimentalismo" as if the reader were acquainted with this combination (*Política femenista*, 14, my emphasis). And near the end of the novel, Pocaterra refers to "uno de *esos* ramos de flores," again assuming prior common experience of reader and writer (*Política femenista*, 83, my emphasis). Consequently, the issue of complicity and the reader as voyeur is as significant in *Política feminista* as it is in *Santa*.[19]

Pocaterra's satirical barbs are wide-ranging, for he uses satire throughout the novel. The omniscient narrator, for example, occasionally intervenes to explain and clarify matters of social and political importance. Nevertheless, he offers no consistent political message or consistent ideological base for his critiques. On the surface, he seems to suggest that the solution to Venezuela's problems is education, which, of course, promotes reading and good manners. In the fictional world of *Política feminista*, however, Pocaterra criticizes all values—traditional and modern—and all social classes, as well as both old and new political discourses. Consequently, the reader reaches the conclusion that Pocaterra's vision and aesthetic do not go beyond the entertainment value to be found in his satire.

Carlos Riga, the twenty-year-old protagonist in *El mal metafísico*, also faces crises in values and belief systems. The first part of this three-part novel presents Riga's literary interests and conflicts with his father, who wants his son to become a lawyer. Riga not only wants to be a poet, but he desires to modernize Argentine letters by innovating poetry along the lines of *modernismo*. By the end of the first part, Riga publishes a new literary magazine, *La Idea Moderna*, with the hopes of moving Argentine literature toward the innovations in which he holds interests. The second and third parts relate Riga's increasing problems and failures. His literary efforts go relatively unrecognized, his economic life continually worsens, and the final stages of his story tell of his isolation, alcoholism, and death.

El mal metafísico deals with the (then) new *modernismo*, but Gálvez is actually as traditional as Gamboa in terms of narrative technique. He carefully describes the characters upon introducing them, and the prose style corresponds to the elegant writing of traditionalists such as Azuela and Gamboa. Gálvez seems interested in modernity as a topic to consider, but his heart clearly lies with the traditionalists. Gálvez also reveals his fundamentally conservative worldview in the third part of his novel: characters who have adopted conventional ideas and lifestyles—abandoning literature—do well; those who do not, suffer. Thus, Gamboa would seem to embrace the patriarchal order.

> The multiple and often contradictory ideas embodied in *La idea moderna*, Riga's literary magazine, are central to an understanding of *El mal metafísico* as an example of the early-twentieth-century Latin American novel. The narrator offers the following description of the magazine when it is about to be launched: it is to look for the "regeneration of the republic, to restore old ideals."[20]

Aside from the narrator's ironic and mildly derisive tone, his comments about the magazine's proposed role for the nation are noteworthy. In his introductory description of the magazine, it seems to propose a conservative—even reactionary—role similar to the equally conservative work of the intellectuals and political leaders of the Regeneration in Colombia (see chapter 1). Indeed, the idea of restoring old ideals sounds like a conservative proposal. With this introduction, the reader is wary of the unnamed ideology that might bring "unity" to the nation. Carlos Riga and his cohorts are not at all consistent, however, in their apparently conservative ideals for the nation. In later discussions, these same intellectuals embrace the cultural modernity of Germany, Great Britain, and the United States, rejecting the more traditional cultural and linguistic values inherited from Spain. Thus, those three nations are described by one of the characters as "civilizados" and Spain as a "barbarian" nation (*El mal metafísico*, 214), in part because Spaniards still worried about the rules of grammar. Clearly, these young writers are not entirely in line with the conservative agenda of the Regeneration in Colombia, for the latter did indeed fervently follow the rules of Spanish grammar.[21]

In addition to the numerous contradictions in the aesthetic and ideological program of *La Idea Moderna*, this novel stands out as a synecdoche for the discursive mode of most of the discussions of value and belief systems. More specifically, most of the ideas, values, and beliefs are conceived in the broad context of nation—as national values rather than those of an individual or a human collectivity smaller than a nation. Thus, the vicissitudes of Carlos Riga and his peers are conceived and presented as national vicissitudes. And ongoing discussions of culture are really debates about the past, present, and/or future of Argentine culture.

Both the implied author of *El mal metafísico* and the protagonist Carlos Riga seem to aspire to be modern, but that is not a consistent pattern either. Clearly, Riga is fascinated with many aspects of what was considered new and modern: his poetic writing rings much like Rubén Darío's, and his persona has much of Tulio Arcos from *Sangre patricia*. The implied author seems equally fascinated with what is new, modern, and in fashion culturally. There are regular references throughout the text to *la vida moderna*, making it obvious that among all the new and old values, *lo moderno* is an overriding concern.

In the final analysis, however, Gálvez seems suspicious, at best, of modernity and the bourgeois values associated with modernity in the new Argentina. His protagonist, who embodies modern literary values, dies of alcoholism after a series of devastating rejections by the cultural establishment. At the end of the novel, the narrator describes him as someone not capable of adapting to "la bajeza de nuestra vida moderna" (the lowness of our modern life; *El mal metafísico*, 226). Here the narrator intercalates himself *(nuestra)* as one of the critics of modern life and, implicitly, as a supporter of the status quo.

The reader of *El mal metafísico* concludes, despite the contradictions, that both modern literature (here, *modernismo*) and modernity are a failure in turn-of-the-century Argentina. The reader is also invited to conclude that Riga's problem is his *mal metafísico*—his "sickness" of dreaming and creating as it is described in the fifth chapter of the novel. Even this idea, which is so clear early in the text, becomes clouded by the end because of Riga's severe alcoholism. This disease is described in such convincing detail that the reader is invited to speculate along at least two lines: (1) Is Riga's most serious ailment *el mal metafísico* or, in reality, alcoholism? (2) Is *el mal metafísico* in fact just one external manifestation of his alcoholism? Whatever the conclusion might be concerning the exact nature of Riga's sickness, it is evident that his demise has much more to do with his individual problems than with a nation that is either too traditional or too modern.

Pocaterra had implied that many of Venezuela's ills could be improved upon or cured by good taste and good manners within the national culture. Gálvez is not nearly as consistent or explicit, but he does occasionally suggest his admiration for good taste. His narrator comments negatively on the bad taste of the bourgeoisie and presents characters who demonstrate *buen gusto* in a positive light. Gálvez, then, implicitly reinforces the patriarchal order as much as did Pocaterra.

Despite the strengths and weaknesses of these five novels that critics have freely and openly pointed out, these works have survived literary scrutiny in a variety of ways. *Los de abajo* was read and commented upon widely in the 1920s in Mexico and became a model for the novel of the Mexican Revolution that dominated Mexican fiction for several decades. *Santa* was a best-seller in the early part of the century in Mexico and by the late 1930s had sold sixty thousand copies.[22] *Sangre patricia, Política feminista,* and *El mal metafísico* do not have quite the same marketing record, but they have remained solidly entrenched, as have *Los de abajo* and *Santa,* in the scholarly histories of the Latin American novel.[23]

Of these five novelists, the most traditional with respect to form and the least critical with respect to modern society was Federico Gamboa. Gamboa was essentially a product of the *porfiriato* himself, having served in the diplomatic corps under Porfirio Díaz's government, having had the luxury of writing his novels while on Díaz's payroll abroad, and having written to a small upper-middle-class reading public that was fundamentally pro-*porfiriato.* Writing in 1914, after the downfall of the pro-Díaz Huerta, Gamboa stated in a conference on *La novela mexicana* the following: "Hoy por hoy, la novela apenas si se permite levantar la voz. Muda y sobrecogida de espanto, contempla la tragedia nacional que hace más de tres años nos devasta y aniquila."[24] Having made this declaration of the novel's inertia, he goes on to declare its death: "La novela, de luto ya, como el país entero."[25] Making this statement in 1914, Gamboa was declaring the symbolic death of the nineteenth-century novel. This statement and Azuela's *Los de abajo* mark a symbolic end of the predominance of nineteenth-century fiction writing in Latin America. *El mal metafísico,* too, was a strong statement in favor of traditionalism. Yet these novels also opened the door for the innovations of the 1920s and the decades that followed.

In these five novels, a masculinist aesthetic predominates; both masculinity and the masculine nation, nevertheless, are fragmented, incoherent, and fragile. The early part of the century is dominated by male writers who were insecure about their roles as novelists in nations whose patriarchal and oligarchic order was disappearing before a new bourgeoisie they did not uniformly find attractive. In the end, these writers all suggested that life was marked by futility: the ideal exoticized female other was unattainable, and the protagonists were either unable or unwilling to function as good citizens within the framework of the new bourgeois order.

These five turn-of-the-century Spanish American novels exhibit both the diverse interests and contradictions of the Latin American writer of the period, particularly with respect to modernity. They are still strongly oriented toward science and religion, as well as toward the realist-naturalist novel that predominated in the previous century. But at the same time that these novelists were attracted to some aspects of modernity, they tended to reject the modernity of U.S. capitalism that they all considered, in different ways, basically vulgar. In their texts, Díaz Rodríguez and Pocaterra were most explicitly negative toward U.S. capitalism; Gálvez criticized the bourgeois values, the same values that he embraced later in his life. These novelists embraced rather than criticized a patriarchal, heterosexist nineteenth-century order. Even the masculinist aesthetic, however, was fragile: the novelists were insecure about their roles, and none of their works, with the possible exception of *Los de abajo,* became the monument to the respective national literary tradition their authors hoped they would become. All five writers ostensibly desired to be modern, although Gamboa and Pocaterra occasionally resisted modernity, exhibiting nostalgic attitudes toward the conventional values and lifestyles of the late nineteenth century.

Part II **Traditional and Modernist Aesthetics, 1922–1940**

Three **Novelistic and Cultural Contexts
in the 1920s and 1930s**

$\mathbf{M}$any of the Latin American writers publishing before the 1920s were so deeply concerned about national culture debates and so intensely engaged in political dialogue that aesthetics
were secondary. This was not the case for short story writer Horacio
Quiroga or for many of the novelists of this second moment of desiring to be modern who were publishing in the 1920s and 1930s. Some
of these novelists were more gifted in dealing with questions of aesthetics and creating viable experience for readers than most of their
predecessors and many of their peers. A group of established novelists as well as beginners with modernist aesthetics published noteworthy fiction during this period. The desire to be modern took the
Latin American writer in two general directions—toward a traditionalist's reaction against modernity and toward an embracing of modernity in the mode of the *vanguardia.*

Among novelists interested in modernity were the writers interested in exploring the possibilities of New Worldism or *criollismo*
who were profoundly concerned with issues of national identity and
cultural autonomy.[1] This and related cultural movements in Latin
America promoted the idea of a "new" person of the Americas who
represented a racial and cultural mix previously unknown in Europe.
This idea of a new person was particularly promoted in Mexico and
Brazil, but similar ideas circulated throughout Latin America. In the
indigenous areas of Indo-Afro-Iberoamerica, the promulgation of the
cultural ideals of *mestizaje* also promoted the ideas of New Worldism and *criollismo.* Out of this general context came the three now

canonical novels of the period: the Colombian José Eustasio Rivera's *La vorágine* (1924), the Argentine Ricardo Guiraldes's *Don Segundo Sombra* (1926), and the Venezuelan Rómulo Gallegos's *Doña Bárbara* (1929). In addition, women writers such as Teresa de la Parra, author of *Las memorias de Mamá Blanca* (1929), published novels meritorious of more recognition than they received at the time. The presence of de la Parra and other women writers offered an initial feminine response to what was still a predominantly masculinist aesthetic.

On the other hand, the second group of writers and intellectuals conceived of being modern as the appropriation of European avant-garde modernist aesthetics, particularly as they were practiced in France, Spain, and Italy. They were motivated by the surrealist writings of André Breton, the futurist writings of Marinetti, and the like. For some Latin American intellectuals and in some of their texts, these two basic concepts of being modern operated dialogically. Guiraldes, for example, has been associated with both groups, and his *Don Segundo Sombra* (1926) contains stylistic registers of both types of fiction.[2] From this group came novelists who have been far less recognized than Guiraldes, Gallegos, and Rivera, such as the Peruvian Martín Adán, the Chileans María Luisa Bombal, Vicente Huidobro, and Juan Emar, the Cubans Enrique Labrador Ruiz and Dulce María Loynaz, the Mexicans Jaime Torres Bodet and Xavier Villaurrutia, the Argentine Adolfo Bioy Casares, and the Colombian José Felix Fuenmayor.

The cultural debate was most often articulated in Manichean terms as one between civilization and barbarism. Following a discursive mode and conceptualization of national culture from the nineteenth century, the civilization versus barbarism debate articulated issues of national identity in simplistic terms. The basic idea was that Latin America's identity crisis and national crises were to be resolved only when the conflict between the (supposedly) barbaric rural society and (supposedly) civilized urban society would somehow elevate the former from its backwardness. In the 1920s, the *criollistas* maintained that a key to establishing an authentic national identity was to be found and celebrated in local and regional values. Consequently, *criollista* novels tended to exalt local and regional customs. Paradoxically, some aspects of rural culture that had been associated with barbarism became positive values in these novels. In contrast, novelists with more urban and cosmopolitan interests looked to the European model of the modern nation-state. Their novels tended to reflect this enthusiasm for modernity and the cultural innovations of modernism. Both the *criollistas* and the *vanguardistas* believed that their formulas would lead to the production of a literary culture of universal value.

The widespread effort to redefine national identity and cultural autonomy was led in Latin America by José Vasconcelos and Samuel Ramos in Mexico, Fernando Ortiz and Jorge Mañach in Cuba, and Ezequiel Martínez Estrada in Argentina. In Puerto Rico, Luis Lloréns Torres and the intellectuals of the Generation of 1930 worked along these lines, which included essayists, poets, and novelists. Consequently, the cultural criticism of Antonio S. Pedreira and the literary criticism of Margot Arce and Concha Meléndez, as well as the novel *La llamarada* (1935) by Enrique Laguerre, made important contributions to this dialogue on national identity. The poet Luis Palés Matos contributed by conceiving of the culture of the region as a mulatto one, thus working with ideas parallel to those promoting *mestizaje* in Mexico and the Andean region. Lloréns Torres brought the idea of national literature to Puerto Rico, as well as Puerto Rico's participation in broader questions of national identity delineated in the island as a matter of *lo puertorriqueño.*

The *Revista de Occidente,* founded in Spain by José Ortega y Gasset in 1923, was essential to an understanding of how the cultural dialogue in Latin America unfolded in the 1920s and 1930s. As González-Echevarría explained, it would be difficult to exaggerate the enormous impact that Ortega and his *Revista de Occidente* had on Latin America.[3] By means of this magazine, Ortega's thought permeated the continent, as did the many translations of German philosophers that the magazine's publishing house disseminated. Most importantly, Ortega and his cohorts translated, discussed, and popularized the ideas of Spengler, whose book *The Decline of the West* was much in vogue throughout Latin America. It appeared in Spanish translation in 1923 and was an immediate best-seller. Ortega y Gasset was also responsible for an ongoing dialogue on the European avant-garde in his book *La deshumanización del arte* (1925).

Spengler's ideas also served the purposes of both groups. He offered a view of universal history in which Europe was no longer the center; it was simply one more culture.[4] Thus, Spengler offered a strong argument for Latin America's cultural autonomy, one with which both the nationalist *criollistas* and the promoters of avant-garde modernism could agree and one they could appropriate. The Cuban Jorge Mañach, an advocate of a new *vanguardia* in Cuba, read Spengler and spoke of the "physiognomy" of Cuban culture, the Cuban Fernando Ortiz was lecturing in 1924 on *la decadencia cubana*, and Vasconcelos published his view of a future *mestizo* culture under the title *La raza cósmica* in 1925.

Most of the groups of *vanguardia* were inspired by the aesthetic programs of the avant-garde in Europe, and the writers they mentioned most often were Joyce, Proust, and Benjamín Jarnés.[5] In their typically brief fictional experiments, they pursued innovative narrative forms, exploring the possibilities of interiorization of characters, for example through interior monologues, and the use of multiple points of view and striking imagery. Some, such as Torres Bodet and Arqueles Vela, were more effective in undermining the conventions of traditionalists than in constructing their own fully developed novels. Throughout the major urban centers of Latin America, there were groups of writers—often held together by a magazine or journal—who promoted modernist aesthetics. Among these groups were the "Florida" circle in Argentina, those associated with the magazine *Contemporáneos* in Mexico, and those artists associated with the *Revista de Avance* in Cuba. Similar, earlier organs were *Martín Fierro* (founded in 1924) in Argentina, and *Horizontes* and *Irradiador* in Mexico.

With respect to modernism and the avant-garde of cultural aesthetics, in Brazil the aesthetics of European modernism were quite well received. The Semana de Arte Moderna of 1922 was a celebration of the new modernist aesthetics, with particular emphasis on the poetry and the arts. The event took place at São Paulo's municipal theater, with iconoclastic exhibitions and proclamations by the avant-garde of Brazil's artists, musicians, and writers.

Indeed, 1922, the year of the celebrations in Brazil, was a landmark year for avant-garde literature. That year, César Vallejo published his iconoclastic book of poetry *Trilce,* Joyce published *Ulysses,* and T. S. Eliot came forth with *The Wasteland.* Joyce was of great interest to the writers of the *vanguardia,* and the stylistic innovations of *Ulysses* were evident in the fiction of Juan Filloy, Agustín Yáñez, and several of the major novels of the 1960s.[6]

In Cuba, the *Revista de Avance* appeared in 1927 under the direction of Jorge Mañach and four others. Yet another outgrowth of the Spanish *Revista de Occidente,* the *Revista de Avance* featured avant-garde poets César Vallejo and Jaime Torres Bodet, as well as Miguel

Angel Asturias and a host of Spanish writers considered by critics to have embraced universal interests: Américo Castro, Miguel de Unamuno, Eugenio D'Ors, and others. One of the key figures of the Cuban avant-garde, Mañach, had joined a group of equally irreverent young intellectuals to form the Grupo Minorista in 1923.

The cultural dialogue in Argentina took the form of a debate between the groups known as Florida and Boedo. They were not in direct opposition, however, for there was an evident crossover between the groups, and many personal friendships. In general terms, the Florida group promoted cosmopolitan attitudes toward literature and culture, and its adherents tended to equate sophistication with cultural trends in vogue in Europe. The Boedo group was generally less elitist in attitude and more associated with the general populace; novelist Roberto Arlt was the principal influence in this group.

Some of the essayists and thinkers of this period formulated ideas about nation, identity, and cultural autonomy that drew upon the ideas that were in vogue, but their contributions to the broader dialogue were relatively minor and highly derivative. In Argentina, Ricardo Rojas, obviously drawing from Vasconcelos, predicted in *Eurindia* (1924) that the New World would find its emancipatory expression in a new race of people. As Masiello has observed, Rojas uses sexual metaphors to describe Latin America as the passive female, and thus his essays contributed to the masculinist aesthetic that was still powerful in Latin America during this period.[7]

The reviews *Horizontes* and *Irradiador* were organs of *estridentismo*, which arose in 1921 with the affirmations and exaltation of the new technology and new urban lives as promoted in Mexico by Arqueles Vela, Manuel Maples Arce, and Germán Luis Arzubide in their magazine *Actual*. For the most part, the *estridentistas* were poets, but Arqueles Vela wrote the novel *El Café de Nadie* (1926). From 1928 to 1931, the *vanguardia* in Mexico coalesced around the journal *Contemporáneos* and through it promoted the ideas of artistic renovation. The *Contemporáneos* group attempted to open Mexican culture to the latest trends in European art. Its most active members were Jaime Torres Bodet, Gilberto Owen, Salvador Novo, Xavier Villarrutia, and Carlos Pellicer.[8]

In Central America, the most active movement of *vanguardia* was in Nicaragua. The avant-garde manifesto of sorts in Nicaragua was José Coronel Urtecho's sardonic poem "Oda a Rubén Darío." Coronel Urtecho was joined by Pablo Antonio Cuadra, Joaquín Pasos, and

Luis Alberto Cabrales in the publication of several avant-garde periodicals: *Critero* (1929), *rincón de vanguardia* (1931), and *vanguardia*
(1931–1932). By the end of the 1930s, the group was known as the *movimiento de vanguardia*.[9]

Puerto Rico produced numerous groups of *vanguardia*, even
though most of the writers themselves have remained relatively obscure outside of Puerto Rico. The poet Evaristo Rivera Chevremont
brought *ultraísmo* from Spain to Puerto Rico, thus serving in the
intermediary role (between Europe and Latin America) for Puerto
Rico that Borges served in Argentina and Huidobro in Chile. Nevertheless, the roots and reach of the avant-garde movement in Puerto
Rico were more local than international.[10]

Awareness of the different magazines associated with these groups
is important because, as Unruh has argued, Latin America's *vanguardias* are best understood not in terms of individual works or specific
authors' careers.[11] Rather, they need to be viewed as a multifaceted
cultural activity, expressed in a variety of creative endeavors. Women
played a key role in this as *salonnieres*, directors of cultural magazines, and supporters of the arts. Norah Lange and Victoria Ocampo,
for example, moved in elite lettered circles in Argentina, exercising a
notable influence in the formation of national culture. Along with her
companion Oliverio Girondo, Lange published the magazine *Martín
Fierro;* her prose and verse contributed alternative views of feminine
participation in national culture. Ocampo directed the influential and
prestigious magazine *Sur;* she and Lange functioned as "bridge" figures of the avant-garde.[12]

Political movements in the 1920s and 1930s highlighted the urgent
need for social and political change, and leftist and radical movements
organized with the intention of realizing that change. There was widespread conflict among rising economic groups, new political movements, and the oligarchy that had generally exercised power throughout much of the previous century. In Mexico, power struggles and
conflicts between the state and the church made it impossible to realize the programs of social, economic, and political change implied
in the Constitution of 1917. Uruguay attempted to enact social and
economic reforms similar to those of Mexico, promulgating a constitution in 1917 that provided for a commission-type government,
but a lack of land reform and other problems limited the success of
the Uruguayan experiment. In Argentina, an oligarch with alliances
with Hipólito Irigoyen of the Radical Party, Marcelo T. Alvear, was

elected president in 1922. The reign of the Radical Party was brief, however, for Alvear's alliances with key elements of the Radical Party broke down within three years. The Communist Party of Chile arose in the 1920s, corresponding to the election of conservative Arturo Alessandri. Unable to carry forth a successful political program for either the left or the right in Chile, Alessandri was deposed by the military. Class conflicts and strikes led to devastating massacres of workers in several Latin American nations in the 1920s, two of the most controversial being the ones in Ecuador in 1922 and Colombia in 1928.

In the Caribbean region, widespread economic crises and poverty led to uprisings, new political organizations, and union organizing. In Puerto Rico, Albizú Campos headed a nationalist movement in the 1920s that led to the formation of the Partido Unión. This nationalism promoted political independence from the United States and the importance of the Spanish language. Populism, modernization, and political realism (i.e., negotiation with the United States) resulted in the rise of two elements in Puerto Rico: the Partido Popular Democrático and the concept of the Estado Libre Asociado, which was born in 1928. Rebellions took place in St. Kitts, St. Vincent, and St. Lucia in 1935 and in Barbados in 1937. In 1938, the Barbados Progressive League was formed and soon thereafter the Barbados Labour Party and Barbados Workers Union.

Following the Semana de Arte Moderna in 1922, Brazil entered a period of cultural nationalism and intense creativity. With the rise of modernism, Brazilian novelists such as Oswald de Andrade and Mário de Andrade transgressed the norms of traditional fiction with multiple kinds of formal and linguistic experimentation. Two of Oswald de Andrade's most experimental works of this type were *Memórias sentimentais de João Miramar* (1924) and *Serafim Ponte Grande* (1933). Mário de Andrade's *Macunaíma* (1928) was a valuable and exceptionally well-conceived contribution to avant-garde fiction.

With respect to the novelists of this period, there was a growing awareness of both their modernity and their immediate surroundings. The latter produced an increasing interest in regionalist novels. The masters of the traditional (realist-naturalist) forms were Ricardo Guiraldes, Teresa de la Parra, Rómulo Gallegos, and José Eustasio Rivera. These four novelists published their major works in the 1920s, and by the 1940s Guiraldes, Rivera, and Gallegos were recognized in their respective homelands not only as masters of the art of fiction but,

more important, as the creators of national identity, authentic representatives of a national literary tradition, and leaders in the quest for
cultural autonomy. In each case, there were significant cultural and
political reasons—the momentum of nation building provided cultural and political justification for promoting their works as part of
a national literary culture—that their works were much-needed cultural artifacts of what was promoted as authentically national literary
culture. In this sense, Guiraldes's *Don Segundo Sombra,* Rivera's *La
vorágine,* and Gallegos's *Doña Bárbara* were the foundational novels
in Argentina, Colombia, and Venezuela.

Noncanonical novelists such as the Colombians César Uribe
Piedrahita and Bernardo Arias Trujillo as well as the Argentine Benito
Lynch wrote fiction that was part of the *criollista* dialogue popularized in the novels by Guiraldes, Rivera, and Gallegos. These were
writers who also thought of themselves as modern but were concerned with how cultural autonomy and national identity might be
found in the growing tensions between rural and urban life, or in
essence, tradition versus the modern. In their work, they had different responses to this question. Uribe Piedrahita's *Toá* (1933) and Arias
Trujillo's *Risaralda* (1935) are also novels of social criticism.

Uribe Piedrahita's project is similar to many of that period in Latin
America in that the author contributes to the New World identity
by focusing on a social group that is "less sophisticated, less cultivated [in the European sense] than the city-dwelling members of the
ruling class."[13] Sophisticated and cultivated in the European sense
here refers to one's knowledge of writing culture. In *Toá,* the basic
model is clearly set forth: the outsider Antonio (to whom the narrator
refers even late in the novel as "visiting doctor") experiences a series
of lessons as part of his possible integration into this New World.
Early in the novel the difference between this world and his previous
cosmopolitan life is vividly delineated, as the narrator explains how
the protagonist desires to experience the "strange landscapes of that
new world." The adjectives "strange" and "new" obviously promise
the reader a New World encounter.

Despite Antonio's fascination with this new world, his sympathy
for its exploited people, and his love for Toá, his process of learning is,
in fact, a failure. During the second half of the novel, when he is active
in this new context, he does not fit comfortably with the locals nor is
he physically strong enough to withstand the environment. Near the
end of the work the narrator describes Antonio as "exhausted from

the trip to the jungle."[14] *Toá* follows a typical model of the New World protagonist who becomes so lost in nature that he ceases to function as a social human being.[15] This work is considerably closer than many Spanish American novels of the period to the *criollista* novel.[16]

Arias Trujillo was more explicitly interested in being modern than was Uribe Piedrahita. In his *Risaralda*, Arias Trujillo promises in its subtitle to revolutionize the local obsession with classical humanism, announcing it as a "film written in Spanish and spoken in *criollo.*" He only partially delivers on this promise of modernity combined with local culture. With respect to the potential film (and modernity) in this novel, the promise remains virtually unfulfilled. The only exception is chapter 30, which includes the subtitle "(Projected in slow motion)" and does change in narrative technique. Arias Trujillo, like Guiraldes, Rivera, and Uribe Piedrahita, was committed to defining a national identity by appealing to regional values.

Benito Lynch wrote several books of fiction during this period that were also part of the dialogue on national identity. The short novel *La evasión* (1922) is a continuation of Lynch's interest in portraying authentic Argentine society as *gaucho* life on the estancia. Lynch characterizes protagonist Jaime Frasser as the ideal physical presence in an idealized rural setting. Lynch was a typical author of masculinist aesthetics, and Frasser is described early in the novel as projecting "perfect" and "harmonious" masculinity.[17] The novelette tells the story of this strong-willed protagonist and his young love, Mabel.

In his fiction, Lynch promotes traditional and rural values and, in turn, the importance of oral culture, just as do many of these *criollista* writers.[18] In *El inglés de los guesos*, Lynch portrays the life of a kind of tenant farmer *(puestero)* named Juana Fuentes who works the land while the owners dedicate themselves to business in the city. A British student of anthropology appears on the *estancia* to carry out research and excavations on a fossil bed. The foreign student has a love affair that ends in the suicide of his lover. Through this narrative Lynch is able to provide his idea of the intimate relationship between the *gaucho* and this land, as well as regular digressions for the portrayal of local customs and folklore.

As the dialogue on identity and nationhood intensified into the 1930s, so did the relative sophistication of narrative technique and form. Two novels that joined in the cultural dialogue yet were also a step closer to the modernism of the Latin American novel of the 1940s were *Vidas secas* (1934) by the Brazilian Graciliano Ramos and Demetrio Aguilera Malta's *Don Goyo* (1933). Both novelists demonstrate their technical mastery of structure. *Don Goyo* is set on islands off the coast of Ecuador and deals primarily with two fishermen, Don Goyo and Cusumbo. Aguilera Malta uses a harmonious three-part structure that involves flashbacks to characterize the two characters fully. The author's use of the strategies of both modernist fiction and oral tradition creates some effects that became associated with "magic realism" decades later, making Aguilera Malta yet another important forerunner to the rise of modernist fiction in the 1940s and the more recognized Boom of the 1960s.[19]

In addition to a growing interest in the immediate physical surroundings and nation building, there was also a growing awareness of the social and economic consequences of Latin America's troubled modernity, an increased interest on the part of the writers in these social problems, and early attempts to portray class conflict in fiction. The fiction of Edwards Bello, such as the novel *El roto* (1920), exhibits some of these ongoing concerns. *El roto* tells the story of a young boy, Esmeraldo, and portrays his environment—urban slums in Chile. The center of the story is a bordello. Written with the documentary detail of the realist-naturalist tradition, *El roto* is one of numerous indicators that the realist-naturalist mode had reached its apogee in Latin America in the 1920s.

Leónidas Barletta, Martín Luis Guzmán, and José A. Osorio Lizarazo were also writers with social and political interests. In his novel *Royal Circo*, Barletta's message is unclear and his narrative strategies simple, while his thematic interest is the suffering of common people. Guzmán regales his readers with an insider's view of Mexican politics. His fictions *El águila y la serpiente* and *La sombra del caudillo* are more nuanced political novels than Barletta's. In the former, he reveals the character of Mexican political leaders, and in the latter he fictionalizes the supposedly real happenings in the Mexican political scene after the Mexican Revolution. Its plot centers on the individual in conflict with the collectivity. Osorio Lizarazo published numerous novels of social protest; his main contribution in Colombia was the fact that he was an urban writer. In *La casa de vecindad* (1930), he focuses enough on the characterization of the protagonist to save his work from an overly simplistic presentation of class conflict. In this case, the individual is overwhelmed by the collectivity.

Some of the most classic novels of protest were of *indigenista* themes, and two such texts are Jorge Icaza's *Huasipungo* (1934) and

Gregorio López y Fuentes's *El indio* (1935). In *Huasipungo*, the reader is made privy to the exploitation of the Indians in Ecuador, where they are driven off their parcels of land or *huasipungas*. Fictionalizing the classic power structure triangle of the government, the church, and the local oligarchy, Icaza portrays the human dimension of individuals in the situation. The ugly and extreme violence of the novel shocks the reader into an understanding of the social circumstance. López y Fuentes takes a different approach in *El indio*, characterizing the collectivity as an archetype rather than characterizing the individual. Set in postrevolutionary Mexico, this novel suggests the history of Indians since the time of the conquest.[20]

Huasipungo and *El indio* are stories of cultural resistance, as are Chicano narratives published during this period. An early predecessor to the first Chicano novels to be published decades later, Américo Paredes's story "The Hammon and the Beans" (ca. 1939) is set in the Lower Rio Grande Valley of South Texas, an area of intense border conflict. The story is about an individual's experience in this conflict in the aftermath of an armed uprising by Mexican Americans seeking justice with pistols in hand.

Two masters of the traditional art of storytelling who were just as accomplished in their art as de la Parra, Guiraldes, or Gallegos—yet as concerned about society as Guzmán and Osorio Lizarazo—were Mariano Azuela and Arturo Uslar Pietri. These two, along with Aguilera Malta, published some of the most nuanced and successful fiction of the 1930s. Azuela shows a control of narrative techniques more associated with the new aesthetics of the avant-garde in *La luciérnaga*. In this story, a young man from the provinces attempts to survive in the city, where the changes in postrevolutionary Mexico created numerous social problems. By using a variety of techniques of interiorization (such as interior monologue), Azuela reveals the protagonist's sense of confusion and helplessness in the new urban space. The reality of postrevolutionary Mexico is as ambiguous for this protagonist as it is for the two main characters of *Las lanzas coloradas* (1931), which is set in the period of the war of independence in Venezuela. The two main characters, however, are unclear and ambiguous about their reasons for fighting in the war.

Novelists of the *vanguardia*, such as Dulce María Loynaz, Gilberto Owen, Macedonio Fernández, Jaime Torres Bodet, Xavier Villaurrutia, Vicente Huidobro, Juan Filloy, and Enrique Labrador Ruiz, published novels with an obvious awareness of modernism and the incipient modernity of Latin American, North American, and European societies. Beyond being strictly novelists, they were engaged in the broader activity of modernizing Spanish American fiction. María Luisa Bombal and Adolfo Bioy Casares wrote with an interest in storytelling and awareness of modernist technique that brought them closer to the *vanguardia* than Aguilera Malta and Uslar Pietri. The main character in Loynaz's *Jardín* (1935, published in 1951) is a young woman, Bárbara, who lives with her black maid, Laura. The setting is an old home with a garden in Havana. In the second half of the novel, the story moves back to the nineteenth century and relates the relationship between another Bárbara (great-grandmother of the protagonist) and an adolescent. After the return to the twentieth century, the protagonist goes to Europe with a lover and suffers a tragic death with him at the end. Described by Sklodowska as a hidden jewel of avant-garde narrative, *Jardín* is also an early feminist novel that questions the values of traditional patriarchal society.[21]

Loynaz, Owen, Fernández, and many others of these novelists of *vanguardia* often related the stories of the interior lives of their characters rather than dwelling on their immediate surroundings. Owen's *Novela como nube* is the story of the protagonist's search for the ideal woman. The author uses surrealist imagery to communicate the moods of this protagonist; in the end, the vague imagery blurs what is real about the women and blurs the novel's meaning. Fernández's *Papeles de Recienvenido* (1929) is even more radical in its irreverence toward everyday, empirical reality, for the narrator's perspective is frequently incongruent with standard perceptions of reality. The special and particular feature of this book, however, is its tone, for Fernández found humor in the irrational and in paradox.

Enrique Labrador Ruiz and José Felix Fuenmayor also adopted playful and humorous stances toward reality in their novels of *vanguardia*. In *Laberinto de sí mismo* (1933), Labrador Ruiz portrays pencils in playful dialogue with each other. It is a surprisingly self-conscious and introspective novel for the period and one in which everything is in a constant process of disintegration. Fuenmayor's *Cosme* (1927) is equally playful in tone, although not as self-conscious and introspective. This novel is the entertaining and tragic story of the protagonist, Cosme, growing up in the new, modernizing Barranquilla (Colombia) of the 1920s. *Cosme* is not a novel of elaborate characterizations or profound psychological development. In contrast to the excessive emotion in many of the *criollista* novels of this period—such as *La vorágine*—in *Cosme* the characters function as an element of the novel's play, entering with little or no introduction on the narrator's part. The modernity of *Cosme* is not so much in its use of the narrative techniques of modernism as in its dialogue on the conflict between tradition and modernity.

Fuenmayor is not generally recognized as a writer central to the Latin American *vanguardia*. He, Roberto Arlt, and Norah Lange wrote on the margins of both the elite circles of the avant-garde and the mainstream of more popular fiction. In Lange's novel *45 días y 30 marineros* (1933), a ship removes passengers from their everyday lives. The exceptionality of this novel is the fictionalization of female eroticism, although it shares questions of national identity that are common themes of novels of this period. Arlt was also a special case with respect to the avant-garde movements: he shares some of their interests but is different enough from them to not be generally associated with the *vanguardia*. Arlt's three novels, *El juguete rabioso* (1926), *Los siete locos* (1929), and *Los lanzallamas* (1931), are an urban trilogy that gained more of a readership than most fiction of the *vanguardia*. The narrator-protagonist, Silvio Astier, tells of his intellectual interests (which include the works of Baudelaire, Dostoyevsky, and Baroja) and relates the process of growing up. His adolescent adventures involve petty crimes, working in a bookstore, attempting to become an airplane mechanic, and working as a stationery salesman. In all these anecdotes, his uncontrolled imagination seems to interfere with his ability to deal with everyday life. In *Los siete locos*, the protagonist, Erdosain, is an anguished individual whose cohorts are a group of unstable friends (the *locos*) who organize a secret society. Arlt continues Erdosain's story in *Los lanzallamas*; both the protagonist's anguish and his group's insanity become more intense. The most outstanding element (something of an anomaly) of these three novels is Arlt's style: his prose is not as refined and metaphorical as that of either the avant-garde writers (with whom he shares some interests) or the *criollistas*.

Torres Bodet's first three novels—*Margarita de niebla* (1927), *La educación sentimental* (1929), and *Proserpina rescatada* (1931)—were typical examples of *vanguardia* fiction both in terms of theme and technique. *Margarita de niebla* has little of a conventional plot and vague characters that are sometimes difficult to decipher. Torres Bodet wrote essays in favor of a new kind of novel, and among these works of the new novel, in addition to those already mentioned, were

Dama de corazones (1928) by Xavier Villaurrutia and *El joven* (1928) by Salvador Novo.

Villaurrutia's only novel, *Dama de corazones*, is a short work of less than fifty pages. It is virtually plotless and, as Frank Dauster argues, contains a style in which a number of lyrical passages are similar to poetry arranged in prose form.[22] *Dama de corazones* is the story of Julio, a Mexican exchange student in the United States who returns to Mexico for a visit with his aunt and two cousins. He spends much of the novel with questions over the identity of these women, as well as offering numerous digressions on topics such as literature, travel, death, and the very concept of character. As D'Lugo has observed, Villaurrutia eschews conventional notions of plot and character development and invites the reader to consider the process of narration.[23] Like Fuenmayor, Juan Filloy was a marginal figure of the avantgarde, yet his novel *Op Oloop* (1934) has had a small group of devoted readers. Filloy tells the story of a Finnish resident in Buenos Aires; the reader observes the protagonist's disintegration over a period of twenty-four hours. Writing in the Joycean tradition, Filloy is devoted to language play in itself and often with humorous consequences. The novel's outcome—the protagonist's suicide—however, is not humorous and leaves the reader to continue the protagonist's speculations about the rationality of the supposedly harmonious and rational order.

In the 1920s and 1930s, the writers' desire to be modern—as it was played out in the cultural wars of the period—meant a predominance of a realist-naturalist type of fiction that has generally been categorized as traditional with respect to form. In a book published in 1939, the prominent critic Arturo Torres Rioseco wrote: "The purely psychological novel with no external movement, and the metapsychic novel oriented toward the realm of dreams, have had their cultivators in our countries (C. A. Leumann, Torres Bodet, etc.), but they are inappropriate forms of expression for peoples of such an intense objective life and of such limited literary culture."[24] As Pérez Firmat has argued convincingly, vanguard fiction exists between parentheses.[25] From its inception, the novel of *vanguardia* occupied a liminal space—a parenthetical placement—that has been amply documented in the hostile articles and reviews written at the time. The comment by Torres Rioseco is one telling example of this reaction. The questions that interested Torres Bodet, Macedonio Fernández, and these other writers of *vanguardia*—such as characterization in fiction—were of relatively little interest to most readers and critics at the time. Alejo Carpentier and Demetrio Aguilera Malta, in *Ecué-Yamba-o* (1933) and *Don Goyo*, respectively, bridged the gap for many readers and critics who shared some of the interests of the modernists but were also deeply concerned with the debates on identity and cultural autonomy in the New World.

During this period, the mass marketing of novels became an increasingly important factor in the production of literature. For example, the Argentine Hugo Wast's *Lucía Miranda* (1929) offered a plot of action and adventure directed to the new middle-class reading public. In the 1920s and 1930s, all three of the *criollista* classics—*La vorágine, Don Segundo Sombra,* and *Doña Bárbara*—were promoted as best-sellers in their respective nations. At the same time that these novels were being promoted for mass consumption, periodicals such as *La novela semanal* circulated brief fictions for middle-class readers.

The dominance of upper- and middle-class male writers prevailed, to a large extent, well into the 1920s and 1930s. Indeed, the *criollista* classics served not only to build nations but also to reinforce the role of the old oligarchies as well as of those close to these oligarchies. Nevertheless, the presence of oppositional writing of cultural resistance as seen in *Huasipungo* and *El indio* was increasingly evident. Women novelists such as Teresa de la Parra, María Luisa Bombal, Dulce Loynaz, and Norah Lange were a significant response to what had been a predominantly masculinist aesthetic at the beginning of the century.

In the formation of national cultures, a variety of heterogeneous forces were in play by the 1920s and 1930s. Many of the most successful mainline writers of *criollismo*, such as Guiraldes and Gallegos, were among the most competent in incorporating the oral tradition into fiction. They seemed to articulate the case for cultural autonomy most forcefully. The authors who wrote novels fundamentally in opposition to both mainstream fiction and early pulp fiction were the novelists of cultural resistance of *indigenismo*, the innovative fictions of *vanguardia*, and the alternative writings of women. Certainly there were other noteworthy writers of the avant-garde, among them the Mexicans Efrén Hernández, Salvador Novo, and

Arqueles Vela, the Argentine Oliverio Girondo, the Chilean Pablo Neruda, the Ecuadorian Pablo Palacio, the Uruguayan Felisberto Hernández, and the Venezuelan Julio Garmendia.[26]

In the next chapter of the Latin American novel—the 1940s—the modernist novel was finally an "appropriate" form for the culture. The writers' desire to be modern, in effect, had become a more generalized desire in Latin American society in the process of urbanization and modernization of Indo-Afro-Iberoamerican culture. Given the need for a clearly identifiable national literature in each country of Latin America and given the schematic and seemingly incomplete appearance of many of the texts of *vanguardia*, the cultural scene of the 1920s appeared contradictory and occasionally confusing for much of the new middle-class readership. Nevertheless, a new heterogeneity was increasingly evident.

Four **Rereading Spanish American**
Criollista Classics

The traditionalist writers pursued their search for the
modern in the form of *criollista* novels. Canonical works written in
the traditional (realist-naturalist) mode in Spanish America were *La
vorágine* (1924) by José Eustasio Rivera, *Don Segundo Sombra* (1926)
by Ricardo Guiraldes, *Las memorias de Mamá Blanca* (1929) by Teresa
de la Parra, and *Doña Bárbara* (1929) by Rómulo Gallegos. These
writers were seen as Latin American masters of the traditional craft
of fiction, although their works were affected by the *vanguardia*, too.[1]
Their desire to be modern varied; in all cases they held ambiguous and
contradictory attitudes about what they understood as modern. These
four novels were, nevertheless, important texts for nation building
and the search for cultural autonomy, even though they and others
like them were often closely associated with the old aristocracy and
its patriarchal order.[2]

The critical bibliography of these novels is substantive, consisting
of a lengthy list of studies published since the 1920s but primarily
from the 1930s to the 1950s, when the *criollista* novel was still in
vogue. Carlos Alonso has analyzed the discourse of cultural autoch-
thony that has become virtually synonymous with the novelistic production of Rivera, Guiraldes, Gallegos, and many other Latin American writers of the 1920s and 1930s.[3] Alonso argues that the search for
an indigenous cultural identity should be understood as an attempt to
empower the Latin American writer in the face of modernity's threat
to undermine the authority of his discourse.

The writers of the 1960s Boom were modernity's latest and most devastating threat to the authority of the regionalist discourse, which prevailed well into the 1950s. In both their fiction and their critical essays, the writers of the Boom published essays that were devastating for the *criollista* masters. In his widely read *Nueva novela hispanoamericana* (1969), Carlos Fuentes claimed that these classic texts led to essentially the same outcome: the protagonists were devoured by nature (the jungle, the *llano*, and so forth). Vargas Llosa, morever, made numerous references to these novels as "primitive."

For Doris Sommer, on the other hand, these *criollista* novels were an entire canon of "great novels" that the writers of the Boom dismissed all too easily.[4] More importantly for Sommer, they were key texts in the history of nation building. Following the example of Benedict Anderson, Sommer stresses the continuities between this nation building and print communities formed around newspapers and novels. Sommer shows how national ideals are grounded in heterosexual relationships that provided a figure for national consolidation. She reminds readers that before the Boom, Latin American literature had the capacity to intervene in history, to help construct it.[5]

As realist-naturalist writers, as well as for their search for an indigenous identity, Guiraldes, Gallegos, and Rivera were the most recognized novelists of the period. *Don Segundo Sombra* chronicles a young boy's rite de passage in the process of becoming a *gaucho* and an adult. *Doña Bárbara* is the tale of a conflict between civilization and barbarism. *La vorágine* is ostensibly the story of the protagonist's adventure into the Colombian jungle. All three are novels of adventures—the protagonists travel from the city to a rural area. In *Las memorias de Mamá Blanca*, the protagonist eventually travels from her idyllic hacienda to the city, although the novel deals primarily with her experience as a child on the hacienda.

Don Segundo Sombra consists of twenty-seven chapters narrated by the protagonist, Fabio. The general setting is the pampa of Argentina. In the first part, which consists of nine chapters, the orphaned Fabio is fourteen years old and departs with the gaucho Don Segundo Sombra. During these apprenticeship years, Fabio learns the ways of the gaucho from Don Segundo. In the second part of nine chapters, five years have passed and the young boy has become an adult and a gaucho. In the third part, Fabio and Don Segundo are occasionally together, but this part also tells of Fabio inheriting land and learning how to read and write literature. Throughout the novel, Guiraldes describes the autochthonous elements of life on the pampa.

In this three-part structure, Guiraldes uses water imagery with a variety of functions. The novel opens as follows: "En las afueras del pueblo, a unas diez cuadras de la plaza céntrica, el puente viejo tiende su arco sobre el río, uniendo las quintas al campo tranquilo" (On the edge of town, some 10 blocks from the central plaza, the old bridge stretches its arch over the river, uniting the houses to the tranquil country).[6] The young Fabio has come to his fishing spot, but on this occasion he experiences a different feeling: "Mi humor no era el de siempre" (I wasn't feeling normal; *Don Segundo Sombra*, 11). He remembers his separation from his mother in his childhood and the vagabond ways that had led him to this river. In this opening of the novel, then, water imagery is associated with his reflections upon his past or, as one critic has identified this moment, his "taking stock" of his life and situation.[7] At the beginning of chapter 10, five years later, his gaze falls over a river once again, causing him to reflect on his experiences. He reflects on his years of gaucho life.

Fabio explains that he has matured from a young boy to a gaucho. And at the beginning of the novel's last chapter, Fabio approaches water once again—a laguna—and enters into more reflections on his life:

> Está visto que en mi vida el agua es como un espejo en que desfilan las imágenes del pasado. A orillas de un arroyo resumí antaño mi niñez. Dando de beber a mi caballo en la picada de un río, revisé cinco años de andanzas gauchas. Por último, sentado sobre la pequeña barranca de una laguna, en mis posesiones, consultaba mentalmente mi diario de patrón. [It is evident that in my life, water is like a mirror in which images of the past parade by. At the edge of a river I synthesized my childhood. Giving my horse a drink of water in a river, I reconsidered five years of gaucho wanderings. Finally, seated on the small bank of a pond, in control of myself, I mentally consulted my diary as landowner.] (*Don Segundo Sombra*, 182)

In addition to this use of water imagery to create both a sense of coherence and a sense of the protagonist's changes, Guiraldes employs two basic stylistic registers throughout *Don Segundo Sombra*. On the one hand, the author continues in the stylistic mode of traditional *literatura gauchesca* by imitating rural colloquial language, primarily in the speech of characters but also in the language of the narrator-protagonist. This is the language of the oral traditions of rural speech on the pampa. On the other hand, Guiraldes frequently employs the elegant literary language of the most accomplished *buen escribir*, or "good style," as it was called. His use of water imagery is comparable to Azuela's symbols of the Mexican landscape. Guiraldes occasionally uses imagery more associated with the *vanguardia*. These two stylistic registers, one more traditional and one more modern, reveal Guiraldes's ambiguous desire to be modern.

In many ways, *Don Segundo Sombra* is the epitome of the well-crafted fiction in Latin America. The three-part structure constructed around water imagery gives the novel a sense of coherence and unity that is comparable to Azuela's success with the spiral structure of *Los de abajo*; this coherence and unity is not as evident in *Doña Bárbara*. As perhaps the most accomplished piece of traditional fiction of the three classic *criollista* novels of the 1920s, *Don Segundo Sombra* arguably represents the apogee of the realist-naturalist mode that had continued to be written since the nineteenth century.[8] Nevertheless, numerous critics have pointed to its flaws. For example, one prominent critic has observed that Fabio is not a real-life boy; he is a generalization of the urban adolescent with romanticized ideas about life in the country.[9] For this reader, it requires a considerable stretch of the imagination to first accept Fabio's adaptation to the gaucho life, then his equally difficult adaptation to urban life of high literary culture.

For Alonso, *Don Segundo Sombra* is, in reality, the narration of how a boy simultaneously becomes both a landowner and the writer of an autochthonous text.[10] This critic argues that, as Fabio becomes more educated, he "earns" the right to his new status as landowner. He has also mastered the knowledge of the gaucho life, which is a discipline in itself. It could also be stated that it is not just becoming a gaucho that earns Fabio his ultimate success. Rather, it is the dual discipline of learning to write and learning gaucho ways that leads to his final success. In terms of nation building, Guiraldes points to literary education and literature as positive elements for the new nation.

Critical readings of *Don Segundo Sombra* have also emphasized the contradiction between Guiraldes the privileged landowner and Guiraldes the promoter of gaucho values. The privileged author, according to many of these critics, was too elitist in worldview and literary style to successfully tell the story of the gaucho and his values. For these critics, the expression of the national essence is not viable because of Guiraldes's inevitable elitism.[11]

Doña Bárbara is the longest (and perhaps the most unwieldy) of these four *criollista* novels; it consists of three parts and a total of forty-one chapters (432 pages in a Mexican edition of 1971).[12] Despite its title, it is really the story of Santos Luzardo's "heroic" journey.[13] In this journey, Luzardo leaves Caracas and goes to the *llano*, where he hopes to recoup the land of his estate Altamira and sell it. Having heard of the "barbarity" of doña Bárbara, he also intends to "civilize" her and rural Venezuela as part of his civilizing project for the nation.

Like *Don Segundo Sombra*, *Doña Bárbara* consists of three parts, but it lacks the harmonious and unified tripartite structure so evident in the Argentine classic. The lengthy (175-page) first part consists of thirteen chapters in which the author introduces the numerous characters and conflicts that inform the central conflict between *civilización* and *barbarie*. In the opening chapter, Santos Luzardo travels along the Arauca river through the *llano*. The narrator characterizes doña Bárbara as a person about whom terrible things are said, even though she does not appear in the chapter. Equally terrible and threatening is nature, which is omnipresent in this first chapter.

Proceeding in the systematic manner of the realist novelist, the second chapter provides more background to the conflicts over the land and the Altamira ranch: family disputes between the Luzardos and the Barqueros go back to the colonial period, and the "famous" doña Bárbara became involved in land disputes. Santos Luzardo's mission in this *barbarie* is described as a dual task: to civilize the region and to civilize the impetuous doña Bárbara. The third chapter, titled "La devadora de hombres," characterizes doña Bárbara in more detail, describing her "perturbadora belleza" (disturbing beauty) and her being raped in her youth. The narrator freely makes mention of the numerous legends that surround her, including her supposed pact with the devil and her reputation for being a witch. The third chapter concludes with a description of doña Bárbara's character as cruel and superstitious. The remainder of the first part offers more detailed descriptions of the land and nature, the introduction of additional characters (Balbino Paiba, Marisela, El Pajarote, Mister Danger), and descriptions of rural customs and legal battles over the land. Lorenzo Barquero is portrayed as doña Bárbara's pathetic victim, an ex-lover who fathered doña Bárbara's daughter Marisela. Toward the end of Part I, Santos Luzardo falls in love with this distant relative, the now adolescent Marisela. Also introduced here is the infantile and "barbarous" North American, Mister Danger.

In the lengthy Part II (containing thirteen chapters), the conflict over property rights intensifies, and Gallegos further develops his *criollista* interests. Santos Luzardo becomes more committed to the legal technicalities of his right to the land held by doña Bárbara, who proves to be a cattle rustler in addition to engaging in other illegal activities. Luzardo continues his educating of Marisela, who is transformed into an attractive and civilized young woman. Luzardo also rediscovers his own national roots in local customs, being reminded of his former knowledge of cattle and cowboy culture when he observes a rodeo (Part II, chapter 4, "El Rodeo"). Doña Bárbara is also momentarily transformed by Santos Luzardo (chapter 5) and shows a romantic interest in him. A considerable portion of Part II consists of detailed descriptions of customs on the *llano*.

Part III (fifteen chapters) dramatizes the denouement of the conflict between Santos Luzardo and doña Bárbara, between feuding families, and, in a broader sense, between civilization and barbarism. In the end, some of the characters are consumed by nature, killed by natural forces; Luzardo marries Marisela; and doña Bárbara is a transformed person: she gives her land to Marisela and then disappears.

A paradoxical precedent to this novel was the support that the Venezuelan political figure Juan Vicente Gómez had received in 1909 from Gallegos and his peers, populists who favored the application of high-minded principles and an absolute respect for the law. But Gómez turned out to be a ruthless dictator who had alienated intellectuals and local elites alike by the time Gallegos began to write *Doña Bárbara*. At the time of its publication, this novel was read in Venezuela as an attack on Gomez's dictatorship; as Mariano Picón Salas has pointed out: "se vio en la diabólica varona, vengativa, cruel y oscura, la imagen de la tiranía" (in the diabolical figure, vengeful, cruel, and dark, the image of tyranny is seen).[14] In the 1930s and 1940s, *Doña Bárbara* was not only canonized as Venezuela's national novel, but it also served as the opposition intellectuals' narrative projection of a future victory and a future nation.[15] Produced as a film in 1943, *Doña Bárbara* reached a public that elected Gallegos as a populist candidate representing the Acción Democrática.

Gallegos's faith in constitutional principles and respect for the law is indeed evident in *Doña Bárbara*. Santos Luzardo is presented as the most positive and admirable character in the novel, above all because he has the most sophisticated understanding of property law and the most consistent adherence to its principles. Clearly, Gallegos's idea for the new civilized nation is one in which the law is followed to the letter.

For Sommer, *Doña Bárbara* is Gallegos's "fantasy of return and repair."[16] It envisions a liberation from an internal tyrant (Bárbara/the dictator Gómez) and her external ally (Mister Danger/the oil industry). This was a landmark novel for a modernizing program for Venezuela and more specifically for modernizing the nation's ranches. The backward ranches and medieval political and judicial practices effected in the rural areas, in fact, threatened any idea of "progress." Sommer concludes, referring to Marisela, that Santos Luzardo's offer of legal and loving status to Marisela "shows Gallegos trying to patch up the problem of establishing a legitimate, centralized nation on a history of usurpation and civil war."[17]

Doña Bárbara not only is a novel written clearly within the parameters of *criollista* ideals, but it also is the most closely and consistently dedicated to this project of the four novels discussed in this chapter. Like the other novelists, Gallegos invents a narrator who makes use of regionalisms to describe the flora and fauna of the New World.

Gallegos's modernizing mission in *Doña Bárbara* is most evident. If only Venezuela's uneducated could be educated (i.e., civilized) and if only the ranches on the *llano* could be modernized, national life in Venezuela supposedly would improve. Thus, Santos's mission is to educate Marisela. Similarly, Santos's struggle with Bárbara is another aspect of the conflict between the modernizing centralists and the violently independent regionalists in Venezuela.[18]

Guiraldes and Rivera had paradoxically mixed feelings about modernity, and Gallegos likewise exhibits these ambiguous desires to be modern. On the one hand, this Venezuelan author seems to favor modernizing the *llano*, in effect, populating rural Venezuela with people who would provide the accoutrements of modern life. On the other hand, Gallegos celebrates many of the traditional, folkloric aspects of Venezuelan culture that might well disappear upon modernization. Tradition may be a source of national pride, but it is also associated with economic and cultural backwardness.[19]

Interestingly, the implied author of *Doña Bárbara* seems to be in favor of modernity in some passages of the novel and against it in others. He consistently favors progress and the modernization of the haciendas. On the other hand, he exhibits negative attitudes toward the United States, presenting all aspects of modernity of U.S. origin in a negative light. Thus, Gallegos the cultural nationalist undermines his own ideas about progress and modernization.

Doña Bárbara is not only the longest and most unwieldy of these *criollista* classics—it is also the most ambitious. Indeed, unlike *Don Segundo Sombra* and *La vorágine*, this novel attempts to be that "total novel" that would interest the writers of the Boom several decades later.[20] If we examine Robin William Fiddian's outline for the total novels of the 1960s, *Doña Bárbara* shares several of their characteristics.[21] Like the total novel, *Doña Bárbara* aspires to represent an "inexhaustive" reality and cultivates a broad range of encyclopedic references. The encyclopedic effect in *Doña Bárbara* is particularly evident in the numerous passages of *criollista* content, as in the lengthy and detailed descriptions of the flora and fauna of the Americas, as well as in the equally long descriptions of customs of the *llanos*.

Fiddian also proposes that the total novel is conceived as a system contained in itself, or as a microcosm of signification whose main element is ambiguity. In the case of *Doña Bárbara*, the *llano* does become a microcosm of sorts, and Gallegos's efforts to create ambiguity are perhaps more evident than many modern readers—particularly those writers of the Boom themselves—have been willing to recognize. The author does mitigate the potentially extreme opposition between civilization and barbarism and its multiple parallels, such as man versus woman, by including elements of the opposites in the other. One of the most striking examples of this tendency—given the book's date of publication—is the characterization of doña Bárbara as *andrógina*, an exceptional gender bending that breaks down the male-versus-female dichotomy of the period. Gallegos's characterization of doña Bárbara and his development of a plot with numerous ambiguities would seem to imply his interest in creating the ambiguous and "total" novel. His failure as a creator of lasting ambiguity, as well as his failure to create a modern and total novel, however, is evident on the novel's last page, where all the mysteries of the plot have been solved. One needs also to consider the last paragraph: "¡Llanura venezolana! ¡Propicia para el esfuerzo, como lo fue para la hazaña, tierra de horizontes abiertos, donde una raza buena, ama, sufre y espera!" (Venezuelan plains! Propitious for the effort, as it was for feats, land of open horizons, where a good race of people love, suffers, and waits!; *Doña Bárbara*, 423). With this final line, Gallegos unequivocally confirms his nation-building, *criollista* agenda, leaving no room for ambiguity.

Fiddian's third characteristic of the total novel is the fusion of a historical and mythical vision with a transgression of the conventional norms of narrative economy. This characteristic is important because it suggests that total novels are lengthy and ambitious in framework, an element that *Doña Bárbara* shares with many total novels of the 1960s. Indeed, Gallegos does articulate interests in both Venezuelan history and a tendency to attempt to make Doña Bárbara a character of mythical proportions. Both she and nature, in fact, are depicted in the hyperbolic and legendary terms that are the material of myths. Beyond these three points, a comparison between *Doña Bárbara* and the *novela total* of the 1960s begins to break down. More specifically, Gallegos's novel certainly is not a Joycean text with respect to language.[22] It is, nevertheless, a noteworthy predecessor to the ambitious totalizing efforts of the writers of the Boom.

La vorágine is also an ambitious novel that has elicited ample critical response ever since its publication. Critical readings of *La vorágine* portray a flawed work with multiple sources: romanticism, realism/naturalism, or realism/*criollismo*. One critic has claimed that it is in turn "visionary, mystic, realist, modernist, and melodramatic."[23] Many readers have pointed out the work's defects, stressing problems with the plot. Tomás Carrasquilla, a contemporary of Rivera, described *La vorágine* as a shambles; others have found Cova, the protagonist, unbearable.[24] Later readings embody a similar range of reactions concerning the novel's quality: Randolph Pope absolves Rivera's text by judging Cova's narrative one of a decadent intellectual; Sharon Magnarelli, on the other hand, describes the depiction of woman as a "malevolent being in collaboration with the evil forces of the universe."[25] One assertion can be made on the basis of these three readings: Cova functions exclusively within a plane of writing noetics; he is a product of writing culture.

The narrator-protagonist Arturo Cova has been described as a romantic poet.[26] Certainly much of the text fully supports such a characterization, beginning with Cova's initial portrayal as a free spirit who flees society in search of the ideal. The characterization as romantic poet, however, is only a partial portrayal of the total person. Pope contends that Cova shares many qualities of the decadent intellectual. For Magnarelli, Cova is "seriously demented"; she and others consider him an "unreliable narrator."[27] In fact, Cova is neither demented nor unreliable, and the characterization as romantic poet/decadent intellectual is also too limiting. These characterizations project the image of a "writer." The reader observes a patently literary character creating a self-conscious "literary" text.

The first matter to consider, then, is Cova's supposedly demented

character. Several readers have described him as unstable, irrational, or unreasonable.[28] Indeed, his relationships with women and reactions to his surroundings do indicate unorthodox behavior; his de-
cision to flee from Bogota with Alicia, for instance, is not entirely
reasonable, given the social context. What is unique about Cova's supposed irrationality and instability, however, is its self-consciousness.
Cova himself often qualifies his actions as irrational or his thoughts
as malevolent.[29] Two questions arise when observing such commentary: How literally should it be interpreted? And what could possibly
motivate a self-characterization as an insane person? The answer to
both questions lies in Cova's identity as writer. Interpreted literally,
Cova must be dismissed as a ludicrous madman, as indeed many critics have considered him. He should be seen, rather, as a narrator who
employs a series of strategies in order to effect his characterization as
a writer. At the end of the *primera parte,* Cova watches Franco's house
burn and comments: "In the middle of the flames I began to laugh
like Satan!" Magnarelli contends that his reporting this personal reaction highlights his instability.[30] When Cova makes this oft-quoted
statement, however, Cova the narrator should not be seen as either
diabolical or unstable but rather as attempting to characterize himself
as a literary figure.

Cova's irrationality not only corroborates his characterization as a
writer but functions as a positive antidote to the excessively rational
modern world developing in Colombia. An implied criticism of the
rational arises, for example, when, after a caudillo's greed-driven excesses are described, two characters end the section with the ironic
comment "Logic triumphs! Long live logic!" (*La vorágine,* 134). Here
the modern world of commerce and rationality is placed in opposition
to a romantic world of the "irrational" writer. As such, the authentic Cova is not a demented individual who abuses women (as Magnarelli would have us believe), for this status would require the presence of a human being; lacking the ontological status of being, Cova
is only the figure of a writer. Far from functioning as unreliable narrator, Cova is a paradigm of the model romantic-decadent writer: self-
centered, horrified by a world both vital and decaying around him,
constantly vacillating among multiple duplicities. The telltale indicator of Cova's genuine stability, however, is his consistent insistence
on his instability.

What, then, is the subject of this writer's writing? Readings have
stressed the portrayal of the New World as one of the three classic

criollista texts: civilization versus barbarism, "the evil forces of the universe," and social injustice. Such forces do indeed operate in the fictional world of *La vorágine*. The question, however, is whether these are the primary subject matter—the thematic core of this *criollista* text. The predominant subject of *La vorágine* is not a fictional representation of rural Colombia in 1924, but rather the self in the process of writing.

Several problems arise with reading *La vorágine* as a fictionalized replica of a nation's rural story—as has been seen in the national rural stories of *Don Segundo Sombra* and *Doña Bárbara*. One basic difficulty with such a reading of *La vorágine* as a fictionalized simulacrum of Colombia's rural story is, simply stated, the absence of story. As narrator, Cova constantly vacillates between his roles as creator of story and as narrator of himself. Many of the novel's narrative segments begin not with the subject matter of the external story (that is, Colombia's rural story) but with intrusions about the self. The reader observes Cova reacting to the world rather than fabricating a story.

Given the overwhelming presence of the self in the novel, the story is not essentially of a *vorágine*, of natural phenomena in a New World, but of a self in the process of writing, of establishing a writerly identity that interrupts the narration of a story. Interruptions can appear at the most inopportune moments of the narrative's potential as story. The potential story of an adventure is often subverted by Cova's presence from the beginning of the *segunda parte*. The narrator does not present the Indians as human beings but as the literary figures about whom Cova the writer has read: he characterizes them all as being strong, young, and with Herculean backs (*La vorágine*, 56).

Rejecting the traditional subject matter of *Don Segundo Sombra*, *Las memorias de Mamá Blanca*, and *Doña Bárbara*, and subverting the New World *histoire* from transformation into *récit*, Cova develops as his central subject writing itself: the novel's dynamism is found in the narrator's striving for *écriture*. In addition to his reiterative identification of himself as writer, as an exemplary member of writing culture, the narrator signals the literary quality of his text at the outset with the use of exclusively literary constructions such as the Spanish *pidióme* ("he asked me," rendered in special literary form; *La vorágine*, 7).

The multiple ambiguities with respect to author, writer, narrator, story, and text are a function of the ambiguous genre status of the novel in 1920s Latin America. Oddly enough, Rivera's most significant predecessor and literary model was Jorge Isaacs's romantic classic *María*, which contributes to an understanding of the romantic elements in *La vorágine*. Published some six decades after Isaacs's *María*, *La vorágine* shares approximately the same temporal distance from *María* as does *La vorágine* from readers at the end of the twentieth century. Having been published in several successive editions and read throughout the Hispanic world, *María* was still an understandably viable presence in Colombia during the 1920s.[31]

Modernization, industrialization, and a growing middle class in Colombia during the 1920s fostered an expansion of the reading public. *La vorágine*, like *Don Segundo Sombra* and *Doña Bárbara*, did become a best-seller in its time.[32] Any further statement about this novel's status is more problematic. In *La vorágine*, a plethora of literary conventions and languages is also at work, including realism, *costumbrismo*, decadentism, *modernismo*, and *criollismo*. The text suggests that the empirical author Rivera was unsure or ambivalent about the basic elements of the novel: his own role as author, the narrator's relationship to author and character, and *La vorágine*'s relationship to society. An ambiguous attitude toward rural orality is present in the colloquial language of the dictionary at the end.

The contradictions and ambiguities in *La vorágine* result from its complex dynamics of writer and narrator. It is evident that the function of these elements was not entirely clear to Rivera: he was patently insecure in his role as author. The role of the author, the novel, and the reading public was still in many ways undefined in Colombia and throughout Latin America. Thus, the first edition of *La vorágine* included a supposed *photograph* of the protagonist Arturo Cova![33] The reader must recall, nevertheless, that, rather than simulacra of people, novels are universally composed of language.[34] *La vorágine* is a text about writing—the ambiguities, contradictions, and metaphors are all part of a text striving to attain the status of *écriture*. Despite Carlos Fuentes's admonition that all these early-twentieth-century *criollista* classics were simply variations on the theme "they were devoured by the jungle," *La vorágine* does not play out his pattern in a significant way. The meaningful drama is not the death of Cova or anyone else but rather the survival of the text.

Las memorias de Mamá Blanca has not been as widely recognized as one of the canonical texts of *criollismo* as has the work of Gallegos, Guiraldes, and Rivera. Nevertheless, de la Parra has been increasingly recognized as a major writer, and *Las memorias de Mamá Blanca* is a noteworthy contribution to the cultural dialogue of the 1920s. Described by a traditional scholar in the 1970s as "one of the few good women novelists in Spanish America," de la Parra belonged to the aristocracy of Venezuela and took good literary advantage of contact with writers during a stay in Paris.[35]

De la Parra was as unsure and ambivalent about her role as novelist and the genre of the novel as was Rivera. She uses Rivera's ruse of the "found manuscript"; in this case, she explains in her preface that the manuscript, apparently a partial version of what the reader is to read, was found by the fictionalized author figure. Consequently, part of the drama of this work, as in *La vorágine*, is the adventure of seeing a manuscript becoming a novel. The basic story involves a description of life on the hacienda Piedra Azul and the narrator-protagonist's maturation process on the hacienda. In many ways, *Las memorias de Mamá Blanca* is the classic *criollista* text, with its celebration of local and regional customs. This celebration includes a recognition of the value of oral culture; the oral tradition is exalted as much as writing culture. De la Parra also tends to portray Venezuelan reality in the same Manichean terms of her contemporaries—as *civilización* versus *barbarie.*

Even though her characters finally accept modernization, de la Parra is as ambiguous about traditional and modern values as Gallegos. In this context, the lengthy characterizations of Vicente Cochocho and cousin Juancho are revealing. Vicente Cochocho is portrayed as the idiosyncratic intellectual who dresses poorly because these clothes are "más interesantes" (more interesting).[36] Despite his sloppy physical appearance, he is courteous and, above all, well read. Thus, his character seems to be a synthesis of the rural character of *criollista* ideals yet also refined, inasmuch as most others are able to appreciate the refinement of her "rustic" ways (*Las memorias*, 97). Beyond this compromise of civilization versus barbarism, it is noteworthy that nostalgia is part of his characterization. He encarnates not only certain nineteenth-century rural ideals of Tomás Carrasquilla, but also those of a distant Spanish past.

This characterization of Vicente Cochocho reveals the implicit author's fascination with the old ways that preceded modernization. In contrast, the cousin Juancho is portrayed as progressive liberal. Possessing the *don de la palabra,* he is described as an attractive man of words—a person of both eloquence and verbosity. In terms of modernity, Juancho initially seems to personify the liberal in favor of modern progress. For example, Juancho calls the conservatives "ineptos" (inept). But Juancho has little better to say about his cohorts, the liberals: "¡Son unos ladrones sin idea de conciencia!" (*Las memorias*, 70). He also seems to be a nationalist in favor of the anticipated unity of "los futuros Estados Unidos de Hispanoamérica" (the future United States of Spanish America).

In the end, Juancho is an unreliable political voice and an irrelevant commentator on the modernization of Latin America. He is a consummate raconteur who masters the art of the story without content. Despite Juancho's political inefficiency, the implied author does communicate through him a political vision: the vision of a moralist. With improved moral behavior, de la Parra suggests, things would improve for her nation.

De la Parra and Gallegos agree that moral vision, improved moral behavior, and respect for the law are all the signs of civilization that would lead Venezuela to modernity. *Las memorias de Mamá Blanca* and *Doña Bárbara* invite other comparisons. As Sommer has observed, both novels are about women who break gender stereotypes.[37] Doña Bárbara is the occasionally masculine, occasionally feminine, and sometimes androgynous figure. The masculine older sister of Mamá Blanca, Violeta, is as loved by everyone as Doña Bárbara is seemingly hated by virtually everyone around her.

Las memorias de Mamá Blanca and *Doña Bárbara* are also novels whose central focus is the human character viewed as an essence in the face of social, political, and economic modernization of the nation. In both novels, women who are central to the traditional, rural society come into conflict with men who represent many aspects of change, modernization, and urban society. Rivera seems to fear the rational, while Gallegos is committed to it, seemingly unaware of the multiple contradictions inherent in the vision of his implied author. On the other hand, de la Parra provides more space than either Rivera or Gallegos for both the rational and the irrational, in a fictional world seemingly "doomed" by positive and national change.[38] In her acceptance of the rational and the irrational, de la Parra offers a fictional counterweight to the writing of Rivera and Gallegos.

Like *La vorágine*, *Las memorias de Mamá Blanca* is an unstable fictional text with ambiguous roles for the author, the narrator, and the reader. The novel begins with a prologue in which a young woman explains that she is the de facto editor of Mamá Blanca's posthumous memoirs. The editor-friend was twelve years old, and Mamá Blanca seventy when they were friends. The editor-friend explains her work:

No he podido resistir más tiempo la corriente de mi época y he empren-
dido la tarea fácil y destructora de ordenar las primeras cien páginas
de estas memorias, que Mamá Blanca llamó "retrato de mi memoria" a
fin de darles a la publicidad. [I haven't been able to resist any longer
the currents of my times, and I've undertaken the easy and destructive
task of ordering the first one hundred pages of these memoirs that Mamá
Blanca called "portrait of my memory" in order to give them publicity.]
(*Las memorias de Mamá Blanca,* 13)

The reader is necessarily left speculating exactly what the editor-
friend means by the act of "ordering," as well as speculating why the
task is so "difficult" and "destructive." Given these three words (*ordenar, difícil,* and *destructora*), the reader must assume that the text at
hand is considerably revised from the original memoirs. As such, the
text is an unstable and ambiguous relating of Mamá Blanca's life along
with the editor-friend's subjective story of her *alma* (as she explains
in this preface). Like *La vorágine, Las memorias de Mamá Blanca* is
not only a *criollista* novel of a region, but also the story of an unstable text.

The decade of the 1920s is a period of cultural transformation in Latin America, a period of change from oral to writing culture as the predominant mode of communication. As writers
aware of the oral tradition, these novelists were important precur-
sors for a more successful integration of oral culture in the fiction
of, among others, Carpentier, García Márquez, and Vargas Llosa.[39]
Indeed, in accordance with Alonso, the four novels discussed above
represent a search for indigenous cultural identity in the face of the
threat of modernity. The extent to which this search is truly significant in these texts, however, does vary. This search is quite significant in *Don Segundo Sombra* and *Doña Bárbara* and far less so in *La
vorágine* and *Las memorias de Mamá Blanca.*

All four of these novels were, indeed, important contributions to a
process of nation building. They offered a vision of Argentine, Colombian, and Venezuelan identity during a period when this identity was
not only in doubt, but formed part of a much larger polemic. Clearly,
Rivera and de la Parra were the least willing to define identity in fixed
terms; they were also the most interested in telling other stories besides the national story, such as the stories of their texts. Certainly no
critical readings of the *criollista* classics have had more impact than

the devastatingly negative comments by writers of the Boom. These novelists have been so uniformly critical not only because they view these novels as aesthetically deficient, but also because the novels contained two additional defects: they failed as modernist fiction, and they failed as "total" novels. On the other hand, they were successful as traditional fiction written in the naturalist-realist mode, and they played a central role, as Sommer argues, as contributions to the dialogue on nation, identity, and cultural autonomy.

The desire to be modern led these four writers to confront modernity and modernization in their novels. They were simultaneously attracted to modernity at the same time that they yearned for an idyllic past. These ambiguous attitudes toward a past and a future society were particularly evident in Guiraldes, Gallegos, and de la Parra. For all four writers, being modern also meant being universal, even though their ideas about universality differed vastly from the writing of *vanguardia*.

Five **Rereading Novels of *Vanguardia***

The avant-garde fiction writers of the 1920s and 1930s were a cultural minority who nevertheless pursued a modernist aesthetics inspired by the new European and North American modernist trends. For them, this new writing involved a multifaceted cultural activity. Vicente Huidobro, more recognized as a poet, in fact, wrote what he called a *novela fílmica* and was involved with the film industry; Adolfo Bioy Casares was fascinated with the implications of technology and film in the context of literature, an interest evident in his novel *La invención de Morel*. Modernist works that were either ignored or rejected by the predominant *criollista* and traditionalist literary culture of the time and to be considered in this chapter are *El Café de Nadie* (1926) by Arqueles Vela, *La casa de cartón* (1928) by Martín Adán, *Mío Cid Campeador* (1929) by Vicente Huidobro, *Proserpina rescatada* (1931) *Margarita de niebla* (1927) by Jaime Torres Bodet, *La última niebla* (1927) by María Luisa Bombal, and *La invención de Morel* (1940) by Bioy Casares. Virtually forgotten works in Latin America, they were resuscitated by scholars in the 1970s and 1980s, as well as by postmodern Latin American novelists of the 1970s and 1980s who felt an aesthetic alliance with these frequently marginalized writers.[1] They offer different degrees of innovation and experimentation with time, plot, and character, clearly distancing themselves, in the process, from the traditional (realist-naturalist) modes of Rivera, Gallegos, and the other *criollistas*.

Deemed "inappropriate" for Latin American readers by one of the most influential literary scholars of the time, Arturo Torres Rioseco, the writers of the *vanguardia* were, in reality, proposing a fundamental change in the cultural paradigm. According to Torres Rioseco, Latin American culture was still too "limited" for the production of psychological or innovative fiction. For David Daiches, the modernist novel in the United States and Europe meant a basic breakdown of the implied agreement between author and reader about what was significant in the human experience.[2] In Latin America, this breakdown began in the 1920s with the publication of the first novels of the *vanguardia* and the cultural debates promoted by Torres Bodet and Arqueles Vela in Mexico, by Huidobro in Chile, by Bioy Casares, Borges, and Victoria Ocampo in Argentina, and by numerous other intellectuals. Whatever the more contemporary assessments and revisions of this fiction may be, most of these works were viewed as failures as novels in their times, despite the aesthetic qualities they offered.

These novelists—Arqueles Vela, Torres Bodet, Adán, Huidobro, Bioy Casares, and Bombal—did not represent a unified cultural or ideological front, nor were they associated with the aristocracies of the patriarchal order. To the contrary, they were a heterogeneous group with limited communication among themselves, holding diverse literary and political agendas. They were all affected (or afflicted) by different degrees of a desire to be modern and held different levels of enthusiasm for the new modernist cultural agenda. They also varied in their acceptance of Macedonio Fernández's assertion that the writer does not copy reality but makes it.

In addition to the magazines and groups that attempted to promote new aesthetics (i.e., *Contemporáneos*, Florida), the contributions of Adolfo Bioy Casares, Borges, and Victoria Ocampo to the modernization of Argentine letters in particular and Latin American literature in general were remarkable. Ocampo founded her seminal cultural magazine *Sur* in 1931; this organ and the diverse writings of Bioy Casares and Borges in the 1930s were important forerunners to the rise of the modernist novel in Latin America in the 1940s. Cortázar has explained this as follows: "*Sur* nos ayudó a los estudiantes que en la década del 30 al 40 tentábamos un camino titubeando entre tantos errores, tantas abyectas facilidades y mentiras" (*Sur* helped us students who were looking for a path in the 1930s, living among so many errors, poor facilities, and lies).[3]

These writers were often more connected to their local settings than many of their critics claimed. Martín Adán and Torres Bodet, for example, made references to specific places in Lima and Mexico City in their fiction. They expanded the national geography in such a way that the urban spaces were now at the center, and this constituted a relatively new approach in Latin American fiction.

Jaime Torres Bodet and Vicente Huidobro are best known as poets; in their efforts as novelists, they wrote inventive works the reading of which requires a new tacit agreement between author and reader about what is significant in the experience of a narrative. Torres Bodet the fiction writer has been long ignored by the general reading public and scholars, although his lot improved in the latter part of the century: a two-volume set of his complete fiction appeared in Mexico in 1985, and his fiction is now generally well known by scholars of Latin American literature.[4] His short novel *Proserpina rescatada* has been the focus of several recent readings.[5] It is a fragmented work consisting of twenty-eight segments that appear in four parts, and they relate the story of the relationship between Delfino Castro Valdés and Proserpina Jiménez. Delfino is a doctor, and Proserpina (also called Dolores Jiménez) is a medical student who becomes his lover. After several years of separation, Proserpina calls him on the telephone, which in turn causes him to remember a variety of events associated with their relationship. The characterization of Proserpina underlines her duality, for she functions not only as a medical student but also as a medium or conduit for the dead. The narrator also suggests that Proserpina has numerous identities, as manifested in her being the voice for many souls. The text jumps from one time and space to another, culminating in Delfino finding her approaching a diabetic coma and, after her pleading, agreeing to inject Proserpina with a drug that will prompt her death.

The main structuring device in *Proserpina rescatada* is memory. Consequently, it is a fragmented novel that follows the illogical pattern of the associative process involved in memory.[6] This basic fragmentation of the structure appears as a parallel fragmentation at other levels of reading. The most consistent and obvious of these levels is the characterization of Proserpina as a fragmented being. She is portrayed as a person with a split personality whose segmentation is communicated by means of temporal and spatial fragmentation. The narrator's discourse is fragmented by pauses and a variety of stylistic devices.[7] He even states directly: "No consigo ya unir todos los fragmentos, todas las páginas sueltas del libro desencuadernado, del almanaque en desorden que esparce sobre mi memoria los recuerdos de nuestra vida de Nueva York" (I no longer manage to unify all the fragments, all the loose pages of the unbound book, of the almanac in disorder that spreads the memories of our life in New York on my brain).[8]

Characterization in *Proserpina rescatada* differs radically from what was standard among Torres Bodet's realist-naturalist contemporaries. Pérez Firmat has postulated that characterization in this novel, appropriately enough, is a process of decharacterization.[9] He points to the fact that Delfino's enterprise ends by dissolving his subject into a background of whiteness that cannot but remind one of the blank page. Proserpina is not only a character of multiple identities: she is also a slight and slender character who, in the end, disappears into death. This outcome is but one indicator of Torres Bodet's relative disinterest in character development and his enthusiasm for other aspects of the creative process.

Torres Bodet's desire to be modern is so overt that it could be described as an anxiety of the modern. The characterization of Proserpina features, in addition to her multiple identities, her modernity. This modernity consists of her interest in universal (as opposed to local or national) art and literature and the fact that she avidly consumes everything from the *Upanishads* and the writings of Rabindranath Tagore to the fiction of Paul Bourget and the art of Latin America. The important detail here is not that the art and literature that she admires are necessarily modern (which they obviously are not), but that it is not local or nationalist. The narrator's characterization of Proserpina also involves frequent use of the new objects associated with modernity. For example, her movements have a "nerviosidad eléctrica" (electric restlessness), and her thin hands "derramaban un fluido magnético" (exuded a magnetic fluid; *Proserpina rescatada*, 190).

The text is a celebration of modernity that describes North Americans as "un pueblo de mecanógrafas, de ascensoristas, de médicos que han hecho su carrera por correspondencia y profesores de gimnasia que dan todos los días sus lecciones de tenis por radio" (A nation of typists, of elevator operators, of doctors who have done their studies through correspondence courses, and gym teachers who give their tennis lessons by radio every day; *Proserpina rescatada*, 202). In accordance with standard modernist procedures, Torres Bodet is particularly fascinated with the juxtaposition of the traditional and the modern.

The fragmentation and the focus on modernity have several implications with respect to the state of Latin American fiction and society in the late 1920s and early 1930s. María Bustos Fernández has set forth a reading of *Proserpina rescatada* arguing that the essence of the work is fragmentation as a way of being.[10] For this critic, Delfino and Proserpina offer opposing versions of the "modern" condition, he being practical and scientific, she impractical and irrational. Indeed, *Proserpina rescatada* is a manifestation of a sense of an unstable and fragmented subject and an unstable and fragmented society. As a modernist text, nevertheless, this novel presents the reader with the task of finding harmony when confronted with an apparent chaos of fragmentation, as D'Lugo has observed: "Since Delfino cannot achieve a sense of unification, then readers are the ones to attempt such a task, by means of a more active participation in the narrative process."[11] By the end, the reader does find something of the unity of the modernist text, for in the end, *Proserpina rescatada* is the minimally unified story of a protagonist's search for a lover who escapes the possibility of any stable relationship until her final escape into death.

Proserpina rescatada is a modernist text and thus an evident forerunner of the rise of modernist fiction the 1940s and 1950s in Latin America. It is also a less obvious forerunner to postmodern fiction of the 1970s and 1980s.[12] Like much postmodern fiction, the main interests of *Proserpina rescatada* are more ontological than epistemological, for the ontological status of Proserpina is frequently ambiguous.[13] Vague in its thematic focus, the main subject of the novel is actually language itself, and self-consciously so, as is the case of much postmodern metafiction published several decades later (see chapter 12).

Unlike *Proserpina rescatada*, Vicente Huidobro's *Mío Cid Campeador* is one of the least-discussed novels of the *vanguardia*. Nevertheless, it is a noteworthy work—a curious cultural artifact already—that was made into a film and translated into English under the title *Portrait of a Paladin*. Like *Proserpina rescatada* and much postmodern fiction published much later in the century, it also places emphasis on language as a theme in itself. The use of a mythical literary figure as the protagonist is also typical of the vanguardist writer who desired to be modern by being universal.

The dichotomies observed by Goic are symptomatic of the numerous dualities that are the main structuring device of the text. Indeed, there are three basic dualities that function as aberrations from a simple anecdote about a hero named El Cid. The first is constructed around the contrast between the Cid as literary myth and the Cid as a real person. In the first two chapters, the anecdote accentuates the mythical and universal qualities of the Cid. For example, when his mother is about to give birth to him, the situation is described as follows: "La madre en su cama entre los linos blancos es el centro del universo en el centro mismo de España" (The mother in her bed between the white linens is the center of the universe in the very center of Spain).[14] The young hero is characterized according to modern clichés, with references in English to "Yankees" and "cowboys" (*Mío Cid Campeador*, 29). The novel vacillates between these two visions: on the one hand, the invincible mythical hero and, on the other, the real person of our everyday world. Huidobro uses this duality to intercalate anachronistic allusions. The novel begins on a specific date (1040), but soon the athletic interests of the Cid appear in a contemporary framework: "El campeón estaba *knock-out*" (The champion was knocked out; *Mío Cid Campeador*, 37). Besides modifying the characterization of the Cid as the mythical character of the *Poema del Cid*, the anachronistic nature of this duality places into doubt the supposed "objectivity" of the realist-naturalist tradition.

A second duality, between actions and words, is set forth by Huidobro in the preface when he states: "no puedo negar mi preferencia por los hombres de acción y de aventura" (I cannot deny my preference for men of action and adventure; *Mío Cid Campeador*, unnumbered page). In addition to the futuristic tone that is also occasionally evident in the fiction of Torres Bodet, the reader notes the contrast between the tastes established by Huidobro and his creative act (a cerebral activity not exactly within the domain of *acción y aventura*). A letter that precedes the preface produces even more ambiguity. This missive is directed to Mr. Douglas Fairbanks for having inspired him to study the Cid: "Me pidió usted que le recopilara datos sobre él y se los enviara a los Estados Unidos, y me habló con tal entusiasmo que su entusiasmo se comunicó a mi espíritu, y entonces nació en mí la idea de escribir algo sobre el Cid" (You asked me to compile facts on him and to send them to the United States, and he spoke to me with such enthusiasm that his enthusiasm communicated itself to my spirit and then was born in my idea of writing something about El Cid; *Mío Cid Campeador*, unnumbered page). The contrast between the *hombre de acción* who knows Mr. Fairbanks and the other person, the writer, is evident in the preface that follows the letter. In this section, Huidobro minimizes the true influence of Fairbanks on his creation.(*Mío Cid Campeador*, unnumbered page). With respect to this second duality, Huidobro's interests do not lie in the action of the traditional (realist-naturalist) novel but in the language that was not widely understood as the possible subject of a novel until the rise of postmodern fiction in the 1970s and 1980s in Latin America.[15] None of these four novels— *Proserpina rescatada, La casa de cartón, Margarita de niebla,* or *Mío Cid Campeador*—has the strength of plot found in *Doña Bárbara* or *Don Segundo Sombra.*

A third duality deals with the narrator. An omniscient narrator presents the actions, exercises complete omniscience over the characterization, and organizes the narrative. The duality is expressed in the difference between this traditional narrative position and its subsequent variations. At times, the narrator limits his omniscience as a rhetorical device, asking, for example, if the character really loves the Cid: "¿Ama al Cid doña Urraca?" In a playful manner, the narrator explains supposed difficulties that arise from attempting to follow the actions of the Cid: "Difícil es seguir ahora las andanzas del Cid." (*Mío Cid Campeador,* 301.) He is supposedly unable to relate the details of a battle because one of the characters has disappeared from his view (*Mío Cid Campeador,* 368).

Proserpina rescatada and *Mío Cid Campeador* are the products of inventive, entertaining, and iconoclastic novelists who were, in effect, proposing a new idea of what was significant (to paraphrase Daiches) in the reader's experience of reading fiction. They were also proposing a new cultural paradigm. Obviously, their modernist projects had neither the ambition nor the depth of the high modernist texts that the novelists of the Boom completed in the 1960s—the brief *Proserpina rescatada* will never compete with Vargas Llosa's *La casa verde* for a place in the canon of the most accomplished modernist texts of the century.[16] Arqueles Vela and Adán were perhaps less entertaining than Torres Bodet and Huidobro but equally committed to new ideas about what fiction might be. Arqueles Vela's *El Café de Nadie* has a central character and a setting, and the latter predominates. There is virtually no plot. The setting is the Café Europa in Mexico City. The novel opens and closes with references to the café, whereas the supposed protagonist, a woman named Mabelina, is not introduced until the third of ten chapters. The novel's fragments focus on Mabelina, seen both in an exterior and interior fashion. Given Arqueles Vela's interest in being universal (i.e., modern), he provides no names for the city or its streets.

Mabelina is a character in ongoing crisis, whose fragmented identity, like that of Torres Bodet's Proserpina, is one of being in itself. This problem of being and the generalized vagueness and anonymity of the other characters places this book, like much postmodern fiction, in the sphere of primarily ontological rather than epistemological interests. In *El Café de Nadie*, however, the author is fully and enthusiastically committed to exploring every possible avenue for subverting any conventional concept of "character." Thus, the waiter is a hypothetical character, and the other characters are more beings in the process of collective and ongoing transformation than subjects of fixed and stable personalities.

The characters of many of these fictions of *vanguardia*, such as those of Torres Bodet and Martín Adán, are constantly surrounded by objects and images of modernity. In *El Café de Nadie*, the characters themselves are portrayed as objects of modernity. Influenced by futurism as much as Torres Bodet and Huidobro were, Vela characterizes these ambiguous beings as machines, *aparatos*, that usually move slowly but occasionally move with the quickness and energy of electric motors.

An intriguing aspect of *El Café de Nadie* is Vela's undermining of the individuals as fixed personalities and the very concept of character in fiction. A secondary and less developed matter in this brief novelette is the very concept of reality. In the opening paragraph, the café is situated in the "último peldaño de la realidad" (last step of reality), placing into question not only the geographical location of the café but also the nature of reality in this novel. Near the end, a character pushes a doorbell *(timbre)* "queriendo llamar a la realidad" (wanting to call reality). Conceptualizing "reality" in this way, Vela makes reality in the broadest sense a subject problematized in this work. Clearly, Vela is quite distant from the *criollistas'* interest in transcribing the reality of the New World and nation building, and it is not difficult to imagine why novels like *El Café de Nadie*, which can be entertaining for the postmodern reader, left many middle-class Mexican readers who had not accepted a new implicit agreement between author and reader either frustrated or confused.

Read as modernist novels, *Margarita de niebla, Mío Cid Campeador*, and *El Café de Nadie* were aesthetically inconsistent. All three, however, were celebrations of the surprising metaphor. *Margarita de niebla* is an experiment in modernist aesthetics that tells more of a story than does *El Café de Nadie*—it deals with a young professor in love with two women of opposite personalities. Margarita Millers is the daughter of a German family residing in Mexico; Paloma is the Mexican friend of Margarita to whom the narrator-protagonist,

Carlos, feels an attraction. Carlos, however, is far more committed to the literary image than he is to either of the women. The novel's twelve chapters are a study in ambiguity and contradiction, with constant jumps in time and space. Verani has suggested that an overflow of refined images, in fact, is excessive for the contemporary reader, and this critic is probably accurate in his assessment of even the modern reader's likely response to a work that obviously was not attractive to many readers at the time of its publication.[17]

Margarita de niebla has only little more conventional plot than the novels of Huidobro or Arqueles Vela, and the depiction of the characters makes them difficult to decipher. Rather than depicting psychological states, Torres Bodet was interested in this novel in creating landscapes, moods, and thoughts.[18] Now the landscapes, however, are not replicas of the jungle, the pampa, or the plains, but of modern urban scenes that appear as both exterior descriptions (of what the narrator-protagonist observes) and interior descriptions (of what the narrator-protagonist perceives, sees, or feels). For example, in a description of his memory of her, he uses images from modern science "tubes" to describe a "motor" inside him that seems to flow like a mechanical engine. He then evokes the image of the streets of asphalt, which the reader assumes he is observing as the "motor" that goes over these streets.[19] In this manner, Torres Bodet moves from interior to exterior-type imagery, frequently using objects associated with modernity to describe the narrator's emotional states and what he is observing.

As has been observed, *Margarita de niebla* should not be read as a novel of character, but as an inquiry into the question of characterization in fiction.[20] Thus, the question of the ontological status of the characters is a central matter and invites further comparisons with more recent postmodern fiction.[21] Character in this novel is not portrayed as a human essence (as is assumed in *Don Segundo Sombra* and *Don Goyo*), nor as something always in transformation (as in Arqueles Vela's work), but as either irrational or as a result of chance. As Forster has observed, the two characters are really a pretext for the study of opposites, and neither ever attains human dimensions.[22]

Unquestionably, *Margarita de niebla* and *Proserpina rescatada* made Torres Bodet one of the most articulate spokespersons for the emergence of a "nueva novela que surge por sobre los escombros de la 'novela de ayer'" (new novel that comes forth from the leftovers from "the novel of yesterday").[23] Indeed, there is a sense of vitality and play in these two novels, as well as in *Mío Cid Campeador*, that places them among the early declarations of the death of the realist-naturalist novel.

The potentially excessive imagery of *Margarita de niebla* is even more cultivated in Martín Adán's *La casa de cartón*. The other aspects of this work, however, are as little developed as they were in much Latin American avant-garde fiction, for *La casa de cartón* is, in fact, another brief novelette, in this case consisting of ninety pages and thirty-eight brief narrative segments. Adán's technical adventure in this novel is a remarkable precursor to modernist novels of later decades that test the limits of technical innovation. Anticipating Agustín Yáñez's innovative stylistic procedures in the opening chapter of *Al filo del agua* ("Acto preparatorio") by two decades, Adán uses images virtually without employing conjugated verbs, thus creating a sense of timelessness and eternity in his description of the docks of Barranco.[24]

The images in the opening of this chapter suggest a brightly lit child's toy, and the sense of timelessness in this passage is indicative of how these fiction writers of *vanguardia* often presented specific and identifiable places. They were accused of ignoring local settings in favor of European themes, but Adán places this novel specifically in the Barranco neighborhood of Lima (then a municipality outside of Lima). The difference between the Barranco of Adán (as well as the Mexico City of Torres Bodet) and the spaces of the *criollista* novel is that these writers of *vanguardia*, rather than assuming that local places are to be celebrated as the site of local folklore and customs, assumed that their task was to somehow universalize their settings. In some cases, the space is neither urban nor rural. Adán attempts to universalize the setting by creating a sense of eternal time and space.

La casa de cartón deals with a young man's experience growing up in Barranco. The narrator-protagonist describes going to high school and everyday life in a small town in the mountains above Lima which they visit, observing everyday life on the streets of Barranco, seeing images from a ride on a streetcar. The novel offers vignettes of his different adolescent loves, as well as a satirical description of Latin Americans in Paris; revelations of the narrator-protagonist's impressions of male and female friends; and descriptions of a variety of other characters (emphasizing imagery and emotions). The narrator-protagonist comments about their readings of modernist writers, including Joyce.

A 1971 reprint of *La casa de cartón* includes a commentary written by Peruvian critic Luis Alberto Sánchez and a postscript by Adán's contemporary José Carlos Mariátegui. Arguing in favor of this fragmented novel's unity, Mariátegui observes that "su desorden está previamente ordenado" (its lack of order is ordered in advance).[25] Mariátegui is correct, for *La casa de cartón* is a modernist text that offers the reader an initial impression of fragmentation and chaos, yet in the process of reading, the modern reader finds continuities and unities in the narrator's style, imagery, fluctuating relationship with the world around him, and attitude toward others, making it a more harmonious modernist text than *Proserpina rescatada, Margarita de niebla,* or *Mío Cid Campeador.*

There is little plot development in this novel, so the reader's task is not the organizing of anecdotal material; the major event in *La casa de cartón* is the use of imagery. Adán's consistent use of metaphors involves physical objects and conditions to describe emotional and psychic states. Unlike the anguished and lost souls of *Margarita de niebla,* the narrator-protagonist of *La casa de cartón* is less profoundly affected by his adolescent setbacks than engaged in a celebration of life as it relates to the word. This novel is, above all, an exceptionally joyful celebration of the act of creation and, more specifically, a celebration of the joy of discovering surprising, iconoclastic, and occasionally humorous juxtapositions of words. Much of the literature of *vanguardia* is an object of celebration; Adán, like Huidobro, believed in Argentine writer Macedonio Fernández's assertion that the word is reality and this linguistic reality is a subject of celebration.

Bioy Casares's *La invención de Morel* and Bombal's *La última niebla* were more viable as cultural products of Latin America in the 1930s and are more successful modernist texts than most of the works produced in the 1920s and 1930s. These two novels are increasingly recognized as well-wrought and significant works despite their avant-garde status. Bioy Casares collaborated with Borges in writing projects, using pseudonyms such as H. Bustos Domecq, B. Suárez Lynch, and B. Lynch Davis. Bioy Casares had already published a series of short fictions in the realm of the fantastic by the time that he wrote what Borges described as a "perfect" novel. Remarkably, in the preface to *La invención de Morel,* Borges concludes with this observation: "He discutido con su autor los pormenores de su trama, la he releído; no me parece una imprecisión o una hipérbole calificarla de perfecta" (I have discussed the details of its plot with its author; I have reread it; it doesn't seem to me imprecise or hyperbolic to call it perfect).[26] In typical Borgesian fashion, this statement remains patently ambiguous: in the last line of this four-page preface Borges offers no explanation for exactly why this novel might be considered "perfect." In fact, the reader is soon subjected to a fiction that few would have considered perfect by virtually any measure of aesthetic quality being used in Latin America in the 1940s. *La invención de Morel* reads as the fragmented, incoherent, and contradictory story of a narrator-protagonist (with a criminal record) on an island who falls in love with a woman identified as Faustine. Technically, the text is a supposed diary or memoir of the narrator-protagonist. If one were to identify a perfect modernist fiction of this period—using as the criteria the aesthetics of modernism—two likely candidates would be *La invención de Morel* and Agustín Yáñez's 1947 novel, *Al filo del agua* (see chapter 7).

The opening lines of *La invención de Morel* offer a radical undermining of traditional concepts of linear time already suggested and elaborated in texts such as Borges's short story "El milagro secreto," the novels of Torres Bodet, and *La casa de cartón*. The novel's first two lines read as follows: "Hoy, en esta isla, ha ocurrido un milagro. El verano se adelantó" (Today, a miracle has occurred on this island. Summer jumped ahead; *La invención de Morel*, 13). After this incredible statement concerning time, the narrator nonchalantly returns to the everyday: "Puse la cama cerca de la pileta de natación y estuve bañándome, hasta muy tarde" (I put the bed next to the swimming pool, and I was bathing myself, until very late; *La invención de Morel*, 13). The narrator explains the situation on the island: some white settlers had built a museum, a chapel, and a swimming pool in 1924 and then abandoned the island. A mysterious sickness, which disintegrates bodies and kills humans, afflicts people who might move there.

From early in the novel, the narrator-protagonist makes statements that invite the reader to question the ontological status of Faustine and himself. For example, early in the novel he refers to summer visitors to the museum as "verdaderos" (real) and then follows "por lo menos tan verdaderos como yo" (at least as real as I; *La invención de Morel*, 15). The ontological status of the text itself also becomes increasingly ambiguous. Early in the work, the narrator affirms that the island is called Villings and belongs to the archipelago Las Ellice. A footnote from a fictitious editor, however, says "Lo dudo" (I doubt it;

La invención de Morel, 17) and then explains inconsistencies between this island and the islands of Ellice.

As *La invención de Morel* develops, it does a quite rigorous—perhaps even "perfect"—job of developing ambiguities concerning the most basic elements of the story: the status of the narrator-protagonist, Faustine, the island, and the narrator's text as "real" are all placed in doubt. In addition, the narrator explains problems in writing this diary, which seems to escape the rules of coherency, consistency, and order. In fact, the narrator places the entire narrative into doubt by stating, approximately in the middle of the novel, that the situation described in the novel's first half is not true: "Ahora parece que la verdadera situación no es la descrita en las páginas anteriores; que la situación que vivo no es la que yo creo vivir" (Now it seems that the true situation isn't the one described in the previous pages; the situation that I live isn't the one that I believe I live; *La invención de Morel*, 71). In the end, it is evident that Faustine is not a "real" fictitious character but instead is made of images projected on a screen by a movie projector. Thus, the narrator-protagonist's affair has been not with a character, but with an image. As has been observed in several of these fictions, and as occurred in some post-modern fiction of the 1970s and 1980s, the very concept of character is subverted.

Given the special qualities of *La invención de Morel*, Borges's statement about this novel as perfect must be interpreted as tongue-in-cheek humor. It is perfect in its undermining of the traditional tenets of fiction and as exploration of the possibilities of modernist fiction. As such, it is an important predecessor to *Ficciones* and the right of invention to be celebrated amply in the 1940s.

Bioy Casares and many of the other writers of the *vanguardia* were clearly misunderstood or misinterpreted by many of their contemporaries with respect to their use of space. The *vanguardista* fiction writers did indeed use their nations—both their urban centers and their rural areas—as settings. Their objective, however, was to be universal, and many of them viewed their cities as more similar to European novelistic spaces than to the pampa or the *llano*. (Clearly, they were not engaged in the same nation building project of Gallegos and Guiraldes.) María Luisa Bombal sets her works in *casas de campo* in Chile. She is yet another special case, for she is not frequently associated with the groups of *vanguardia*. Many of these fiction writers, nevertheless, were exceptions in one way or another, and Bombal actually did interact sporadically with the cosmopolitan Argentine writers of Victoria Ocampo's magazine *Sur* during a lifetime that included several years of residence in Argentina. *La última niebla* is another relatively brief novel, yet it relates a compelling story. The narrator-protagonist suffers a crisis of truth that is a noteworthy precedent to Latin American postmodern fiction of the 1970s and 1980s.[27] She remembers an intense love affair, which compensates for an empty and disappointing relationship with her husband. Both the reader and the protagonist, however, have growing doubts about the veracity of the relationship with the lover; the text leaves this matter ambiguous.

Bombal employs water, mist, and dampness as consistent images of the protagonist's unhappiness and alienation. More importantly, the mist contributes to a pervasive sense of uncertainty concerning what is real.[28] Along these lines, mist serves the function of creating a multiple reality in which dreams, the imagined, and the tangible are interwoven. The novel's events flow back and forth between the subjective, interior reality of the narrator and the empirical reality of the exterior world. As Lucía Guerra-Cunningham has pointed out, the ambiguity of *La última niebla* has two sources: the lack of specificity with respect to external reality and objective time; and the elimination of exact and rational limits between the dreamed world and the objective world.[29] Given the protagonist's ongoing crisis, it becomes the reader's task to attempt to understand the enigmatic relationship between her and her supposed lover.

As a work that rejects the conventions of the realist-naturalist novel, *La última niebla* can be easily associated with all five of these novels of *vanguardia*. Like Arqueles Vela and Torres Bodet, Bombal constructs a fictional world that emphasizes interiorization and imagery rather than the imitation of empirical reality. Like Bioy Casares and Borges, Bombal finds the fantastic in everyday life, and clear connections can be made between *La invención de Morel* and *La última niebla*. The male narrator's diary of his relationship with an invented woman has its parallel in *La última niebla*, in which a female narrator fictionalizes a relationship with an apparently invented man. As an avant-garde text, the specialness of *La invención de Morel* is the fact that the protagonist's lover turns out to be an entirely fictionalized entity; the specialness of *La última niebla* is the ambiguity of the protagonist's lover—textual evidence makes it impossible to ascertain whether he really exists.

In contrast with the tenuous world and ambiguous human relationships of the protagonist, her friend Regina lives in a concrete world with a real human relationship. Like the protagonist, Regina finds it difficult to endure the mediocre reality that surrounds her in her everyday life. Regina commits suicide, making her an important character in the novel. As Borinsky points out, the woman Regina controls the meaning of the relationships that the narrator has with those surrounding her. The protagonist strives for difference: "Her being a woman is rooted in wanting to be a different woman, or be punished with a constant doubt as to who she is."[30]

In *La última niebla*, Regina's story offers a conventional plot, reminding the reader of this virtually missing element in the novel. Many of these novels of *vanguardia*, of course, offer a minimal plot and, consequently, the protagonist's exceptional story of a potential relationship and the minor character's more conventional story distinguish *La última niebla* from much fiction of *vanguardia*. Sharing the interests of both the innovators and the more conventional storytellers of the 1930s, Bombal is a key transitional figure between the most experimental avant-garde writers of the 1920s (i.e., Torres Bodet and Huidobro) and the modernist storytellers of the 1940s (i.e., Asturias and Yáñez).

These five novelists of the *vanguardia* shared a common interest in breaking the conventions of time, plot, and character in the novel. To the limited extent that their characters are recognizable and credible as human beings, these beings, such as Proserpina and the Cid, were identifiably "modern" with the obvious intention of also being "universal." In fact, these writers of *vanguardia* were content to associate their characters with both Greco-Roman antiquity and modernity, with the goal of being universal. More often than creating truly universal human types, however, they simply subverted the very concept of character itself. This was the case of the characters in *Mío Cid Campeador* and *El Café de Nadie*.

The new cultural paradigm suggested by these writers involved a breakdown of the previously accepted tacit agreement between author and reader about what was important in human experience. Unfortunately, no new commonly accepted agreement was forged with respect to this new modernist fiction. Consequently, these new novels were frequently criticized, ignored, or openly rejected. The writers' desire to be modern was momentarily frustrated. In general, the modernist project of the 1920s and 1930s went unrealized with respect to the novel.

As Unruh has pointed out in her discussion of the avant-garde, it could well be that Latin American literature's time has come at the end of the century (rather than in the 1920s) precisely because it has been in tune with the cacophonous disclocation of our postmodern times. Careful rereading of these Latin American texts suggests that the experience of radical discontinuity is a story that the literature of Indo-Afro-Iberoamerica has been attempting to tell about itself for several decades.[31]

Successful as a type of underground promotion of the right of invention, the avant-garde fiction of the 1920s and 1930s began to explore Macedonio Fernández's idea that the writer does not copy reality (as Gallegos and company had attempted), but makes it. If the *criollista* fiction was a celebration of regional customs, the fiction of *vanguardia* was a celebration of the word. The collaborative cultural work of Victoria Ocampo, Bioy Casares, and Borges, as well as the aesthetic achievements of Adán's *La casa de cartón*, Bioy Casares's *La invención de Morel*, and Bombal's *La última niebla* were exceptions to the generally unsuccessful modernist fictions published in the 1920s and 1930s.

The relative "failure" of this early modernist writing, in reality, should be understood as insignificant in the total process involved in the Latin American writers' desire to be modern. In the case of Torres Bodet and his cohorts of the *Contemporáneos* group, their aesthetic and ideological proposal for fiction was in many ways an imaginative and viable response to the realist-naturalist tradition in fiction. They were proposing a heterogeneous fiction that challenged the limits of the conventional masculinist aesthetic. In the cultural wars of the period, however, their opposition was not exclusively an antiquated literary tradition. These writers were accused of distancing themselves from reality, but in fact, their defeat in the cultural wars in Mexico in the late 1920s and early 1930s perhaps had less to do with literary aesthetics than personal conflicts. The legacy and importance of these novels is evidenced not only by their survival in literary history and the attention scholars have accorded these texts, but also by the fact that more contemporary writers such as José Emilio Pacheco and Salvador Elizondo were still writing about Torres Bodet with great enthusiasm in the 1970s. Indeed, the connections between

Latin America's avant-garde of the 1920s and its postmodern fiction of the 1970s and 1980s are reasonably evident and often confirmed by writers such as Pacheco and Elizondo.

In their desire to be modern, many of these novelists were more successful in writing against the conventions than they were in creating fully developed modernist novels. There is no *Ulysses* hidden in the annals of the *vanguardia*, nor is there any truly perfect novel, of course, despite Borges's argument to the contrary. Rather, there are mostly short projects for potential novels such as Vela's brief *El Café de Nadie*. For the postmodern reader, they are provoking and often entertaining experiments. Given the overall unsure and insecure status of the national novel during this period, these brief experiments did little to assure the nascent middle-class reading public that each of the Latin American nations did indeed possess a mature national literary culture.

Part III   **The Rise of the Modernist Novel,
1941–1961**

Six Novelistic and Cultural Contexts of Latin American Modernism

The avant-garde writers of the 1920s and 1930s had laid the groundwork for a modernist novel in Latin America in the 1940s and 1950s. Unfortunately, their work in fiction had little immediate impact on the Spanish American novel, and the more important forerunners for the rise of modernist fiction in Latin America were not writers like Torres Bodet and Huidobro, but rather Proust, Dos Passos, Kafka, and Faulkner, in addition to other foreign modernists. For novelists, wanting to be modern in this period tended to consist of the desire to be the Latin American Dos Passos or the Latin American Faulkner. The seminal Spanish American figure behind the rise of the modernist novel and the reaffirmation of the right of invention in Spanish America was the Argentine poet, essayist, and short fiction writer Jorge Luis Borges. In the case of the Latin American novel, during the 1940s and 1950s, the desire to be modern was played out primarily by employing the strategies of modernist fiction. In this period numerous cultural tensions surfaced, and writers such as the Mexicans Carlos Fuentes and Rosario Castellanos fictionalized attendant issues of cultural conflict, cultural difference, and hybridity.

Borges's promotion of avant-garde aesthetics in Latin America in the 1920s and 1930s, his innovative short fiction of the 1940s in the form of *Ficciones*, and his translations of Faulkner into Spanish, among other contributions, made him a central figure for the rise of the modernist novel in Latin America. Of these contributions, his book *Ficciones* represented not only innovation just in terms of form, but a reaffirmation of the right of invention.[1] Seemingly an obvious right for modernist novelists in Europe and the United States, pure invention had been under attack (and fallen into disrepute) from the traditionalists and *criollistas*. Given this background, Borges's reaffirmation of the right of invention was a cultural revolution in itself. His volumes of short stories *El jardín de los senderos que se bifurcan* (1941) and *Ficciones* (1944) suggested innovative, new paths for Latin American writers. The story "El milagro secreto" deals with time in ways that few Latin American writers other than those of *vanguardia* had dared to explore in fiction. These stories also contain metafictional qualities, a matter considered irrelevant by the traditionalists and nationalists. Subjective concepts of time and space are also common experiences for readers of *Ficciones*. The same had been the case for some of the avant-garde Latin American fiction writers of the 1920s, but now the culture and the society seemed ready for such approaches to fiction and to reality. Huidobro had admonished poets in his "Arte Poética" to invent, and the Latin American and Caribbean writers two decades later were freely fulfilling Huidobro's desire to be modern. Writing in French, Caribbean writer Aimé Césaire stressed the importance of invention, advocating "the drive to invent our own way and to rid it of ready-made models."[2]

Several of the major modernist writers of the 1940s and 1950s had direct contact with the European avant-garde. Guatemalan Miguel Angel Asturias and Cuban Alejo Carpentier had been well versed in European modernist literature since the 1920s. Asturias traveled to Europe in 1923, studying the Mayan collection at the British Museum and then Mayan mythology at the Sorbonne. During this stay in Europe, he also became acquainted with the most prominent French surrealists as well as with European avant-garde writing in general. The poet Robert Desnos had helped Carpentier escape political repression in Cuba and find exile in Paris. In Europe, Carpentier became deeply engaged in European and Latin American culture of the moment and participated in the literary circles of Louis Aragon, Tristan Tzara, and Paul Eluard.

Some Latin American writers conceived of modernity as a challenge rather than a burden. In Brazil, the most prominent novelists of the 1940s and 1950s were social critics who also hewed to the aesthetics of modernism. Since the Semana de Arte Moderna in 1922, Brazilian writers had been dedicated to the modernization of Brazilian fiction. One result of this process was the rise of four renowned novelists from the northeastern region of Brazil: Graciliano Ramos,

Jorge Amado, Rachel de Queiroz, and José Lins do Rego. Independent of these regionalists were the two prominent figures of modernist fiction in Brazil, João Guimarães Rosa, and Clarice Lispector.

Throughout Latin America, the 1940s and 1950s were a period of intense cultural debate as new sectors of Latin American society contributed to the debates on national identity and cultural autonomy. Important foci of these debates were the multicultural Caribbean, indigenous cultures, and African cultures. Disparate cultural forces such as *indigenismo*, Caribbean negritude, and Marxism contributed to this dialogue, and all three of these forces were a response to what was viewed as the degeneration of Western modernity.[3] The Caribbean region called for cultural independence. During this period, some of the most significant cultural texts of this Caribbean dialogue were Alejo Carpentier's *La música en Cuba* (1946) and George Lamming's *In the Castle of My Skin* (1953). Aimé Césaire's *Cahier d'un retour au pays natal* (1939) is a radical text that affirms the cultural independence of the Caribbean region. Nevertheless, *Cahier* is also indebted to European modernist models.[4] Indeed, Césaire used the ecumenical language of high modernism to make his call for a rejection of colonialism. Gikandi explains as follows: "Whatever its limitations, what makes Césaire's poem so remarkable in the discourse of decolonization is its initial conceptualization as a fragment that, nevertheless, exists as the preliminary toward a whole: the poet falls back on the discourse of deracination borrowed from European modernism to explode the colonizer's claim of an integrated Caribbean culture (i.e., one integrated to the empire)."[5] In Caribbean modernism, as throughout Latin America—from Césaire to Fuentes and Cabrera Infante— the master of form also deforms. Césaire was also a prominent spokesperson for international discussions of negritude.

In his book *Caribbean Discourse*, Edouard Glissant proposes that the long history of colonialism in the Caribbean and the construction of its culture under European domination have resulted in the region's irruption into modernity as a violent departure from the colonial tradition. Glissant insists on the "real discontinuity beneath the apparent continuity of our history."[6] Despite the reaction against colonialism among Caribbean writers, they did not totally reject European modernism. As Simon Gikandi has observed, Aimé Césaire is agitated by any notion that he is an "enemy of Europe" or the mere thought that he ever urged colonized peoples to return to "the ante-European past."[7] Near the end of this period, the Cuban Revolution served as a model for the Caribbean intellectuals who had been calling for independence from neocolonial powers.

The Haitian Jacques Stephan Alexis entered into cultural dialogue with Alejo Carpentier and, at the same time, into dialogue with Latin America at large. In 1956, Alexis began theorizing new ideas about Caribbean time and space. For several years preceding Alexis's writings, Carpentier had been articulating a Spenglerian view of history, with regular references to the idea of the decline of the West.[8] Alexis appropriated this view of history from Carpentier along with the Cuban author's concept of Caribbean identity as a New World Mediterranean.[9] Consequently, the cultural autonomy and national identities of the Latin American nations seemed to be assured with the rise of this region and the decline of Europe.

Carpentier visited Haiti in 1943, and this experience had a profound impact on his vision of Caribbean culture. Haiti's popular culture, with its strong African elements, was for Carpentier the authentic source of Latin American identity. As González-Echevarría has explained, "Carpentier searches for the marvelous buried beneath the surface of Latin American consciousness, where African drums beat and Indian amulets rule; in depths where Europe is only a vague memory of a future still to come."[10]

In Puerto Rico, American influence was asserted during World War II as it never had been before. During the 1940s, the military presence on the island increased, and Puerto Rican nationalists were persecuted. With the support of the United States, Luis Muñoz Marín formed a new political party in Puerto Rico (the Popular Democratic Party or PPD), leading to Muñoz being elected the first governor of Puerto Rico. Given the growing anticolonial movements throughout the Caribbean, the government of the United States found a formula that allowed Puerto Rico some political autonomy under the name of the Estado Libre Asociado.

The new modernist fiction in Latin America was published by Asturias and Carpentier as well as by recognized writers such as Agustín Yáñez, Juan Rulfo, and Leopoldo Marechal. Among these modernist writers were Rosario Castellanos, David Viñas, Antonio de Benedetto, Yolanda Oreamuno, Salvador Garmendia, and Haitian Jacques Stephan Alexis. The Caribbean writers George Lamming, Edouard Glissant, Jacques Romain, and Samuel Selvon published modernist novels that questioned the authority and discourse of colonialism. The list of noteworthy modernist novelists could potentially be quite long but should also include, in the 1950s, Eduardo Caballero Calderón, Miguel Otero Silva, and Ramón Díaz Sánchez. In Puerto Rico, the writers to be associated with modernist aesthetics during this period were identified as the Desperate Generation and included José Luis González, René Marqués, Pedro Juan Soto, José Luis Vivas Maldonado, and Emilio Díaz Valcárcel.

The narrative strategies appropriated by these Latin American modernists could be easily associated with numerous European and American fiction writers. These stratagems included the use of interior monologues, stream of consciousness, fragmentation, varying narrative points of view, neologisms, innovative narrative strategies, and frequent lack of causality. Just as important as these narrative techniques, however, were some fundamental changes of attitude that came with modernism. One obvious change was the acceptance of new concepts of time, as well as the promotion of new concepts of space. The basic breakdown of the implied agreement between author and reader about what was significant in human experience (as postulated by David Daiches) was evident: in the 1920s, this rupture had begun to take place in Latin America, but the breakdown became significant, widespread, and successful as promoted, above all, by Borges.[11] In general, modernist fiction tended to present a chaotic and fragmented modern world in seemingly chaotic and fragmented texts. The reader's task with the modernist text was to find a subtle, implicit, or implied harmony—a unity of some sort—in the novel.

The clearest indicator of the rise of the new modernist novel in Latin American—a major shift in the cultural paradigm—was the appearance in successive years of Miguel Angel Asturias's *El Señor Presidente* (1946), Graciliano Ramos's *Insonia* (stories, 1947), Agustín Yáñez's *Al filo del agua* (1947), Leopoldo Marechal's *Adán Buenosayres* (1948), Clarice Lispector's *A Cidade Sitiada* (1949), Arnoldo Palacios's *Las estrellas son negras* (1949), and Alejo Carpentier's *El reino de este mundo* (1949). The parallel phenomenon in the English-speaking Caribbean was represented by Samuel Selvon's *A Brighter Sun* (1952, Trinidad) and George Lamming's landmark novel, *In the Castle of My Skin* (1953, Barbados). An engaging and challenging modernist text in Brazil during this period was *Grande Sertão: Veredas* (1956) by João Guimarães Rosa. Chicano José Antonio Villareal also appeared on the scene during this period, publishing *Pocho* (1959), a novel many critics of the time considered the "first" Chicano novel. With these books, the right of invention is evident; the radical rupture of the implicit agreement about what is important in human experience had taken place.

During this period, Colombian Gabriel García Márquez and several other Latin American writers were intrigued by the possibilities Faulknerian narrative approaches could offer for telling the stories of their respective regions.[12] García Márquez, David Viñas, Di Benedetto, and Rulfo were immersed in the writings of Faulkner in the 1950s and produced modernist texts crafted in the Faulknerian mode: *La hojarasca* (1955) by García Márquez, *Cayó sobre su rostro* (1955) by Viñas, *El pentágano* (1955) by Di Benedetto, and *Pedro Páramo* by Rulfo exhibit clear affiliations with Faulkner. García Márquez had read *As I Lay Dying* with great interest and used three different narrators to relate the story of fictional Macondo—his Yoknapatawpha County—from 1903 to 1928 in *La hojarasca*. Viñas also was a deft technician in *Cayó sobre su rostro*, a novel in which the chapters alternate between the past and the present, but both types of chapters suggest ways in which the past affects the present. It is a historical novel that debunks some of the nineteenth-century military leaders who had been considered national heroes in Argentina. Di Benedetto's *El pentágano* is a novel of a love relationship among five characters, and the author's masterful use of narrative point of view is just as effective as García Márquez's and Viñas's. A master of language, Di Benedetto experiments with a variety of languages and tones that is more ambitious than the styles employed by García Márquez in the 1950s.

García Márquez, Viñas, Di Benedetto, and a host of other novelists of this period use a specific region to create a more universal human experience than had generally been the case for Latin American regionalists before the 1940s. This new type of regionalism, which one critic has identified as transcendent regionalism, is the type of fiction also cultivated by Juan Rulfo.[13] Rulfo had published a volume of well-constructed Faulknerian stories set in rural Mexico, *El llano en llamas* (1953), before the appearance of one of the most accomplished and prestigious modernist novels of the century in Latin America, *Pedro Páramo*[14] (see chapter 7 for further analysis).

José Donoso, Miguel Otero Silva, and Ramón Díaz Sánchez published modernist novels that were less flashy in narrative technique than *Pedro Páramo*. In his first novel, *Coronación* (1957), Donoso employed interior monologues to characterize a protagonist, an aging Chilean oligarch, who narrates a story of frustrated human relationships. The novel is both an engaging character study and critique of the Chilean oligarchy. Otero Silva also uses soft touches, such as special syntactical structures and certain stylistic devices, to characterize the people in a decadent town. His *Casas muertas* (1955) is constructed primarily on the basis of extended flashbacks, and the author avoids the potentially obvious symbolism of the decadence surrounding "dead houses." Otero Silva was just as committed to social justice as he was to subtle narrative strategies, but neither interferes with him or the reader in *Casas muertas*. Díaz Sánchez's *Cumboto* (1950) is also more nuanced than the typical Latin American novel of social protest written in the 1930s and 1940s. Its four-part structure and carefully controlled tone—opening with a tone of mystery—make it as engaging to read as Donoso and Otero Silva of the same period.

Some novelists, such as Donoso, Galindo, Lispector, Onetti, and Mallea, were attracted to modernity in some ways but less interested in modernist techniques. They cultivated novels of human relationships. Like *Coronación, El bordo* (1960) by Sergio Galindo and the stories *Laços de família* (1960) by Clarice Lispector are small-screen fictions of human relationships. Both *El bordo* and *Laços de família* deal with relationships within a single family. *El bordo* focuses on an aunt in the family, Joaquina, who misses her opportunities for self-realization and lives a tragic life.

Eduardo Mallea's *Todo verdor perecerá* (1941) portrays the relationship between a married couple, with the main focus on the woman, Agata Cruz. Mallea uses imagery and variations of third-person narration to communicate a sense of a sterile fifteen-year relationship between the two and the emptiness of their lives. Unable to find any alternative to her solitude and anguish, Agata is seen as frustrated and disoriented at the end of the novel.

Galindo, Lispector, and Mallea changed the focus from the broad and external to the details of the characters' interior lives. In Colombia, a similar and significant change took literature in the direction of modernist aesthetics.[15] This change was signaled particularly in the work of six fiction writers in the 1940s: Tomás Vargas Osorio, Rafael Gómez Picón, Elisa Mújica, Ernesto Camargo Martínez, Jaime Ibáñez, and Jaime Ardila Casamitjana. Novels such as Ardila Casamitjana's *Babel* (1943), Ibáñez's *Cada voz lleva su angustia* (1944), and Mújica's *Los dos tiempos* (1949) carry thematic overtones of reaction against Colombia's process of modernization at the same time that the novelists exhibit interest in modernist fiction writing. *De la vida de Iván el mayor* (1942) by Camargo Martínez relates the protagonist's psychological disintegration. Gómez Picón's *45 relatos de un buró-crata con cuatro paréntesis* (1941) deals with the tedious and stulti-fying life of a small-time bureaucrat; the suffocation the protagonist feels—if seen as typical of the lower middle class—was unleashed in 1948 with the *bogotazo*, when a clash between liberals and conserva-tives led to civil war.[16]

Gómez Picón, Camargo Martínez, and the early Lispector focused on the individual, and these three authors shared some of the interests of European existentialists. Juan Carlos Onetti also fictionalized some of these existential interests in *El pozo* (1939), *Tierra de nadie* (1941), *La vida breve* (1950), and *Los adioses* (1954). They are novels about isolated, alienated, and anguished individuals. The fictional port city of Santa María (an amalgam of Buenos Aires and Montevideo) is the sordid setting of his work. Most readers have agreed that Onetti's major novel was *La vida breve*, a story about the protagonist's real and imaginary incursions into an apartment next to his own, a space occupied by a prostitute who is alcoholic and psychologically warped. The novels' ambiguous conclusions suggest the general meaningless of life. *Tierra de nadie* deals with the human relationships among a small group of characters, creating a sense of chaos. Not an aggres-sive innovator in terms of narrative technique, Onetti did find ways to use the third-person narrator and conventional literary language in unexpected and effective ways.[17]

Many more novelists of this period used less ambitious strategies to create novels of interior dimensions, with incursions into the psy-chology of characters, along the lines of Onetti. Ernesto Sábato pub-lished *El túnel* (1948) and Yolanda Oreamuno *La ruta de su evasión* (1949); these are novels of interiorization, works of the modernist aes-thetic concern over individual consciousness and, just as typical of the 1950s, novels of existential anguish. Sábato develops philosophi-cal ideas and a psychological portrayal of love, jealousy, and murder in *El túnel*, a novel portraying a protagonist isolated from others. The protagonist in *La ruta de su evasión* is equally incapable of estab-lishing relationships with others and also suffers from existential anguish.

The fiction of Elisa Mújica and Yolanda Oreamuno brings to the forefront the fact that by the 1940s and 1950s, women writers were increasingly present in elite Latin American culture. In addition to Mújica and Oreamuno, Antonia Palacios, author of several volumes of short fiction and poetry, published the novel *Ana Isabel, una niña decente* (1949), a bildungsroman that can be read as a metaphor for the decadence of a social class. It consists of a series of sketches in the life of a young upper-middle-class girl in Caracas. The style of *Ana Isabel, una niña decente* can be connected to the fiction of *vanguardia*.[18]

The tradition in Latin America of social literature had numerous manifestations in the 1940s and 1950s, beginning with Ciro Alegría's *El mundo es ancho y ajeno*; three of the most successful novels of this type were Rosario Castellanos's *Balún Canán* (1957), Eduardo Caballero Calderón's *El cristo de espaldas* (1952), and Asturias's *Hombres de maíz* (1949). *Balún Canán* was Castellanos's first novel set in Chiapas, where she initiated her *indigenista* fiction. Despite being white, educated in Mexico City, and upper-class, Castellanos wrote convincingly of the Indian condition in Chiapas. As Franco has asserted, the novel is less successful when the author abandons the child narrator and adopts a third-person narration in order to show the increasing defiance of the Indians.[19] The context for *El cristo de espaldas* is the civil war in Colombia in the 1950s, identified as La Violencia (1948–1956). It tells the story of a parricide in a small town: a son who belongs to one political party kills his father, who belongs to another. The town's novice priest becomes a surrogate victim when he attempts to defend the son's just cause. The plot is clearly a typical scenario of both La Violencia and many novels of this period; Caballero Calderón distinguishes himself from many of these Colombian novelists by creating overtones in this fiction of the venerable tradition of Hispanic literature that dates back to the Spanish Golden Age and *Don Quixote*.

Writing from a position in Peru comparable to that of Rosario Castellanos in Mexico, José María Arguedas wrote the *indigenista* novel *Los ríos profundos* (1958). Arguedas was bicultural, and his young protagonist in *Los ríos profundos*, Ernesto, is reared in indigenous culture even though he is white by birth. His worldview is typical of an oral-culture perception of the world around him. After his father leaves Ernesto in school in the town of Abancay, *Los ríos profundos* becomes the dual story of growing up and of a person from an oral culture learning to adapt to writing culture.

The Peruvian Ciro Alegría's *El mundo es ancho y ajeno* (1941) is the most canonical of these *indigenista* novels yet the least compelling and convincing for the modern reader. This disjointed text portrays the world of Rumi and his people. They suffer from the injustices of the landowners and local power brokers; the narrator offers editorial comments to the potential (traditional) reader who might need such clarifications.

The *indigenista* writer tended to deal with bicultural themes, and this is almost always an explicit or implicit topic of Chicano writing. The bicultural Américo Paredes continued laying the groundwork—with a variety of texts written in the 1940s—for what became the Chicano novel of the 1960s. His story "Over the Waves Is Out" (ca. 1948) deals with the experiences of a young boy who wishes to be a musician against his father's will. The conflict is not between cultures, but between generations. In the end, father and son find reconciliation. Rereading Paredes in the 1990s, Saldívar has observed: "Paredes's story shows how oppositional Chicano narratives attain hegemonic patriarchal force precisely by repressing the threat of its feminist consciousness."[20]

Regional awareness was strong in several areas of Latin America, but particularly in Brazil and Colombia. The 1940s in Colombia witnessed the conception of a fiction based on awareness of regional sociopolitical and cultural realities; the novels of Guillermo Edmundo Chaves, Diego Castrillón Arboleda, and Arnoldo Palacios represented this awareness of a new novelistic project. Chaves's *Chambú* (1946) is a search for identity which recalls similar *criollista* projects of the 1920s, but *la tierra* is now the southern region of the Greater Cauca in Colombia. Chaves demonstrates not only an awareness of this region's tri-ethnic oral and writing culture but also is fascinated with it as the material for establishing an identity.

Diego Castrillón Arboleda likewise pursued a fictional project closely related to the Greater Cauca region in Colombia and, more specifically, its indigenous, black, and mestizo cultures. Castrillón Arboleda wrote as an outsider to the culture, producing the novels *José Tombé* (1942) and *Sol en Tambalimbú* (1944). In both novels a strictly writing culture is the frame of reference for telling stories intimately related to the region's tri-ethnic culture. *José Tombé* deals with the exploitation of the indigenous population by the local power structure in the hands of whites.

Castellanos and Castrillón Arboleda were novelist-anthropologists who studied culture in ways that allied them with scholars of the academic discipline of anthropology. González-Echevarría has argued for the importance of this discipline as "the mediating element in the modern Latin American narrative because of the place this discipline occupies in the articulation of founding myths in order to see itself as the other."[21] Asturias, Carpentier, and Jacques Romain are examples of the novelist-anthropologist; Romain founded the Bureau d'Ethnologie in Haiti in 1941 and later published anthropological studies. Asturias explores Native American folkloric traditions in *Hombres de maíz,* a text in which Asturias synthesizes modernist strategies and folklorist themes. It is an elusive and digressive modernist work in which Asturias himself has admitted he made no concessions to the reader.[22] *Hombres de maíz* is divided into six parts and an epilogue, and the conflict revolves around the cultivation of corn: the outsiders desire to interfere with the Indians' cultivation of corn, even though it is a sacred form of sustenance for them. Here, Asturias incorporates an oral-culture understanding of the world. The language of this novel is also a synthesis of modernist experimentation and oral tradition. As a modernist, Asturias exercises the right to experiment with the word and, by repeating syllables within words, he evokes effects of the oral tale.

The writing of Arnoldo Palacios and Adalberto Ortiz confirms a new social and political awareness of Afro-Latin Americans in the 1940s. Palacios's novel *Las estrellas son negras* (1949) follows a day and a half in the life of Israel, a black boy in the region of Chocó in Colombia who suffers from poverty and the physical pain of hunger. Israel (usually referred to as "Irra") is the first of five children in a family headed by the mother. The omniscient narrator is close to Irra: he follows Irra's thoughts and actions closely during the novel's short span of time. The thematic focus is on Irra's suffering, but in certain key moments he attains the political awareness that his suffering is part of a general condition of class and race. Ortiz's *Juyungo* (1943), like *Las estrellas son negras,* involves a synthesis of social protest and the protagonist's search for individual identity. The novel begins when the protagonist is approximately twelve years old, making this a story of rite de passage. The main interest of the novel, however, arises from his position as a black man in a variety of social contexts.

The publication of novels such as Luis Carlos Flórez's *Llamarada, novela obrera anti-imperialista* (1941) in Colombia was an indicator of the continued thrust of social protest fiction. The Colombian writer in Antioquia who most actively cultivated this type of fiction was Iván Cocherín, whose settings were western Antioquia (the present-day state of Caldas). The circumstance of mine workers in the town of Marmato in Caldas and similar scenarios are to be found in his novels

Esclavos de la tierra (1945), *El sol suda negro* (1954), and *Carapintada* (1959). Already more sophisticated than Cocherín in the use of narrative technique in his first novel, *Tierra mojada* (1947), Manuel Zapata Olivella's thematic interest was the experience of workers in plantations located in the northern Caribbean region of Colombia.

Latin American novelists shared a common bond in their questioning of the modernization, and, consequently, the burden of modernity was an issue.[23] Mariano Azuela questions Mexico's modernization project in *Nueva burguesía* (1941). Here, modernization undermines traditional values, and the satirical tone reveals Azuela's dismay over the postrevolutionary construction of capitalism in Mexico.

As mentioned, Carpentier had visited Haiti in the 1940s and believed that the African roots of Latin America were to be found in the popular culture of Haiti. In *El reino de este mundo,* Carpentier looks at the historical roots of Caribbean culture, here in Haiti. This novel relates the life and character of Ti Noel as they develop throughout the book's four parts. The first part, which consists of seven brief chapters, narrates a rebellion under the leadership of a man named Mac-Kandal. The second, which takes place twenty years later, also contains seven chapters and tells of the historic Bouckman massacre and of a yellow fever epidemic. The seven-chapter third part deals with the rule of Henri Christophe, and the fourth part relates the coming of the mulattos. *El reino de este mundo* does not offer the technical experimentation of Asturias or Yáñez; Carpentier's idea of innovation did not involve the use of fragmented structures or multiple points of view. His method for reaching a layer beneath the surface of empirical reality was not the employment of modernist strategies, but of oral storytelling techniques. As Carpentier understood the right of invention in the 1940s, the Latin American writer's task was to express "the marvelous real."[24]

Carpentier continued his discussion of Latin American culture in *Los pasos perdidos* (1953). In this novel, the characters regress in time as they travel into the jungle. This journey into the past ultimately leaves the protagonist lost—with ambiguous identity—for at the end he realizes that he is a misfit in the city and in primordial nature. It is a novel of failures: the protagonist fails to find any sort of transcendence, and Carpentier fails to fully exploit the ideas suggested in the novel.[25]

In general, the Brazilian novelists Ramos, Amado, de Queiroz, and Lins do Rego were not as committed to experimenting with narrative technique as were many novelists writing in Spanish, such as Asturias, García Márquez, and Rulfo. Nevertheless, these northeastern Brazilian writers had read Faulkner and produced novels of transcendent regionalism comparable in many ways to the fiction of Faulkner, Rulfo, and the early García Márquez.

Amado, de Queiroz, and Lins do Rego were modernists who published a substantial body of fiction during this period. The most productive of the group was Amado, whose commitment to social change was so marked during this period that some critics complained that his novels were too laden with ideas and explicit political messages. He began publishing fiction in the 1930s and subsequently wrote *Serra vermelha* (1946) and *Os subterrâneos da liberdade* (1954). De Queiroz brought women characters and women's themes to the forefront of Brazilian culture. She published her major fiction in the 1930s, although a notable second edition of *As três Marias* appeared in 1943 and a trilogy of previously published novels, *Três romances*, in 1948. Lins do Rego initiated a prolific and successful career as one of Brazil's pioneer modernists in the 1930s. In most of his fiction, Lins do Rego presents human beings in conflict and within a broad social context.

One of the most complex and ambitious modernist novels of the century in Latin America was João Guimarães Rosa's *Grande Sertão: Veredas*, comparable in complexity to Marechal's *Adán Buenosayres*. In addition to *Grande Sertão: Veredas*, several novels of the late 1950s that set the stage for the Latin American and the Latino novel of the 1960s and 1970s were Carlos Fuentes's *La región más transparente* (1958), Salvador Garmendia's *Los pequeños seres* (1959), and José Antonio Villareal's *Pocho* (1959). These novels emerge as a response to the fragmentation of the traditional societies in which they were written. In the case of *La región más transparente*, the new urban society of the postrevolution "Mexican miracle" was in conflict with the traditional and rural values of the prerevolutionary agrarian and hierarchical society. More traditional in narrative technique, *Pocho* is a Chicano novel that emerges as an art form responding to the conflict between traditional social relations of Hispanic society in the United States and a modernizing cultural hegemony in the region.[26] Both novelists focus on individual identity within this context of cultural conflict firmly grounded in history. Like García Márquez and Viñas, Fuentes and Villareal are interested in exploring how the past affects the present.

Like Fuentes, Garmendia explored the possibilities of modernist fiction in an urban setting. *Los pequeños seres* (1959), widely recognized as a pioneer urban novel in Venezuela, is the story of Mateo Martán, told mostly through interior monologues, with multiple levels of time and varied levels of the perception of reality. The exploration of an individual's psyche in this urban setting is something of an innovation in itself in Venezuela, although this type of fiction already had seen exponents throughout Latin America since the late 1940s. *Los habitantes* (1961) is Garmendia's fictionalization of urban working-class life, with a focus on truck drivers. It is the story of an individual's alienation, with subtle changes in time and perspective.

Garmendia's anguished characters tend to be engaged in some kind of existential search, and many novelists of this period, including Marechal, Lispector, and Sábato, published novels of existential search. Villareal's *Pocho* is equally rooted in the events of empirical history as Fuentes's *La región más transparente:* one important character, Juan Rubio, must flee to the United States after having participated in the Mexican Revolution. His son, Richard, however, is the protagonist and *pocho* (a pejorative term for an "Americanized" Chicano). Born in the agricultural lands of California, Richard struggles with belonging to two cultures but not being fully accepted in either. He rejects his father's Mexican values as well as his mother's Catholic values, proclaiming his own sense of identity simply as "I am."

These novels by Fuentes and Garmendia represent an opening for the Spanish American novel in a variety of ways. Fuentes appropriates a full array of modernist strategies to tell a historically based urban story about identity with an ambitious approach that many Latin American novelists continued in the 1960s and 1970s. Clearly, a totalizing impulse is evident in the writing of these authors.

In their desire to be modern, the Latin American novelists of the 1940s and 1950s were well aware of the basic tenets of modernism, and their understanding of the aesthetics of modernism dramatically transformed Latin American fiction. The roots of this novelistic revolution are to be found in the *vanguardia* of the 1920s, the 1922 Semana de Arte Moderna in Brazil, and the fiction of Borges. Like their counterparts in Europe and the United States, these writers searched for new methods to know the world through individual consciousness. Unlike their counterparts, however, many of these Latin American modernists remained somewhat concerned with the world of ideas or things that could be objectively known—the social and political realities that had concerned several previous generations of Latin American writers. Their successful understanding of oral cultural traditions—as seen in Asturias, Carpentier, and others—and their incorporation of it was a major innovation for modernist writing. This use of oral tradition, as cultivated by the novelist-anthropologist, set Latin American fiction apart. Cultural conflict was a common theme in many of the modernist texts of this period, including what was essentially a conflict between writing and oral culture. Asturias, Fuentes, and García Márquez, for example, were experimenting with both individual consciousness and the objective world of cultural conflict. The enthusiastic reception of Faulkner by this generation of Latin American writers was understandable, for these novelists found in Faulkner innovative narrative strategies, new methods for exploring individual consciousness, and a hierarchical, traditional society burdened by anachronistic values similar to those still extant in their own nations.

With the rise of modernist fiction in Latin America, these novelists were writing with confidence. They explored new depths in the reality of the various regions, penetrating the interior of both the individual and the collectivity. The novels of Galindo and Garmendia were representative of the new modernist fiction in Latin America that focused on human relationships as opposed to the broad, muralistic novels such as *La región más transparente*. With their writing, these modernist novelists reaffirmed their right to create a fiction that not only reproduced reality but also invented it. They finally realized the desire to be modern as it had been conceived among the writers invoked with the 1920s *vanguardias.*

The heterogeneity of the Latin American novel was more evident than ever: the writing of women, Afro–Latin Americans, Native Americans, and Chicano writers during this period was evidence of this growing hybridity. The novelistic production of Rosario Castellanos, Antonia Palacios, Yolanda Oreamuno, and Elisa Mújica were testimony to the significant fictional contributions written by women. The masculinist aesthetic was challenged in a wide range of texts written by men and women who questioned authority and traditional discourses. Afro-American writers such as Arnoldo Palacios and Adalberto Ortiz contributed to the heterogeneity of discursive practices.[27]

The desire to be modern is played out with modernist aesthetics and with a new focus on problems of identity and cultural conflict. Generally speaking, identity was sought in a universal context. Many of the novelists carried this out with the strategies of transcendent regionalism, while others pursued the effects of oral culture and, in turn, what was identified as magic realism.[28] In retrospect, it is evident that some of the major modernist texts of the century appeared during this period, one of the most remarkable being Nobel laureate Asturias's *El Señor Presidente*. Another Nobel laureate, Gabriel García Márquez, published his first novel and stories in the 1950s, as did Fuentes. The Chilean poet Gabriela Mistral was awarded the Nobel Prize in literature in 1945. In a variety of ways and because of several unrelated circumstances, by 1961 the scene was set for the 1960s Boom of the Spanish American novel.

Seven   **Rereading Spanish American**
Modernist Novels

In addition to the short fiction of Borges, the unequivocal indicator of a cultural shift in Latin America toward modernist
writing was the publication in the 1940s of the landmark modernist novels of Miguel Angel Asturias, Agustín Yáñez, Leopoldo Marechal, and Alejo Carpentier.[1] Important and representative novels of
the 1940s and 1950s to be analyzed in this chapter—all of which demonstrate an urgent desire to be modern—are Asturias's *El Señor Presidente* (1946), Yáñez's *Al filo del agua* (1947), Marechal's *Adán Buenosayres* (1948), Juan Rulfo's *Pedro Páramo* (1955), and Carlos Fuentes's
La región más transparente (1958). Among these writers, Marechal
has been the least recognized. Nevertheless, they all were fully engaged in a new modernist aesthetic, and they were interested, to different degrees, in fictionalizing universal archetypes or myths, such
as the quest. Three of these novelists were ostensibly political in their
writing.

When the Latin American writer entered the decade of the 1940s,
readers and critics were not readily prepared to set aside their conventional expectations for fiction and to embrace the modernist novelistic enterprise. The modernist novel as explored, written, and promoted by the different groups of *vanguardia* had not satisfied the
cultural context. The situation seemed to confirm what García Canclini declared decades later: "Latin America: where traditions have
not yet departed, and modernity has not yet arrived."[2] The novelists of this period, like those of today, made García Canclini's remark
as questionable as was Torres Rioseco's in 1929 with respect to the

fiction of *vanguardia*.[3] These novelists realized interests of the *vanguardia* writers of the 1920s and 1930s; indeed, there were several direct connections between these novelists and the *vanguardia*. Asturias was involved with the avant-garde in Europe in the 1920s, and Yáñez published in the avant-garde magazine *Bandera de Provincia* in Guadalajara. Fuentes's connection to this *vanguardia* was through his mentor Alfonso Reyes.[4]

Borges's claim that Bioy Casares's novel of 1940, *La invención de Morel*, was the perfect novel is noteworthy within the context of the novels that appeared during the remainder of the 1940s. It is difficult to guess what Borges's criteria might have been to reach this conclusion, which the reader is invited to assume must have been stated with tongue in cheek, perhaps because, by the conventional standards in place in Argentina at the time, the novel was a grossly imperfect aberration of known literary practices. But in the 1940s and 1950s, several novels, including *El Señor Presidente, Al filo del agua,* and *Pedro Páramo,* were in some ways perfect, at least as manifestations of modernist aesthetics in fiction.

Many modernist writers in Europe and the United States implicitly accepted a divorce between aesthetics and politics. Asturias, Fuentes, and most of the other Latin American modernists refused to recognize this supposed separation between art and ideology. Continuing in the path of their Latin American forerunners, they considered themselves political writers, and they were. *El Señor Presidente* is an explicitly political novel in which Asturias denounces a historical dictator in Guatemala as well as Latin American dictators in general. The politics of writing held different meanings for Marechal, Yáñez, and Fuentes. For Marechal, who was known as a Peronist writer in Argentina, literary politics meant marginalization from his lifetime friends of the Florida and Martín Fierro groups. In the influential organ *Sur,* for example, *Adán Buenosayres* was summarily dismissed as a poor copy of *Ulysses.* For Yáñez, politics meant participating in the political establishment (Mexico's PRI) at the same time that he wrote novels critical of the status quo in the Mexico of earlier years. Carlos Fuentes, on the other hand, vigorously questioned the political and literary establishment in Mexico in the 1950s, and his early novels *La región más transparente* and *La muerte de Artemio Cruz* explicitly set forth his rebellious attitude and revolutionary politics of the late 1950s and early 1960s.

The most ostensibly modernist and explicitly political of these novels are Asturias's *El Señor Presidente*, Yáñez's *Al filo del agua*, and Fuentes's *La región más transparente*. Having been fully committed to the modernist enterprise since the 1920s, Asturias employed a broad range of modernist strategies of fiction in the creation of *El Señor Presidente*. He utilizes interior monologues and stream of consciousness, for example, with mastery. Asturias also uses techniques that associate this novel with expressionism, surrealism, and cubism. Asturias relies on expressionistic stratagems to suggest irrational mental states in moments of panic. Indeed, Asturias filters the thoughts of characters whose extreme fear distorts their vision of reality, producing expressionistic effects. The author's exploration of dreams and use of dreamlike imagery (especially the image of a single eye that appears in one dream) connect the novel to surrealism, and the surrealist effects are constant in this work.

In all five of these novels, authority figures are under siege. The authority figure in *El Señor Presidente* is a fictionalized version of Manuel Estrada Cabrera, the early-twentieth-century strongman in Guatemala, even though neither Estrada Cabrera nor Guatemala is ever specifically named in the novel. The time frame is approximately the first half of the century, and the novel begins with the assassination of a military officer, Colonel José Parrales Sonriente, when a deranged person kills him as an instinctual reaction on the street. The dictator, identified only as "the President," uses this death to eliminate two men, the lawyer Carvajal and General Canales. Colonel Parrales Sonriente has Carvajal arrested, tried in court, and shot. He plans to have Miguel Cara de Angel persuade Canales to flee his home at night in order to have him shot. Cara de Angel, however, creates an escape scheme that allows the general to flee from his home and into the mountains. Back in the city, Canales's daughter becomes ill, and Cara de Angel falls in love with her and marries her. In the end, he is imprisoned and eventually dies. Despite this outcome and the attendant setbacks for the small group of essentially well-intentioned individuals, this denunciation of the amoral dictator intimates that there is some hope for the citizens of this nation and for humanity. The dictator himself appears rarely—only six times—and usually briefly. Rather than operating as a visible character, he is a shadow presence that pervades virtually everything; Estrada Cabrera was a similarly invisible omnipresence in Guatemala.

This résumé of the plot does not provide a sense of Asturias's strategies as a storyteller. Like García Márquez, Asturias maintains a rapid flow not only of language, but of plot, too, with chapters that function well as entities in themselves, as in *Cien años de soledad*. Lacking the hyperbole of García Márquez's novel, Asturias overwhelms the reader with ugly scenes of grotesque human behavior. The reader is not a spectator to an incredible celebration of life (as in *Cien años de soledad*), but to the spectacle of horrific human behavior and the attendant moral dilemmas.

Readings of *El Señor Presidente* have tended to emphasize the universal qualities of one of Latin America's most widely read and canonical novels. Many of these readings have focused on how Asturias achieves widely appreciated effects through the use of language. Indeed, the opening chapter invites the reader to join in a universally understood and primordial order of linguistic effects—as opposed to rational communication. The arresting first chapter offers an impressive linguistic texture in which sensory perceptions, especially the sense of smell, dominate. The novel begins with the narrator's incantation "Alumbra, lumbre de alumbre, Luzbel de piedralumbre!" (referring to lights and the devil) and the sound of church bells. The chapter's initial setting involves a group of beggars on church stairs and a dark street at night; it culminates in the madman's attack and murder of Colonel José Parrales Sonriente. The narrator evokes both Christian and Arabic religious traditions with his language, and after these words of invocation, he closes with a brief final sentence: "Estaba amaneciendo." This understatement creates a striking contrast with the powerful language and lengthy sentences of the remainder of the chapter.

By creating a strong sense of closure to this first chapter, Asturias demonstrates his subtle handling of his craft as a traditionalist. In a similar use of a conventional device, Asturias creates a circular structure in the novel through the presence of a student and a sacristan at the beginning of chapter 2 and in the last chapter. The author employs other time-tested strategies in *El Señor Presidente*, such as the regular use of conventional images of darkness and light to suggest pessimistic and optimistic moments in the novel. Many aspects of Asturias's novel can be associated with traditional cultures and writing and several others with modernity and modernism. With respect to the modern, Naomi Lindstrom considers *El Señor Presidente* the most cosmopolitan and urbane of Asturias's novels and observes how many of the book's features relate directly to the experimentation of the European avant-garde that had been so important for Asturias in the 1920s.[5] She points out that the word "nightmare" appears frequently, and the novel generates an atmosphere of nightmarish fear and uncertainty. It replicates certain spatial and temporal distortions characteristic of uneasy dreams. *El Señor Presidente* can also be read as a cyclic struggle between fertility and destruction: the president embodies sterility and death, and Cara de Angel represents the generative forces of nature. Some of the novel's scenes can be related to Mayan mythology; thus, Asturias juxtaposes Babylon, a symbol of corruption and cruelty since biblical times, with a modern city suffering a cruel dictatorship. Asturias's mythic vision can be related to Rulfo's desire to be modern and universal through the use of myths.

These simultaneously conventional and modern approaches to fiction and reality help define the specialness of *El Señor Presidente*. In many ways, this novel is a summa of traditionalist and modernist aesthetics and interests in Latin American fiction since early in the century. Paradoxically, this is a work that uses high modernist narrative strategies, yet contains a dictionary of vocabulary at the end that the reader associates with the *criollista* text. Similarly, *El Señor Presidente* contains, on the one hand, an incorporation of oral storytelling techniques of traditional cultures and the stream of consciousness of high modernism. The result of Asturias's synthesis is exactly what Torres Bodet and Guiraldes attempted and failed: the universal text. To use Borges's reference to Bioy Casares once again, this synthesis could be used as an argument for how *El Señor Presidente* indeed is the perfect novel.

Yáñez and his generation of writers in Mexico were equally interested in participating in what they called "universal" literature. For Joseph Sommers, Yáñez was fully successful, affirming that *Al filo del agua* is a work of "universal interest."[6] Like Asturias, Yáñez had an ear for oral culture as well as contact with the *vanguardia*. In *Al filo del agua* he evokes special effects with stylistic maneuvers with language and interior monologues. Rarely does one find a modernist novel with such a seemingly perfect harmony between form and content; it is a technical masterpiece of modernist fiction in Mexico and Latin America in general. If *El Señor Presidente* represents a synthesis of traditional and modernist aesthetics, *Al filo del agua* is its peer in modernist aesthetics and the novel for which Borges might have made the argument about perfection, at least within the context of modernist fiction. As a modernist with universal interests who used a specific regional setting, Yáñez was a pioneer in creating the transcendent regionalist text.

The setting for *Al filo del agua* is a small town in the provinces during a year-and-a-half period leading up to the Mexican Revolution in 1910. Early in the novel, it is apparent that the Catholic Church dominates all aspects of life in the town. In the second chapter, "Ejercicios de encierro," for example, the reader is privy to seven characters' digressive thoughts about the church and spiritual matters. The omniscient narrator describes the characters' thoughts, which, in turn, are intercalated with interior monologues of the seven characters. As the novel progresses, however, it is also evident that the church is losing its influence among the townsfolk. Secret lives and relationships also develop in the town. Micaela and the northerner Damián have a secret affair. After Micaela experiences life in Mexico City, she cannot accept the strict social morés of the town. At the end of the novel, the young woman María rejects her upbringing and the town's patriarchal values by fleeing with the revolutionaries who sweep through the region.

One reason that *Al filo del agua* produces the effect of moving from chaos to harmony is the structure. The novel contains sixteen chapters that unfold into a pattern of two parts. The first part consists of eight chapters, the first of which is the "Acto preparatorio." In this chapter, which offers a static vision of life in the town, Yáñez employs few verbs—including many sentences with no verbs at all—to create a sense of timelessness. A series of repetitions, such as the mention of "mujeres enlutadas" four times throughout the chapter, creates a sense of tediousness and monotony that are the essence of life in the town. The minimal sense of the flow of time operates in contrast to the forces of repression and reaction against change.

Stylistic suggestions of the opposition between change and repression of change set up, in effect, the entire first part of the novel's structure; the next seven chapters operate on the basis of a series of oppositions or dualities. Chapter 3, for example, contrasts Marta and María, sisters who are characterized as opposites in everything from their physical appearance to their personalities, like their New Testament namesakes. Marta is cautious and conservative; María is bold, progressive, and interested in modern life beyond the town. María reads foreign novels and dreams of traveling to modern cities, from Aguascalientes (Mexico) to Rome and Constantinople. The seventh chapter,

"Los norteños," introduces characters who have been in the United States and bring back modern ideas about life and politics in opposition to the fixed ways of the townsfolk.

Yáñez did not have quite as deep an interest in oral culture as Asturias, but traces of oral culture are evident in this first part of the novel. In this context, a chapter titled "El viejo Lucas Macías" stands out. The old man Lucas Macías, the repository of oral culture in the town, remembers and relates the town's past and its traditions—the conventional role of the storyteller in oral cultures. He is an illiterate who bridges the gap between oral and writing cultures, since much of his knowledge actually comes from what the townsfolk have read to him.

In the role of the oral storyteller, Lucas Macías is the synthesizer of the stories he hears from others and a central figure in the town. As storyteller, his stories contain some of the formal qualities of the oral tradition and lack some of the qualities of writing culture. Yáñez imitates his oral style in Lucas's story about a circus that came to town, which is transcribed in one sentence that extends over two pages in length. In another type of reproduction of oral storytelling, this same chapter contains a minutely detailed description (of almost two pages in length) of the coffin in which don Timoteo's wife, Tacha, is buried. The copiousness of this description recalls the oral tradition as defined by Ong.[7] In the last chapter, as the news of the revolution reaches the town, Lucas recognizes that he belongs to an earlier (preliterate) order and states "¡Eh! yo ya soy más del otro mundo que de éste" (Oh! I'm now more from the other world than from this one).[8] When the revolution has overtaken the town near the end of the novel, it is the wise Lucas Macías who announces "¡Estamos al filo del agua!" (We're at the edge of the storm! *Al filo del agua*, 376) and then dies, thus signaling a changing of the guard in the town, in essence, the shift from a preliterate to a modern world.

In his role as oral storyteller, it is notable that Lucas is also something of an author figure for Yáñez, articulating the role of the modern writer. This is not really an idea cherished by the oral storyteller, who either likes to see the events or feign having seen them. Here, rather, Lucas plays the role of the modern (Yáñez figure) who affirms the right of invention.

The eighth of the seventeen chapters, "Canicas," functions as a type of intermezzo, recapitulating some of the novel's themes and prefiguring the revolution.[9] This chapter prefigures the upcoming change in the town, which is about to be drawn into the larger scene in Mexico. The chapter also introduces Gabriel, the bell ringer whose music is central to the town's entire daily rhythm and life. The narrator associates Gabriel's creative force with the revolution.

"Canicas" begins with the arrival of the new political boss *(director político)*, who attempts to negotiate political support from don Dionisio and the church. But the first segment suggests that rather than being subject to the will of either the political director or don Dionisio, the townsfolk will find their future in "rodar de las canicas" (rolling the dice; *Al filo del agua*, 163). Soon thereafter, in the second narrative segment of the "Canicas" chapter, Yáñez uses the image of the *canicas* (dice) in the town as a synecdoche for the nation: "Mientras ruedan lentamente las oscuras canicas de la parroquia, se precipita la vida del país" (While the black dice roll slowly, the country's life goes on; *Al filo del agua*, 164). The remainder of the chapter continues developing a vision of life as simply a process of seeing how this game of chance—this *canicas*—plays itself out. A "dark" player is in the background, too, the *canica oscura* that is the figure of Gabriel the bell ringer (*Al filo del agua*, 166). In this "Canicas" chapter, then, three intangible, subjective forces are in operation: the unpredictable *canicas*, the conservative forces of the church, and the growing political tensions that are entering the town from the outside. The image of the *canicas* is repeated in oral storytelling fashion throughout the chapter, and the chapter ends with the statement "Va rodando la bola" (The ball rolls on), suggesting that the future of Mexico is as uncertain as a game of chance.

In the novel's second part, the ninth chapter, entitled "Gabriel and Victoria," functions as an overture to the novel's second half and thus has a function parallel to the "Acto preparatorio" in the first half.[10] This chapter relates the relationship of Gabriel and the attractive Victoria, but the relationship becomes an abstraction, for Gabriel is characterized not only as a bell ringer but also as the artist in the abstract: he is not interested in merely imitating the styles of other bell ringers in other churches but is so committed to his art that he is not capable of such betrayal of his artistry. Gabriel's mysterious origins contribute to his specialness as a character, giving him mythic qualities.

The novel's last seven chapters function as a mirror image of the first part, creating a symmetrical structure. They continue to portray relationships among the people of the town as well as the growing rebellion. By the end, the hermeticism of the town is broken by the revolution. The mirror-image effect with the first part is created by repeating elements similar to those seen in the first part. María, for example, continues reading foreign novels and continues dreaming of life in such remote cities as Paris, Vienna, and Constantinople. Gabriel is characterized as an individual who mirrors María. This characterization, in turn, contributes to Gabriel's identity as a mythic character—the other-worldly artist. In Yáñez's constant play of opposites and mirrors in the novel, he presents María and Gabriel, interestingly enough, as parallel characters who erroneously think they are opposites (*Al filo del agua*, 182). With this characterization, Yáñez invites the reader to question the validity of extreme opposites: oppositions can also contain parallels and harmonies, so reality cannot necessarily be reduced to simplistic oppositions.

One of the most subtle mirror images of the first part is stylistic: certain passages in the second half of the novel reflect back stylistically on the first part. For example, in the narrator's description of the third time that Gabriel and Victoria saw each other, the narrator creates a stylistic mirror image of the "Acto Preparatorio," with short sentences and without the use of conjugated verbs, as in the "Acto Preparatorio." The effect of this passage is to recall the novel's opening, to evoke the long-term static quality of the town, and to place the sprouting relationship between Victoria and Gabriel in this context.

The meaning of *Al filo del agua* is multileveled. The Catholic Church is an overwhelming presence, affecting all aspects of life and thought in the town. At the novel's conclusion, the church's domination of the town is ended with the coming of the revolution from the outside. Near the beginning of the last chapter, the priest, don Dionisio, feels tired and wants to die, a symbolic characterization suggesting the overall malaise of the church. The outcome of the church's role is signaled by the statement near the end of the chapter with the priest's demise: "El cura se derrumba sin sentido en el pavimiento" (The priest falls down unconscious on the pavement; *Al filo del agua*, 386). In its totality, however, the novel is less about religion than tyranny, as Brushwood points out: "Yáñez's novel is not antichurch or even anticlerical, as some have wished to make it; it is very much anti the tyrannies men allow themselves to create and then suffer."[11] It is also a novel that creates oppositions and dualities while inviting the reader to question any sense of reality that reduces individuals and events to simple and consistent dichotomies: in the end, the world of *Al filo del agua* is too nuanced and complex for the reader to accept all such reductions.

Rarely does one encounter a modernist novel with such a seemingly perfect harmony between form and content as *Al filo del agua*. The two-part structure leads the reader through a process from fragmentation to harmony; the content of the novel also points to the fragmentation of the characters in the first half and their harmonious fulfillment of desires when they join the revolution.

Rulfo's *Pedro Páramo* has many connections with *Al filo del agua*, both as modernist text and as a novel set in a rural ambience in which oral culture is important. Like *El Señor Presidente* and *Al filo del agua*, *Pedro Páramo* is the transcendent regionalist text that uses a regional setting for a microcosm to relate a story of broader, universal interest.[12] In Spanish, in fact, the title itself has universal implications.[13] A short novel, *Pedro Páramo* consists of seventy brief segments (ranging in length from three lines to eight or nine pages) that tell the story of Juan Preciado, one of the many children of Pedro Páramo.[14] The setting is the fictional town of Comala, a small town in the desert that is similar to the rural areas of Jalisco where Rulfo was reared.

This is a novel of a quest: Juan Preciado comes to Comala in search of his father, and the reader soon discovers that Páramo is dead; in segment 37, about sixty pages into the novel, it is evident that all the characters of Comala, in fact, including Juan Preciado, are dead. The narrative alternates between first-person accounts of Juan Preciado and narratives related by an omniscient narrator. In their totality, the brief segments and the numerous voices (of the two narrators and the characters) provide a portrait of Pedro Páramo as a ruthless cacique. There are eight different first-person narrators and at least seventy-three characters. The lack of causality is extreme for a novel published in 1955: only near the end do all the pieces come together well enough for the reader to ascertain that Páramo had forced Dolores Preciado to marry him, then abandoned her after gaining control of her fortune. Embittered by the loss of the one woman he apparently loved, Susana San Juan, Pedro Páramo pursued women and power and eventually left town.

Pedro Páramo does not offer the precise and systematic structural duality of *Al filo del agua*. The first half of the novel deals primarily with Juan Preciado's search for his father, as well as conversations with deceased residents of Comala and anecdotes from the past, including the funeral for Páramo's son Miguel. In the second half, it is revealed that Comala has suffered because Páramo wanted to punish the town after it celebrated the death of Susana San Juan. It also becomes apparent that Páramo's illegitimate son, Abundio, killed Pedro.

The matter of exactly who narrates each of the novel's segments has been much disputed; it is generally accepted that Juan Preciado narrates most of the first half of the novel (segments 1–37). In fact, he narrates eighteen of the narrative segments to an old woman, Dorotea, in their common tomb, and the second narrator of importance is Pedro Páramo himself, who narrates seven segments.[15] Since there are multiple narrators and a variety of temporal levels, the reader experiences an initial impression of facing a chaotic and potentially confusing text. Nevertheless, a certain order and sense is gained as the text advances. The fact that Juan Preciado and Dorotea speak in a state of death does not need to imply, for example, that all of their lives or that all the conversations they hear are from the dimension of death.[16] In addition, *Pedro Páramo* is not as completely atemporal as some critics have suggested. To the contrary, there is an important chronology of events at the temporal level, and there are enough time indicators for the discerning reader to reconstruct many of the stories in time.[17]

Like Yáñez, Rulfo was a master of style who seemed to imitate rural speech but who in fact used stylistic nuances that meant innovating conventional literary language and everyday speech. As Lindstrom has observed, Rulfo's accomplishment was to develop a type of speech that seems plausible in the mouths of uneducated characters yet is unmistakably poeticized.[18] Similarly, Brushwood has explained that Rulfo captures and uses the essence of rural speech so that we accept his language as authentic, but Rulfo allows it to remove us from a folkloric plane to a mythic plane where we observe not customs but symbols of customs.[19] In *Al filo del agua*, the language of the omniscient narrator and characters such as *el viejo*, Lucas Macías, is copious and repetitive; in *Pedro Páramo*, the language of the omniscient narrator and the characters tends to be sparse. The effect of this sparse language and neutral tone is a certain mythic quality that permeates *Pedro Páramo* and makes it the transcendent regionalist text that seems to belong to a specific regional setting, yet it has much broader thematic overtones.

In addition to language, several other facets of *Pedro Páramo* create mythic effects. The basic story line contains the mythic dimension of a son's search for his father. In addition, the entire story offers certain analogies with classical myths, beginning with relatively obvious biblical allusions. In Juan Preciado's introduction to Comala in the novel's first segment, for example, there are several suggestions that the characters are in hell, including the statement by one character that Comala is "en la mera boca del infierno" (in the very mouth of hell).[20] Páramo's life can be associated with the biblical Fall. Rulfo returns to some of the most basic forms of myth, but without creating characters with the solemnity of many mythic characters.[21]

The novel's mythic qualities offer a level of unity to this fragmented work, giving the reader the opportunity to find order in the reading of the novel as allegory. In addition, the use of certain imagery, such as water imagery, creates a sense of unity. Rulfo uses water imagery to lead the reader into flashbacks, telling key events in the past in connection with raindrops, for example. The narrative segments dealing with Páramo's lover Susana, for example, are flashbacks introduced with water imagery. By offering the reader unities in the form of allegorical readings and imagery, Rulfo created one of the most subtle modernist texts to have been written in Latin America by mid-century.

The competent modern reader finds unities in *Pedro Páramo* in the process of reading and is presented with an allegory in the character of Juan Preciado, whom one critic has identified as a "surrogate" for readers.[22] This competent reader assumes a task—indeed, a search—parallel to Juan Preciado's, actively attempting to establish identities and find order. Arriving at halfway through the text (segment 37), the reader must make adjustments, accepting the new reality of a fictional world that is entirely deceased. Despite all the adjustments that the modern reader must make, readers have not questioned the basic verisimilitude of this text; once the reader moves beyond segment 37, the novel's mythic truths require the reader to set aside conventional ideas of causality and logic.

The novel's final image of Pedro Páramo as a "montón de piedras" (pile of stones) can be seen as a symbol of both the unity and fragmentation of the text, thus capturing the essence of the reader's experience of the work's early chaos and final unity.[23] Indeed, from the first narrative segment to the last line, Rulfo has constructed a masterpiece that the competent modern reader might conclude is indeed the perfect novel (within the parameters of modernist aesthetics). If *Al filo del agua* offers the perfect structure, Rulfo uses the perfect set of ambiguous fragments and language.

Rulfo creates characters of specific individual identity that is in line with modern concepts associated with the singular and the existential. The identity of Pedro is of macho and cacique, and the other males in *Pedro Páramo* tend to fit the paradigm of the classic macho personified by Pedro. The women in the novel have their identity defined and limited by societal conventions. Susana San Juan is one exception: she stands forth as an individual who is unconventional, who celebrates her sensuality and sexuality, and who can be linked with the spirit of life. Like Gabriel in *Al filo del agua*, she is a creative force.

Pedro Páramo is a noteworthy book in the context of more recent discussions of the masculinist aesthetic that predominated in much Latin American fiction of the first half of the century. The destructive and repressive actions of Pedro underline the worst that a conventional patriarchal society can produce. His desire for total possession of his lover's body is a description of a patriarchal hold on the female body. The counterpart to this patriarchal scheme, however, is Susana: as the sensuous and sexual individual, she is the voice of life and regenerative element in this fictional world. The counterpoint of Susana makes it possible to view *Pedro Páramo* as a transitional text between the masculinist aesthetics of writers such as Guiraldes and the postmodern and feminist aesthetics of later writers such as Eltit, Piglia, and Molloy.

Leopoldo Marechal and Carlos Fuentes, in contrast to Asturias, Yáñez, and Rulfo, are urban writers with distance from oral cultures, from folk traditions, and from transcendent regionalism. Their settings for the novels *Adán Buenosayres* and *La región más transparente* are Buenos Aires and Mexico City. In Argentina, Marechal suffered marginalization because of his politics (his association with Perón), one of the principal reasons his novel *Adán Buenosayres* did not receive the recognition it deserved in Argentina (or Latin America) during the 1940s and 1950s. Like Asturias, Yáñez, and Carpentier, Marechal was interested in European avant-garde writing; he participated in the cultural activities of the "Martín Fierro" group in Buenos Aires in the 1920s. Since the 1960s, there has been a Marechal revival in Argentina; writers and critics of several generations have expressed their admiration for his creative work.

Lengthy, complex, and sometimes daunting, Marechal's *Adán Buenosayres* had its genesis in Paris in the 1930s, when, according to Marechal, he was suffering a profound spiritual crisis and wrote a first draft. The novel consists of seven *libros* that are divided into three parts. The first part, which contains five of these books (368 pages), centers on Adán Buenosayres and his cohorts. The second part, book six (36 pages), is Adán Buenosayres's "Cuaderno de tapas azules" (Notebook with blue covers). The third part, book seven (239 pages) is entitled "Viaje a la oscura ciudad de Cacodelphia" (Trip to the dark city of Cacodelphia). In the first five books, Adán Buenosayres engages his intellectual and writer friends in a lengthy dialogue. In a "Pró-logo indispensable" (Indispensable prologue) preceding these books, the narrator tells of the burial of Adán Buenosayres, an act that is de-scribed less as the death of a man than as the material of a "poema concluido" (finished poem). The narrator-author then explains that Adán had given him two manuscripts on his deathbed: "Cuaderno de tapas azules" and "Viaje a la oscura ciudad de Cacodelphia." After re-viewing them and deciding that they merited publication as valuable contributions to Argentine letters, the narrator-author decides to pro-vide a portrait of the author and protagonist of these two pieces. After further consideration, however, he opts to portray the protagonist in the context of the conflicts and crises in his own life. The result is the five books that follow the prologue, covering one day in the life of Adán Buenosayres. The narrator-author sets the tone for the novel by mentioning that he himself wrote the first draft for this work in Paris in 1930 and then suffered a spiritual crisis. *Adán Buenosayres* can be read as an important satirical novel dealing with the world of avant-garde literati in Buenos Aires in the 1920s.[24] An intellectually induced circumstance created by the personalities in the novel is the basis for the work's style. For Lindstrom, Adán is a metaphor and can be seen as a figure of man at the outset of life, or a representative of the human quest, and he incarnates the Argentine, the man of Buenos Aires, or the city itself figured in human form.[25] Adán, however, alternates be-tween metaphorical and realistic traits, just as the novel alternates between abstract and realistic modes of representation. The novel's themes follow a similar dual pattern, involving the reality of Buenos Aires as well as neo-Platonic and Christian philosophical concerns.

The first book, which begins on an April 28 sometime in the 1920s, tells of Adán Buenosayres's life in Buenos Aires as a poet and intellec-tual fascinated with Greek and Roman literature. Like Pedro Páramo, he suffers from an idealized love for a woman (Solveig Admussen) as well as from a general existential anguish. There is mention of the "Cuaderno de tapas azules," Adán's prized work that he gives to Sol-veig. In this chapter, the narrator also introduces Samuel Tesler, a Russian emigré from Odessa who practices philosophy.

The second, third, fourth, and fifth books continue the story of Adán, his love for Solveig, and his intellectual friends. Adán's walks around Buenos Aires are portrayed in the epic terms of the hero involved in a quest. He participates in a lengthy literary *tertulia* with his friends—a soirée at which they discuss Argentine and world literature, particularly the former. At another level, the text functions as a roman à clef that satirizes certain Argentine intellectual figures of the 1920s; these, in turn, criticize and satirize Argentine society of the time, particularly its bourgeois values.

The sixth book (and second part of the novel), "Cuaderno de tapas azules," is Adán's notebook in which he has recorded the history of his soul and his emotional states since childhood. To some extent, it is also a history of his insanity: he probes into the depths of his afflicted soul, letting his imagination run free, and reveals his dreams. At the end of his tortuous spiritual quest, he concludes his notebook by observing that his life finally has a clear direction and hope.

The seventh book (and third part of the novel) is Adán's surreal trip through the nine levels or circles of the dark city of Cacodelphia (a name that plays with the word for excrement in Spanish). The astrologer Schultze serves as Adán's guide, explaining in the beginning that Cacodelphia is not a mythological city but a real one. After approaching a foggy part of town, they descend into its center. (The reader is warned early in the book either to return to Buenos Aires or to continue the trip.) During the playful and satirical journey, Marechal continues his critique of Argentine literature and society. Numerous allusions throughout the novel also make it a parody of classical Greek texts.

The humorous effects and remarkable style in *Adán Buenosayres* depend to a large extent on Marechal's use of language. The text's standard discourse is an elegant literary style into which Marechal occasionally inserts colloquial or vulgar words and phrases, thereby creating a farcical effect. The vulgar language tends to emphasize the anal, and the humorous consequences tend to deflate the pretentious.[26]

An ambitious modernist novel, *Adán Buenosayres* is distant from the oral tradition and transcendent regionalism of *Al filo del agua* and *Pedro Páramo*. Like *La región más transparente*, however, this novel prefigures some of the impulses toward the "total" novel seen in the 1960s Boom. Indeed, this lengthy and Joycean text shares several of the characteristics of the total novel, certainly making it a much more viable example than had been seen in ambitious yet conventional works such as *Doña Bárbara*.

Fuentes's *La región más transparente* shares Marchechal's totalization impulse. The urban setting for *La región más transparente* is a Mexican city similar to the Mexico City of the 1950s, when the nation was in a process of ongoing modernization. *La región más transparente* deals with the nation in this context and the issue of identity. Fuentes's desire to be modern is exhibited both in modernist technique and in the work's dealing with modernity as a theme: Mexico's modernity is fictionalized within a context of rapid capitalization and promotion of industrial and technological change as questionable progress. Like Pedro Páramo and Adán Buenosayres, the characters are representations of the modern individual subject; progress is fictionalized in a context of the successes and failures of individuals, with their respective ascents and descents in Mexican society. Identity, in fact, is frequently conceptualized in this novel in opposition to progress: the modern Mexican is portrayed as an uprooted individual who has lost much sense of past and identity.

La región más transparente appeared at a time when identity was more of an issue for Mexican intellectuals than it was for Marechal in Argentina. In Mexico, the essays of Samuel Ramos and Alfonso Reyes in the 1930s and Paz's essay *Labyrinth of Solitude* (1950) set a discursive direction for many Mexican intellectuals. Thus, in *La región más transparente*, Fuentes appropriates and fictionalizes many of Paz's themes, such as the characterization of men as violators and women who are violated and Mexicans' use of masks to hide their identity.[27] It deals self-consciously with the conventional macho paradigm and is overt in its questioning of masculinist aesthetics.

Fuentes began this first novel by establishing a distinction between "novel" and "history" more clearly delineated: a page appears at the beginning with a chronological outline of the *novela* and another with the events of Mexican *historia*. After this six-page chronological overview, Fuentes offers a four-page guide to all of the eighty-three characters, with brief, one-line descriptions of the role of each. They are classified, to a large extent, by social status. The wide range of characters includes the de Ovanda family, the Zamaconas, the Polas, a bourgeois group, intellectuals, foreigners, socialites, a lower-class group, and representatives of the Indians—Ixca Cienfuegos and his mother Teódula Moctezuma. For Fuentes, the numerous individuals and social groups have intricate and seemingly endless connections and contacts. Thus, what might appear to be a chaotic presentation of a large panoply of characters eventually becomes a huge network with connections that provide one of the numerous levels of unity to *La región más transparente*.

In *La región más transparente*, Fuentes fully exploits the technical devices pioneered by First World modernists as well as by Rulfo and Yáñez to explore the past and present of modern Mexico. In this novel, he uses the multiple points of view and collage effects of this work's most important predecessor, *Manhattan Transfer*. Fuentes employs the possibilities of the first-, second-, and third-person narrations, thus moving Mexican narrative one step beyond Yáñez and Rulfo strictly in terms of narrative technique. Like Dos Passos, Rulfo, and Yáñez, Fuentes the modernist moves from a fictional world of an apparent fragmented chaos to one of order and harmony.

These novels share several commonalities as modernist texts written in the 1940s and 1950s. Asturias, Marechal, Rulfo, Yáñez, and Fuentes were engaged in a search for truth. Each of these authors created characters who were involved in a quest of mythic proportions. With respect to characterization, these five authors portrayed characters who are modern rather than postmodern individuals: they tend to be singular and existential rather than the multiple self that breaks ontological barriers.[28] These five modernist texts question many of the assumptions of the masculinist aesthetic that preceded them in Latin America; in *El Señor Presidente*, *Al filo del agua*, *Pedro Páramo*, and *La región más transparente*, the authority figures of patriarchal society are questioned.

The relative lack of communication among the Latin American nations and its writers in the 1940s and 1950s—at least compared to the 1960s and 1970s—was one of the main reasons there was no internationally acclaimed "boom" of the Latin American novel with the publication of these ambitious, historical, and intensely modernist novels in the 1940s and 1950s. With the exception of small groups of well-informed writers and intellectuals, local critical reaction to these novels tended to range from negative to a kind of neutral puzzlement. One exception was Julio Cortázar, who, in 1949, wrote in laudatory terms about *Adán Buenosyres* (and a generally marginalized Leopoldo Marechal).[29]

In the 1940s and 1950s, Latin American writers successfully confronted what Alonso has identified as a burden of modernity.[30] Paradoxically, as they faced their modernist task, they began to incorporate oral culture into fiction more successfully than had ever been seen in Latin American fiction, thus realizing the task which the *criollistas* failed to fully understand as an essential part of their labor as writers committed to telling the autochthonous stories of their respective regions. Of these five novels, *El Señor Presidente*, *Al filo del agua*, and *Pedro Páramo* incorporate oral culture most successfully.

Some of these novelists prefigured the Boom by demonstrating a totalizing impulse that Fuentes associated with the writing of the Boom. Fuentes himself exhibited this totalizing interest in *La región más transparente*, but the explicitly totalizing project was *Adán Buenosayres*. Yáñez and Asturias also reveal some interest in the total novel as described by Fiddian, for *Al filo del agua* and *El Señor Presidente* contain several characteristics of this same elusive novelistic experiment.

This modernist project began to form the new, modern, active reader who will be so important to the novelistic process in the novels of the 1960s Boom. The text that fictionalizes a reader most carefully and systematically is *Pedro Páramo*. After the publication of the short fiction of Borges and this novel by Rulfo, anything was seemingly possible in the Latin American novel, and this was clearly evidenced in the novels that came forth in the 1960s. Each of these five novelists successfully used the strategies of a modernist aesthetic to become the first generation of universal Latin American novelists.

Part IV **Modern and Cosmopolitan Works, 1962–1967**

Eight **Novels and Contexts of the
Boom and Beyond**

The Boom of Spanish American fiction during the
1960s began with international recognition of the remarkable quality
of the fiction written by a select few talented Latin American modernists—Carlos Fuentes, Mario Vargas Llosa, Gabriel García Márquez,
and Julio Cortázar. Notably, a modernist of the previous generation,
Miguel Angel Asturias, received the Nobel prize in literature precisely in 1967—at what might be considered the apogee of the Boom.
What a few writers and critics have viewed as a burden of modernity
was for these four writers and many others a celebration of heterogeneity and the right of invention in fiction. By 1967, the indicators of
a radically modern—or postmodern—fiction were also evident.

This fourth moment of the desire to be modern was evident well
beyond the writings of these four novelists. In each of their respective nations—Mexico, Peru, Colombia, and Argentina—these novelists had compatriots equally dedicated to the modernist enterprise,
writers such as Rosario Castellanos, Elena Garro, and José Emilio
Pacheco in Mexico, Julio Ramón Ribeyro in Perú, Manuel Mejía Vallejo, Alvaro Cepeda Samudio, and Héctor Rojas Herazo in Colombia,
and David Viñas and Ernesto Sábato in Argentina. In addition, novelists such as José Donoso in Chile (who was closely associated with
the Boom), Salvador Garmendia in Venezuela, Clarice Lispector, Jorge
Amado, and Autran Dourado in Brazil, Jean Rhys, Rosa Guy, and José
Lezama Lima and Guillermo Cabrera Infante in the Caribbean participated in the creation of a new, modernist novel in Latin America.

In their desire to be modern, these writers of the Boom produced some of their most complex and totalizing novels during this period, as did their contemporaries throughout Latin America. Julio Cortázar published *Rayuela* (1963), the Cuban José Lezama Lima wrote *Paradiso* (1966), and the Mexican Fernando del Paso created *José Trigo* (1966), all three lengthy works with many qualities of the "total" novel that writers of the Boom found attractive.

Many of the novelists of the 1960s continued in the search for the universal through the creation or re-creation of Western or indigenous myths. Continuing in the path of Asturias and Carpentier, writers such as García Márquez, Vargas Llosa, and Rosario Castellanos created new myths or further elaborated known ones. Some novelists continued writing in a Faulknerian mode and using the procedures of transcendent regionalism. García Márquez, Viñas, Cepeda Samudio, and Rojas Herazo published novels with both regional and universal overtones. Cepeda Samudio's *La casa grande* (1962) and Rojas Herazo's *Respirando el verano* (1962) are neo-Faulknerian texts set in small towns in Colombia, and both were key novels for the rise of modernist fiction in Colombia. In *En noviembre llega el arzobispo* (1967), Rojas Herazo continues the family story initiated in *Respirando el verano*, although he characterizes a broader spectrum of society than in his first novel.

This Boom of the Latin American novel in the 1960s was the result of the fortunate confluence of numerous individuals, institutions, and circumstances, among them the Spanish literary agent Carmen Balcells, the appearance of a brilliant translator (Gregory Rabassa), the Cuban Revolution, publishers Harper and Row in the United States and Seix Barral in Spain, the rise of international Latin Americanism as an academic discipline, and the publication of the literary magazine *Mundo Nuevo* in Paris. In his book on the subject, *Historia personal del Boom*, Donoso observes that Carlos Fuentes was the catalyzer who promoted the unity of the group.[1] Donoso, in fact, wrote a novel while living in a bungalow on Fuentes's property in the early 1960s.

The social, cultural, and political context of the early 1960s was dominated by the Cuban Revolution and other radical and anti-establishment movements, such as the international youth rebellion that emanated from the United States and Europe. Puerto Rico was in a process of change caused, to a large extent, by the transformation of the island from an agricultural to an industrial economy. This transformation, in turn, resulted in the increased social mobility of many Puerto Ricans, even though the U.S. Project Bootstrap is generally considered a failure. Puerto Rican intellectuals became increasingly critical of the island's dependent status, and the political crisis in Puerto Rico reached its apogee when Governor Luis Muñoz Marín stepped aside from his position, and his party, the PPD, lost its first election in more than two decades. In this period, writers Luis Rafael Sánchez, Edgardo Rodríguez Juliá, Ana Lydia Vega, Rosario Ferré, and Manuel Ramos Otero became visible on the Puerto Rican cultural scene for the first time.

At the outset of the 1960s, the Cuban Revolution became a rallying point for most Latin American intellectuals, and the writers of the Boom uniformly supported Fidel Castro's revolutionary ideals. When Castro arrived triumphantly in Havana in January 1959, Fuentes was awaiting him to offer his congratulations and support. García Márquez was also an early ally of the revolution, and soon thereafter Vargas Llosa and Cortázar offered their solidarity, as did Caribbean intellectuals such as C. L. R. James.

The symbolic moment in which the ideology of the Cuban Revolution and the politics of the Boom were united occurred in 1962 at a literary conference in Concepción, Chile. There, Fuentes declared to Donoso and other prominent Chilean writers that the Latin American intellectual should be *engagé* and join in support of the Cuban Revolution. As Donoso has explained in his history of the Boom, never before had he heard a writer express such political positions so stridently.

In Spain, literary agent Carmen Balcells and the Seix Barral publishing firm also contributed to the rise of the Boom. Balcells set high professional standards for Latin American writers and their writing; in doing so, she was highly influential in the rise of Latin American novelists as full-time professional writers. Before Balcells, the vast majority of them had to make a living in other professions and write as a sideline when they could.

By the 1960s, the Latin American novel had numerous masters besides García Márquez, Fuentes, Vargas Llosa, and Cortázar. José Donoso published an impressive set of novels and, as a personal friend of these writers, was sometimes associated with the Boom. Salvador Garmendia was perhaps the exemplary novelist who was not part of the Boom: he has written a long and uninterrupted series of novels since the 1960s but has remained basically ignored by critics and readers outside of Venezuela. The Brazilians Clarice Lispector and

João Guimarães Rosa were recognized primarily by a growing number of scholars, although they have been translated into Spanish and on occasion into English. Jorge Amado, however, enjoyed considerable commercial success with *Dona Flor e seus dois maridos* (1967).

Novelists such as Donoso, Lispector, and Garmendia wrote a type of modernist fiction that differs markedly from the major novels of the Boom. These novelists generally did not write the works of expansive geographies and histories observed during the Boom. Their work has little or none of the magic realism or broad historical vision of García Márquez. Donoso's early novels, including *El lugar sin límites* (1966) and *Este domingo* (1966), were more closely associated with the realist tradition and interior, psychological spaces than with the modernists' right of invention. Many of his main characters are aristocrats; Donoso's family belongs to this upper class in Chile. In *El lugar sin límites*, a small rural town is a symbolic hell where the arrival of a transvestite cabaret performer destabilizes local relations. The setting (a brothel) and the personalities of the main characters (among them a biological father who also is a psychological mother) make this an early example of Donoso's very particular understanding of human beings. *Este domingo* is a return to the problems of the old aristocracy and class differences in Chile. In it, Donoso is once again concerned with the subtleties of human relations, often with existential overtones.

Lispector's daring narrative experiments began to gain international attention in the early 1960s and have since been translated. Garmendia has published more than fifteen books of fiction since the late 1950s; like Lispector, he is a small-screen novelist who is a master of narrative technique. In the early 1960s, he was in the avant-garde among a small group of Latin American writers—including Fuentes—who were successfully using the narrative strategies recently pioneered by the French *nouveau roman*. In addition, in the 1960s Garmendia was using techniques from film. The protagonist of *Día de ceniza* (1964) is a frustrated writer suffering a crisis, and Garmendia employs the strategies in vogue in the *nouveau roman*, such as the narrator with a camera-lens perspective.

What Eduoard Glissant has identified as the Caribbean region's "irruption into modernity" was increasingly evident in the 1960s and part of a cultural process of which Caribbean writers were acutely aware. This process was seen by some Caribbean intellectuals as an important stage beyond colonialism; others focused on the interaction among the diverse cultures of the Caribbean region. Writing in 1962, the Trinidadian C. L. R. James set forth a teleological view of Caribbean history as a quest for national identity initiated in 1804 with the Haitian Revolution and culminating in 1959 with the Cuban Revolution.[2] As Dash has explained, James did not see the Caribbean as a collection of static, victimized nations, but as cultures in dynamic engagement with global history.[3] Writing in 1964, Wilson Harris of Guyana conceived of the Caribbean as "overlapping contexts of Central and South America as well." For Harris, the Caribbean's early models of the modern nation-state were a groping toward alternatives, possibilities, and relationships which remained unfulfilled in the early 1960s.[4]

The writing of Guillermo Cabrera Infante and José Lezama Lima embodies some of these cultural analyses. Cabrera Infante began writing in his native Cuba, then went into exile in the 1960s. He has published a continual flow of books since then, most of which escape easy genre definition. *Tres tristes tigres* (1967), a disperse and witty book set in prerevolutionary Cuba, was of major impact for at least two reasons. On the one hand, it opened the door to humor in the Latin American novel; on the other hand, its Joycean play with language proved important for postmodern novelists of the 1970s and 1980s. After a prologue-like opening set in a Havana nightclub, *Tres tristes tigres* is narrated by three characters who take the reader through a zany world that seems to be nearing an end. As such, the predominant tone is one of nostalgia. Epistemological problems are not the main concern of certain sections of this novel, and the shift from an epistemological focus to an ontological one is a primary characteristic of the transition to postmodern fiction.[5] Given the focus on language and the ontological, *Tres tristes tigres* is a key text for the publication of many postmodern novels in Latin America in the 1970s and 1980s.

José Lezama Lima also placed considerable focus on language as a theme in itself. Best known as a poet, his novel *Paradiso* (1966) was a major work of the 1960s that was praised by Fuentes, Vargas Llosa, and Cortázar soon after its publication. It is the story of José Cemí, but the dense language and digressive style make any clear sense of plot questionable. Its language is intensely metaphorical, justifying Lezama Lima's own description of it as a "poem-novel." As he develops both the time-bound story of the Cemí family and the time-free elements of metaphorical language, Lezama Lima confronts the contradictions of time and language throughout this text.[6] Neither the chapters of *Paradiso* nor its characters are linked to a particular time frame. Rather, the characters themselves are metaphors who are in constant search of origins, a search that is the primary theme of the novel.

The "overlapping contexts" of which Harris spoke are evident in the novels of the French, English, Spanish, and Dutch Caribbean. Sylvia Winter set her novel *Hills of Hebron* in her native Jamaica, continuing the quest theme set forth in several Latin American novels of the 1950s, such as *Pedro Páramo*. This quest involves Afro-American people seeking their own physical space and their own black deity. As a novel of Afro identity, *Hills of Hebron* heralds a time of "radical reorientation" in the Caribbean.[7] Rosa Guy set the novel *Bird at My Window* (1966) in the United States; its theme—the African desire for liberation and authentic identity in the Americas—is of interest in much of Latin America as well as in the United States and the Caribbean.

The heterogeneity of the Latin American novel was increasingly evident in the 1960s with the breakdown of conventional norms of sexual relations and gender. Cortázar's *Rayuela* played a major role in the subversion of these conventional mores. Rosa de Lima's *Tomorrow Will Always Come* was an exceptional piece in its presentation of sex roles between the protagonist and his male lover. The transvestite central character in Donoso's *El lugar sin límites* also breaks down traditional roles in Latin American fiction. An early novel with homosexual themes in Mexico was Miguel Barbachano Ponce's *El diario de José Toledo* (1964). Chicano writer John Rechy has been ignored in some circles because he is openly gay and writes about gay characters, even though he has published several significant novels, including *City of Night* (1963) and *Numbers* (1967). *Rayuela* and the works of writers such as Donoso, Barbachano Ponce, and Rechy signaled the demise of a masculinist aesthetic in the Latin American novel.

In Brazil, in addition to Lispector, Autran Dourado, Carlos Heitor Cony, Erico Veríssimo, Jorge Amado, Dalton Trevisan, Rubem Fonseca, and other writers contributed to the heterogeneity of the Latin American novel of the 1960s. Several Brazilian novelists responded to the ambitious projects of the Boom. Dourado's *Opera dos mortos* (1967) resonates of Faulkner and García Márquez, and Amado's *Dona Flor e seus dois maridos* relates the entertaining story of the female protagonist's erotic fantasies, but it has also been read as a political allegory.[8]

A prominent fiction writer, poet, and essayist in Mexico, Rosario Castellanos, unlike Donoso and Lezama Lima, was generally ignored by the writers of the Boom. Nevertheless, she did publish twenty-seven books before her death in 1974. Castellanos is a writer associated with feminism and the Indian world in which she grew up—Chiapas, Mexico. Her major novel, *Oficio de tinieblas* (1962), based on a historical uprising of the Chamula Indians in Chiapas in 1867, had an unusual protagonist: a female Indian. Although Castellanos was not as interested in language per se as Lezama Lima or Cabrera Infante, *Oficio de tinieblas* exhibits a mastery of narrative technique.

Manuel Mejía Vallejo, like Garmendia and Castellanos, has been the antithesis of the jet-set public intellectual of the Boom. He spent much of his life writing in his farmhouse in rural Antioquia, Colombia, rarely traveling beyond nearby Medellín. Mejía Vallejo's major novel, *El día señalado* (1964), depicts political violence in Colombia in the 1950s, incorporating both oral tradition and the aesthetics of modernism. The action takes place in a small provincial town, reminiscent of the setting for Juan José Arreola's *La feria*. Using a series of narrative segments to create a mosaic, Arreola characterizes a series of individuals and the town as a whole. The narrative segments produce a generalized understanding of the town; Fanny Buitrago uses narrative segments and multiple voices for similar effects in *El hostigante verano de los dioses* (1963). It is a small-screen novel that communicates a sense of boredom among a group of a younger generation. Brushwood describes small-screen novels as fiction with a limited scope. They typically involve a small group (such as a family) in a limited physical space (such as a home). These novels tend to deal with human relationships rather than broader issues of nation, history, or the like.[9]

The small-screen fiction of Donoso and Lispector focuses on the subtleties of human relationships. Sergio Galindo, Jorge Edwards, and Silvina Bullrich are additional specialists in small-screen fiction. Galindo's *La comparsa* (1964) is set in Xalapa, Veracruz. As in *La feria*, the novel portrays the whole town, focusing on the celebration of carnival. *La comparsa* offers a view of Mexican society across classes and generations. Edwards's *El peso de la noche* (1965) changes in focus between two male characters, Joaquín and Francisco, to describe a clan's matriarch, mostly through the memories and dreams of the two males. In Bullrich's *Los burgueses* (1964), a first-person narrator—who is never clearly identified—relates the story of a family on an Argentine *estancia*. The ambiguity of the narrative voice and the transformation of society provide the novel's dynamic quality.

The small-screen fiction of Bullrich and Donoso portrays human relationships in the context of upper-class decadence. In the case of *Los burgueses* and Donoso's *Este domingo*, the aristocracy is in decline. *Este domingo* dramatizes crises both on the personal and class level, underscoring not only the decline of an aristocratic family, but its exploitation of and symbiosis with the servant class.

Adalberto Ortiz and Gabriel Casaccia produced well-wrought small-screen novels dealing with human relationships that expanded in focus beyond the typical limitations of small-screen fiction. In Ortiz's *El espejo y la ventana* (1967), the scope begins as broad and historical and then becomes more limited to a family and one of its members. In *La llaga* (1964), Casaccia probes the relationships among a mother, her son, and her lover, but the plot then expands beyond the family to a revolutionary uprising in Asunción.

In the mid-1960s the first signs of a radical experimentation with modernist aesthetics were evident, the first indicator of what would become the postmodern novel of the 1970s and 1980s in Latin America. Cortázar's *Rayuela* (1963) was a late modernist experiment but also opened the doors to many subsequent postmodern exercises. The writer figure in the novel—Morelli—proposes a series of radical innovations that were, in effect, a call for a postmodern novel in Latin America. In *Rayuela*, Morelli questioned the assumptions of the realist novel as well as many of the operations of modernist fiction.

A first wave of Mexican postmodern writing emanated directly from Borges and Cortázar, writers whom José Emilio Pacheco and Carlos Fuentes had promoted among Mexican intellectuals in the early 1960s. An early reaction against the modernist tradition in Mexico came in the form of the irreverent young writers of the Onda, such as Gustavo Sainz and José Agustín. They were associated with counterculture in the United States and rebellious attitudes of the 1960s. Vicente Leñero was also one of the novelists who helped set the stage for later postmodern fiction in Mexico.

In his novel *Los albañiles* (1964), Leñero questions the possibilities of truth, and his play with versions of truth was a predecessor to postmodern fiction. *Los albañiles* deals with the identification of a murderer, but it ultimately questions the epistemological constraints that define truth in a social context. Salvador Elizondo's *Farabeuf* (1965),

Sainz's *Gazapo* (1965), and Agustín's *De perfil* (1966) constitute significant early contributions to the Mexican postmodern.

Farabeuf is one of the most hermetic novels of the period, narrating over and over again a limited number of the same episodes. Devoid of significant action and of characters with fixed identities, *Farabeuf* places the reader in a vague space, involved in the novel's main image: Dr. Farabeuf dissecting a live body while gazing at someone else. In a postmodern fiction that discards action and also discounts characters and content as worthwhile elements, it privileges language itself to such an extent that, in a world in which only language remains, human cruelty is neither an issue of morality or immorality, but simply an amoral, neutral act. Consequently, the title character, Dr. Farabeuf, executes the specialized techniques of Chinese torture, techniques of no more and no less moral content than those highly specialized narrative gestures of Salvador Elizondo and José Emilio Pacheco and the equally specialized roles the fictionalized reader must play in order to execute the reading of *Farabeuf*.

The fiction of Gustavo Sainz and José Agustín questioned the traditional boundaries between high and low culture, a common strategy of postmodern writers. Like *Farabeuf*, Sainz's *Gazapo* affords the reader a sense of fiction and empirical reality as versions and possibilities but shares little else with Elizondo's fiction. An early text of the Onda, *Gazapo* was a notable innovation for the Mexican and Latin American postmodern: it brought the language of adolescents into the Mexican novel, as well as the new technologies of communication—especially by means of tape recorders and other media. Above all, the fiction of Sainz was an irreverent contrast to the dominant modernist practices in Mexico in the early 1960s. A story of adolescent relationships and trivial actions, it seems apparently distant from the historical and political fiction of Fuentes and Pacheco. The history of *Gazapo*, however, is the history of a continual present in which the narrative transpires, for *Gazapo* also privileges memory: what human memory might forget is recorded in precise detail on tapes. Agustín shares many of Sainz's attitudes in *De perfil*, and it also relates a young man's process of maturation. Both novels are notable—and attractive—for their humor and their portraits of rebellious youths of the 1960s.

By 1967, signs of the early postmodern were evident with the publication of novels like Cabrera Infante's above-mentioned *Tres tristes tigres*, José Emilio Pacheco's *Morirás lejos*, and Fuentes's two novels *Zona sagrada* and *Cambio de piel*. The four works have some of the epistemological qualities of modernist fiction and some of the onto-logical qualities of postmodernist writing. Like *Morirás lejos*, *Cambio de piel* is a historiographic metafiction and a novel in which charac-ters have no fixed identity. Set in Mexico in the 1960s, *Cambio de piel* relates the story of two couples who spend a weekend together in the Mexican town of Cholula, although there are numerous digressions into the past and other continents, including the Nazi period covered in *Morirás lejos*.

Cambio de piel is one of Fuentes's early experiments with char-acters of multiple (rather than just double) identities. When it is ulti-mately revealed that the voice telling the story is that of a madman in an asylum, it is apparent that Fuentes's fiction has moved from con-cerns over the epistemological *(La región más transparente* and *La muerte de Artemio Cruz)* to the ontological.

Despite its unresolved contradictions and metafictional qualities, *Cambio de piel*, like Fuentes's other postmodern fiction, is deeply his-torical and political. His postmodern work is a "transhistorical carni-val" (as McHale calls it) in which characters in their projected worlds interact with those of empirical reality.[10] Simultaneously, Fuentes en-gages in multiple intertextual boundary violations, injecting charac-ters from other novels into his texts. Thus the reader of Fuentes's postmodern fiction experiences an even more complex confrontation with history than does the reader of Fuentes's overtly historical and political modern texts.

Many Latin American novelists of the 1960s accom-plished what their predecessors in the 1920s and 1930s had failed to do in their modernist writings. On the one hand, novelists of the 1960s wrote the harmonious, unified works that tended to develop from chaos to unity, from fragment to harmony, in effect, the perfect mod-ernist texts. On the other hand, these writers of the 1960s actively promoted the new agreement between author and reader that Daiches had set forth with respect to the modernist novel. Fuentes, Vargas Llosa, and many of their contemporaries published essays and granted interviews that were all part of this new contract. The most success-ful of these promoters of a new contract were Fuentes (above all in his book *La nueva novela hispanoamericana*) and Vargas Llosa, in his multiple stories about his stories, communicated in the form of interviews, lectures, and essays.

By 1967, the heterogeneity of the Latin American novel was more of a possibility than ever before. The publication of *Rayuela*, the presence of women writers such as Castellanos, Garro, and Lispector, and the appearance of overtly gay writers opened the door to new approaches to issues of sex and gender and the parallel demise of the predominant masculinist aesthetics.

García Márquez's *Cien años de soledad*, as well as works by Fernando del Paso, Vargas Llosa, and Fuentes, contributed toward a body of "total" novels of a sort that modern writers aspired to produce. Less-known novelists such as Héctor Rojas Herazo and Elena Garro manifested their desire to be modern by engaging in the aesthetics of modernism and the search for the total novel.

A few of the writers who never were recognized as part of the select group of the Boom nevertheless occupied ambiguous positions inside and outside its parameters. Donoso, Cabrera Infante, Amado, and Lezama Lima, to varying degrees, participated in the Boom, interacted with its members in the private and public sphere, and perhaps even benefited, albeit in minor ways, from the rise of the Boom as a cultural phenomenon in Latin America.

On the other hand, numerous gifted writers in Latin America were either unable or unwilling to assume such a public identity; Mejía Vallejo, Garro, and Castellanos are just a few of the writers in that category of the "writer's writer" who did not venture into the public sphere. The list of talented and productive writers in Latin America whose work has passed by with far less recognition than it deserves stretches far beyond the authors presented here.[11] An overview of Latin American fiction of the 1960s does indicate that by 1967 the aesthetics of modernism were pervasive, and the initial signs of the postmodern were evident. Indeed, on the international scene, not only were some of the most talented masters of Spanish American fiction at their apogee, but also several others were writing in ways never before imagined.

Nine Rereading Novels of the Boom

Carlos Fuentes, Julio Cortázar, Mario Vargas Llosa, and Gabriel García Márquez have written a large corpus of outstanding fiction, and each has published more than one novel that has garnered broad critical acclaim and a large international readership. Fuentes, Vargas Llosa, and García Márquez have published several best-selling novels in the United States and Europe. Among the most recognized Spanish American works of fiction to appear during the 1960s were Fuentes's *La muerte de Artemio Cruz* (1962), Cortázar's *Rayuela* (1963), Vargas Llosa's *La casa verde* (1965), and García Márquez's *Cien años de soledad* (1967). These works have had considerable impact among readers and writers in Latin America. Indeed, many scholars and writers already consider them modern classics. In each of these novels, the author uses a variety of approaches to express his desire to be modern and to assume his modernity.

These four novels and a few others were the initial cause for the discussions by Latin American writers and critics in the 1960s and 1970s of the "total novel." The total novel aspires to represent an inexhaustible reality; it is conceived as a microcosm of signification; it is characterized by a fusion of mythical and historical perspectives.[1] Indeed, these four novels were ambitious modernist works that contained many of the elements associated with the total novel. For example, all four cultivate an encyclopedic range of reference as a means toward representing an inexhaustible reality; at the same time, all four were conceived as self-contained systems or microcosms of signification.

Fuentes had been writing short fiction since the early 1950s, and *La muerte de Artemio Cruz* appeared after *La región más transparente* and *Las buenas conciencias*. With the publication of these novels, Fuentes confirmed what he and many of his young contemporaries were stating in their cultural magazine *Revista Mexicana de Literatura:* Mexican literature needed to be more modern and universal. For Fuentes, being modern meant joining in the international modernist movement in fiction. *La región* had considerable impact in Mexico, where it created quite a stir, but it was not until *La muerte de Artemio Cruz* that Fuentes became well known beyond the borders of Mexico. With this novel, Fuentes assumes not only his modernity, but also his own national history.

Fuentes himself considers all his fiction one work, a lifetime writing project he has organized around fourteen cycles that he has entitled "La edad del tiempo"—a lengthy reflection on time. The four works that Fuentes calls "El mal del tiempo" comprise the first of these fourteen cycles, and they deal with the problem of time itself. In them, any sense of Western linear time is blurred; in different ways, they undermine and destroy time.[2]

Narrated in alternating segments of first, second, and third person, *La muerte de Artemio Cruz* is the story of one man as well as of twentieth-century Mexican history. As a prototype modernist fiction, it consists of a series of fragments that the reader places together in the process of reading in order to find an implicit unity of the novel. Paradoxically, as the reader finds progressively more order, the protagonist and the nation suffer greater fragmentation. Cruz's story is a reconstruction of his life that parallels the rise of the new order that took power in Mexico during and after the Mexican Revolution.

As Faris has observed, four specific failings of postrevolutionary Mexican society recur throughout *La muerte de Artemio Cruz:* class domination, Americanization, financial corruption, and the failure of land reform.[3] In the early scenes of the novel, Fuentes takes the reader through a series of brief portrayals of Cruz as an individual devoid of feelings for his wife and family and of the entire family's hierarchy of dominance. For Cruz and his family, there is always something more important—a business deal or a shopping trip—than the masses of people suffering from the domination of the upper class to which Cruz belongs. Clearly, Cruz and his class represent a betrayal of the ideals of the Mexican Revolution and the 1917 Constitution that was to bring it to institutional fruition.

In the end, the implied author of *La muerte de Artemio Cruz* shares many of the ideas set forth by Octavio Paz in *The Labyrinth of Solitude*. Mexico is divided between the powerful (the *chingones*) and the weak (the *chingados*), the rich and the poor, the Spanish and the Indian. Despite the critical tone and pervasive pessimism of the novel, however, Fuentes does offer some hope for Artemio Cruz and for Mexico. Fuentes represents memory as power, and to some degree (at least temporarily), Cruz's memory triumphs over his circumstance.[4] This note of optimism defies critics' claims that the writers of the Boom are systematically pessimistic.[5]

A constant pattern in Fuentes's fiction is that of a character trapped within the confines of an architectural construct, desiring or needing to escape. Such is the basic circumstance of Artemio Cruz and of the protagonists of several other Fuentes fictions. In some, characters find the enclosed space sacred, as is the case of the protagonists of *Zona sagrada* and *Terra Nostra*. Fuentes was smitten by the desire to be modern with readings of Dos Passos, Borges, Kafka, and Faulkner at a young age and soon by certain postmodern elements of Joyce, Borges, and Cortázar as well. The most powerful of Fuentes's modernist works are *La región más transparente, La muerte de Artemio Cruz*, and *Zona sagrada*. In these three novels, Fuentes fully exploits the technical devices pioneered by First World modernists to explore Mexico's past and present. The structure and the narrators of the fiction of Faulkner and Butor are evident in *La muerte de Artemio Cruz*; Fuentes the modernist moves from a fictional world of an apparent fragmented chaos to one of order and harmony. For McHale, *La muerte de Artemio Cruz* represents a variant of the modernist novel of interior monologue that focuses on a grid which each mind imposes on the outside world or through which it assimilates the outside world.[6] This early Fuentes, like his modernist predecessors and the other writers of the Boom, was still searching for truths and still producing the totalizing grand narrative.

Vargas Llosa was well advanced into his own totalizing project by the time he wrote *La casa verde* in the early 1960s: he already had published the ambitious and totalizing modernist novel *La ciudad y los perros*, an immediate bestseller that catalyzed the international recognition of the Boom. With *La casa verde*, Vargas Llosa assumes his Faulknerian modernity and attempts to assume his nation's multicultural makeup as well as the contradictions of Peruvian society. Like Fuentes, Vargas Llosa had read Sartre well, considered himself fully *engagé*, and was interested in novelizing his nation's history.

Like *La muerte de Artemio Cruz, La casa verde* offers a complex yet systematic structure. This novel consists of four parts and an epilogue. Parts 1 and 3 and the epilogue contain four chapters; parts 2 and 4 have three chapters each. The chapters of parts 1 and 2 contain five narrative segments; those in parts 3 and 4 have four narrative segments. Numerous stories are woven through this novel, but the work offers two broad settings that correspond to two general plots.

As in *La muerte de Artemio Cruz*, the logic of cause and effect in a sequential, conventional story line is systematically undermined in *La casa verde*. Incidents leading to the development of conflicts as well as those pertaining to their resolution are revealed before the exposition of a climactic moment for each character. For example, Bonifacia's story involving the mission in Santa María de Nieva has not been fully developed when it is revealed that she has become a prostitute in Piura.

La casa verde is a patently dialogic novel in several ways. First, the novel is richly dialogic in its incorporation of multiple layers by means of telescoping. The novel is also dialogic in its use of many-layered discourses from different spheres, such as religion and various social classes. The reader is in constant contact with a changing sense of the real in continual flux. Since the variant communications of languages are in opposition, reality takes on a capricious quality that the reader becomes accustomed to questioning. Reality becomes so innately relative, in fact, that the nature of truth and even the possibility of truth are called into question. And this type of questioning created by the techniques specific to *La casa verde* is essential to the experience of the modern Vargas Llosa reader, who also comes to question the possibility of attaining a complete understanding exclusively through rational means. Using a variety of strategies, Fuentes and García Márquez question this possibility in their novels of the Boom, too. In many ways, *La casa verde* was an early version for Vargas Llosa of the total novel.

Vargas Llosa is a storyteller in the Faulknerian tradition that so pervasively affected Latin America during the 1940s and 1950s; of the writers of the Boom, he and García Márquez were the most loyal to Faulkner in this stage (the 1960s) of their careers. This type of fiction, identified as transcendent regionalism in Spanish American literature, has been practiced in a variety of ways since the rise of modernist fiction in Latin America in the 1940s. Unlike Cortázar and some postmodern writers, Vargas Llosa has never questioned the value of storytelling in itself but rather has sought to clarify in his fiction, essays, and plays how the writer creates and what function the story and storytelling have in society.

The writers of the Boom all sought—using differing strategies— to be universal. Several characteristics of Vargas Llosa's themes and techniques contribute to this universality. The interest in the total novel makes him comparable to Faulkner and Fuentes. The successful development and incorporation of literary romance—from the early stories through *La casa verde* and later novels—distinguish Vargas Llosa from many Latin American writers who share his political and social perspectives but who produce a more overtly "social" literature.

García Márquez, like Fuentes and Vargas Llosa, grew up idolizing Faulkner. Perhaps the most intensely committed to the idea of being modern of these four writers of the Boom, García Márquez grew up in Colombia, which historically has resisted modernity and change in culture. His major novel, *Cien años de soledad*, is the culmination of his cycle of Macondo, which consists of the novels *La hojarasca* (1955), *El coronel no tiene quien le escriba* (1961), and *La mala hora* (1962). *Cien años de soledad* is the story of the Buendía family and the story of the town of Macondo.

Cien años de soledad might seem at first like a book of fantasy, but it is one of the most historical books of the Boom, and it abounds in social and political implications. Colonel Aureliano Buendía, who fights endless battles in the novel, is modeled after a late-nineteenth-century figure, General Rafael Uribe Uribe, who was a leader of the liberals who suffered numerous defeats in Colombia. The strike of banana workers, which is related as one of the most fantastic events in the novel, is in fact one of the most historical. In November 1928, Colombian workers declared a strike against the United Fruit Company, and the massacre of several hundred workers ensued. García Márquez was among the first to relate and popularize this lamentable episode.

One consistently used technique of oral storytelling in *Cien años de soledad* is overstatement or exaggeration when referring to the commonplace and, in contrast, an absolute coolness or understatement when describing incredible situations. The narrator regularly reacts to the most marvelous and fantastic events with utter passivity— a technique García Márquez learned from the oral tradition of the northern coast of Colombia where he grew up. In the first chapter, José and his children witness a man vanish upon drinking a special potion. Neither the narrator nor the characters pay particular attention to this extraordinary occurrence.

Walter Ong has observed that many cultures and subcultures, even those immersed in advanced technologies, preserve much of their original and primary orality.[7] García Márquez, a sophisticated product of writing culture, juxtaposes print culture with much of the residually oral milieu of his youth in Aracataca. Both a primary oral culture and sophisticated writing culture permeate *Cien años de soledad*, often in hilarious juxtaposition.

This transition from orality to different stages of literacy is essential to the experience of *Cien años de soledad* and is particularly evident when one compares the initial chapters with the ending. In the first chapter, the mind-set of a primary orality predominates; in the last chapter, the most intricate exercises of a writing culture are carried out. In the first chapter, these two extremes are represented by Melquíades, who is of a writing culture from the outside, and by Ursula, who possesses a mind-set of orality. The Macondo of the first paragraph is a place of paradisiacal and primary orality in which stones are "white and enormous, like prehistoric eggs." The *prehistoric* associates Macondo with a prehistory, prewriting stage. It is not only a prewriting stage but also one that borders on prespeaking. José Arcadio Buendía, between the two extremes of Melquíades and Ursula, serves as a special link in this chapter between oral and writing cultures. He also paradoxically belongs to both, reacting in some circumstances as an oral culture person. Oral culture persons tend to view many of the modes and concerns of a writing culture as irrelevant or even ridiculous. Similarly, Ursula, in the first chapter, is uninterested in definitions and loses her patience with José Arcadio Buendía when he defines the world as round like an orange. The oral mind-set is also situational rather than abstract, the former being Ursula's constant mode of operation. When José Arcadio Buendía attempts to convince her to move from Macondo with his (abstract) fantastic stories and the (abstract) promise of a prodigious world, her response is to bring him down from this high level of abstraction to the concrete reality of the present, admonishing him to think less about crazy inventions and more about taking care of his sons. Thus, the first chapter emerges as an orality (Ursula), a writing culture (Melquíades), and a humorous semi-orality (José Arcadio Buendía) that bridges the gap between the two.

After the first chapter, Macondo moves from preliteracy to literacy. The narrator's mind-set also shifts from the feigned preorality of the first chapter to the historicity of the second. In the first chapter, he had used the preliteracy image of prehistoric eggs; in the first line of the second chapter, he uses the historical discourse of writing— "When the pirate Sir Francis Drake attacked Riohacha in the sixteenth century, Ursula Iguarán's great-great-grandmother became so frightened with the ringing of alarm bells and the firing of cannons that she lost control of her nerves and sat down on a lighted stove."[8] In the final chapters, *Cien años de soledad* announces itself not only as writing but also as an example of the highly sophisticated forms of self-conscious fiction.

Much of this novel recreates the shift from orality to writing, changes hitherto labeled as shifts from "magic" to "science" but which can be more cogently explained as shifts from orality to stages of literacy. What often has been identified in this novel by the term "magic realism" can be more precisely described as a written expression of this shift. The effects of the interplay between oral and writing cultures are multiple. García Márquez has fictionalized numerous aspects of his youth in the oral culture of rural Aracataca in Colombia. The unique traditionalism and modernity of this novel are based on various roles the narrator assumes as oral storyteller in the fashion of the tall tale, as narrator with an oral person's mind-set, and as the modern narrator of a self-conscious (written) fiction. With roots in oral culture, history, and myth, *Cien años de soledad* exhibits a tendency toward the novel as Archive.[9] It is the total story (and history) of Macondo.

Cien años de soledad, La casa verde, and *La muerte de Artemio Cruz* are now classic modernist works of Latin America. The most radically modern of now-classic novels of the Boom, however, is Cortázar's *Rayuela.* The very structure of this novel was radical in the Hispanic world in 1963 because it offered the possibility of reading at least three different novels, as Cortázar explains in a prefatory note. The first consists of chapters 1 through 56, which tell the story of Horacio Oliveira, a bohemian Argentine expatriate in Paris (chapters 1 through 36), and his relationship with a woman named La Maga. Oliveira lives in constant emotional crisis and does not seem capable of understanding himself or his role in life, despite his sophisticated intellectual repertoire. His physical, romantic, and intellectual wanderings lead him to emotional and moral dead ends that eventually take him to Buenos Aires (chapters 37 through 56), where he continues his quest. Once in his homeland, he connects with his old friend Traveler and Traveler's wife, Talita. The three of them join a circus and engage in increasingly unorthodox activities and relationships. They eventually end up in an insane asylum, and the denouement offers an ambiguous situation in which Oliveira might or might not commit suicide. This first novel within *Rayuela*, then, relates the story of Oliveira in a basically chronological fashion.

The first novel, if it were the complete text of an entire novelistic work, would be an attractive and intriguing fiction in the modernist vein, replete with its use of multiple points of view, fragmented structure, and language play associated with the stratagems of modernism. As a modernist text, the first novel contains the characteristic search for the ineffable and the fascination with ambiguity as a value in itself. In this sense, it is comparable to *La muerte de Artemio Cruz*, *La casa verde*, or Héctor Rojas Herazo's *Respirando el verano*.

Recalling modernist texts of the 1950s such as Rulfo's *Pedro Páramo*, the principal theme of chapters 1 through 56 is the quest. Read as such, these fifty-six chapters constitute a novel of Oliveira's search for some kind of authenticity or substantive meaning in life. The novel begins with the question "¿Encontraría a La Maga?" (Would I find La Maga?) and thus announces the point of departure. Indeed, the search for an authentic relationship with La Maga constitutes much of the story in Paris. In addition, Oliveira's search is played out on a variety of other levels: as a metaphysical search, as a search for intellectual superiority, as a search for true artistic expression. In the end, his inconclusive quest leads him to ridiculous situations and impending suicide.

The second novel proposed in *Rayuela*, as suggested in Cortázar's prefatory note, consists of chapters 1 through 56 and ninety-nine more, chapters 57 through 155. But these chapters do not appear in numerical order; rather, the reader moves back and forth among the previous chapters and the new "expendable" ones, jumping, for example, from 56 to 73, then 1, 116, 3, 84, and 4. In this second novel, Oliveira's story is expanded; several chapters further develop his story in Paris and Buenos Aires. This novel also has numerous chapters about literature, art, philosophy, and the like, as well as a few short narratives that on first reading seem like non sequiturs. With more consideration, however, it becomes evident that each diverse element has its respective function in the novel.

Some of these playful narrative fragments have the function of distancing the reader from the events at hand, inviting the modern reader to pause and reflect on actions and ideas in a fashion comparable to Brechtian theater. Occasional comical passages serve the same function. The long-term strategy with this distancing effect is to invite the reader of this second novel to reflect not only on the actions and characters but also on the novel form itself as well as on the assumptions of traditional readers and writers of fiction in general. Paradoxically, then, the most playful and apparently frivolous aspects of the novel turn out to be the most provocative and perhaps even revolutionary.

With respect to content, however, even more important are the expendable chapters that introduce the writer figure Morelli and his theory of the novel. Morelli questions not only the assumptions of the realist novel but also many of the operations of modernist fiction as well; in this sense, Rayuela differs from the other novels of the Boom and most other outstanding modernist texts of the 1960s published in Latin America. He invites writers (who soon became known as postmodern) to undermine Western concepts of representation and time and, similarly, the very idea of linearity and plot. But one of his most radical proposals is for an entirely new role for the reader— as an active (macho) participant. The postmodern reader of much of the innovative fiction that has been published in Latin America since Rayuela is fundamentally Morelli's idea of the active reader.

In addition to proposing a new, postmodern role for the reader, Rayuela undermines the concept of author. Lucille Kerr has argued convincingly that Rayuela poses questions about the figure of the author and the attribution of authorship.[10] One also finds evidence that this book's propositions about the author's authority both affirm and undermine authorial privileges. In this second reading of Rayuela, the figure of the author seems to reclaim its own privilege under the names of several authors—Cortázar, Morelli, and others. By the end of the second reading, authorial figures and the very concept of authority are questioned.

The postmodern active reader also is offered a third reading of Rayuela, although this reading is implied rather than clearly delineated, because it is only hinted at in Cortázar's prefatory note. Cortázar suggests that the third reading is one the reader constructs; this is the radical novelistic adventure of the type proposed by Morelli. This form of reading generates the open novel that Cortázar seems to desire but that is never actually attained in the first or second reading.

Many aspects of more complete (second and third) readings of *Rayuela* inevitably bring the postmodern reader back to questioning the fundamentals of Western culture, writing, and even thought. With this novel, Cortázar opened the door for two generations of postmodern fiction writers in Latin America and explored the possibilities and limits of radically undermining some of the most venerable assumptions of Western culture and thinking. Among these assumptions is what Cortázar (and Fuentes) considered the Western tendency to conceive of many issues in strictly dualistic terms. Manichean thought, for Cortázar and Fuentes, is one of the Western traditions in most need of radical subversion. This radicalizing aesthetic and political agenda became the new literary and political program of much postmodern and feminist fiction published in Latin America after the appearance of *Rayuela*. Paradoxically, the novel that spoke of the *macho* reader became the work that contributed significantly to feminist writing in Indo-Afro-Iberoamerica during the last three decades of the century.

These four novels of the Boom represent the successful realization of a century-long desire to be modern. Indeed, the four novels have become classic modernist texts, widely read in numerous languages. For the modern reader, Latin America finally had what Borges two decades prior was calling the perfect novel. With *Rayuela*, Cortázar assumes his modernity and rejects all forms of the traditional. He saves Latin American literature not only from its traditionalism, but also from its modernity—by promoting ideas that would bloom in later postmodern fiction. In *La casa verde*, Vargas Llosa assumes his Faulknerian modernity and attempts to assume, just as well, his nation's multicultural identity—its class and cultural contradictions. With the culmination of his cycle of Macondo, García Márquez assumes his modernity and his tradition (both oral and literary). In this sense, *Cien años de soledad* represents the culmination of a century-long search for the authentic and the autochthonous; the Colombian novelist carries out successfully the project that interested the *criollista* novelists but that they were far less able to realize.

In different ways, each of these novelists wrote "total" novels in the 1962–1967 period, although Vargas Llosa and Fuentes would more fully realize their ambitions of the total novel later—with *Conver-*

sación en La Catedral (1969) and *Terra Nostra* (1975), respectively. During this period, Cortázar and Fuentes began the successful undermining of a masculinist aesthetic, which they questioned in a context of revolutionary politics, literary experimentation, and a recognition of the cultural politics of heterogeneity and difference.

Ten   **Rereading the Spanish American**
Novel beyond the Boom

The international recognition and commercial success
of the Boom tended to obscure the writing of numerous outstanding
modernist novelists who published fiction in the 1960s. The Colombians Alvaro Cepeda Samudio, Héctor Rojas Herazo, and Manuel
Mejía Vallejo, as well as the Mexicans Rosario Castellanos and Elena
Garro, published remarkable transcendent regionalist novels. Important works to appear during this period included Cepeda Samudio's *La
casa grande* (1962), Rojas Herazo's *Respirando el verano* (1962), Castellanos's *Oficio de tinieblas* (1962), Garro's *Los recuerdos del porvenir* (1963), Mejía Vallejo's *El día señalado* (1964), and José Emilio
Pacheco's *Morirás lejos* (1967). All six writers shared a desire to be
modern and labored actively to modernize their national literature.
Pacheco also exhibits certain postmodern tendencies that became
more pronounced in the Latin American novel in the 1970s and 1980s.

In the early 1960s, Alvaro Cepeda Samudio and Héctor Rojas
Herazo were masters of modernist narrative technique and considered innovators in Colombia.[1] Cepeda Samudio and García Márquez
shared a great enthusiasm for William Faulkner, as well as a common
history: both were from the Caribbean coastal region of Colombia
that had been the United Fruit Company's site of operation during the
first quarter of the century.

La casa grande and *Respirando el verano* are books of similar origins (Faulkner and Colombian history), comparable dimensions (each
are family stories of approximately 150 to 200 pages), and an identical
focus (a home, *casa*). They were the first novels for each of the respec-

tive authors, although Cepeda Samudio had published *Todos estábamos a la espera* (1954), a volume of short stories, and Rojas Herazo had been publishing poems since 1952. Cepeda Samudio set his only novel in the *costeño* area of Ciénaga, the site of a 1928 strike and massacre of banana workers. Rojas Herazo was born and reared in the Colombian *costeño* town of Tolú, the setting of all three of his novels, beginning with *Respirando el verano*.

In addition to the 1928 banana workers' strike, *La casa grande* tells the story of a family that dominates the town and occupies *la casa grande* (the big house). A narrative tour de force, this novel consists of ten unnumbered chapters, each with a different method of developing a story set in a time frame immediately preceding and following the massacre. The principal characters are members of the family that has dominated the entire town from the *casa grande*, an imposing edifice visible to all. The first chapter, "Soldados" (Soldiers), consists almost entirely of dialogue between two unidentified soldiers traveling to a zone in rebellion. Ten of this chapter's seventeen sections are the soldiers' dialogue (only voices with no intervening narrator), and seven are sections conveyed by a third-person omniscient narrator. The first sixteen sections take place prior to the massacre, and the last after the tragedy. This handling of events is Cepeda Samudio's first innovation of narrative technique: the history and story of the massacre are told without actually depicting the major event itself, a technique radically different from the typically sanguinary novels about La Violencia, the Colombian civil war that began twenty years after the banana workers' strike and massacre.[2]

The second chapter, "La hermana" (The sister), consists of an interior monologue that one sister directed (in the form of *tú*) to another. The time frame for this chapter is after the massacre. The third chapter, in which townspeople kill the father, begins with an omniscient narrative about the father and then moves to nine numbered sections of dialogue among unidentified people who speak of the killing. In the tenth section of this chapter, instead of relating the father's death directly, the omniscient narrator relates what the girl hears — in effect, news of the father's death. The fourth chapter, "El Pueblo" (The town, or The people), contains two and one-half pages in which an omniscient narrator describes the town, always in simple and direct language. The fifth chapter is unique: it is a textual reproduction of "Decreto No. 4" (Decree No. 4) dated December 18, 1928, and is the only historical document in the novel. Elsewhere, the conflict is generalized with no specific names, places, or dates. "Jueves" (Thursday), the sixth chapter, consists of three sections: two feature omniscient narrators, and the third is exclusively dialogue. The time frame is immediately before the massacre.

The seventh chapter, "Viernes" (Friday), contains six sections related by an omniscient narrator, and the last of these sections presents the generalized reaction of the townsfolk. This last section can be seen as a counterpoint to the dialogue between the soldiers in the first chapter; here is the view of the townspeople, who know nothing of the dialogue or the intentions of the soldiers. Yet another narrative technique appears in the eighth chapter, "Sábado" (Saturday). Here a dispassionate and objective omniscient narrator provides a minute-by-minute account from 5:10 A.M. to 10:10 A.M. of the day of the massacre. "El hermano" (The brother), the ninth chapter, is narrated entirely by a brother in the family. The nine sections of this chapter alternate between the brother's account in the present (through an "experiencing self," as Stanzel notes) and his relating of past events (through a "narrating self").[3] The last chapter, "Los hijos" (The children), is exclusively dialogue, identical to the beginning of the novel, but the speakers are children, part of the generation that has survived and will be the future of the *casa grande*.

Respirando el verano is also a family story. In *La casa grande*, as in García Márquez's *La hojarasca*, the generalized hatred of the townsfolk toward the principal family is evident. *Respirando el verano* is also similar to *La casa grande* in that both works deal with intense hatreds, but these powerful emotions in Rojas Herazo's work are directed among members of the same family. The two central characters of Rojas Herazo's three novels are Celia, the aging matriarch, and her grandson Anselmo. Celia lives a bitter life of solitude, apparently despising virtually everyone except one of her children, Horacio. She also appears to be fond of one of her sons-in-law. The grandson Anselmo is portrayed during the years he is discovering the world through some of his special experiences beginning in childhood. In this connection, an important passage occurs in the fourth chapter, when Anselmo climbs the church tower to observe his town as a whole for the first time. *Respirando el verano*'s twenty-three numbered chapters are divided into two parts, "Las cosas en el polvo" (The things in the dust) and "Mañana volverán los caballos" (Tomorrow the horses will return), both of which are conveyed for the most part by an omniscient third-person narrator. In addition, Rojas Herazo develops the characters through the use of synesthesia. For example, one character is described as "listening to the mist in the patio."[4] Rather than literally seeing or hearing events, characters often feel them intuitively: "She felt more than she saw" (*Respirando el verano*, 95).

As Colombian novels published the same year, *La casa grande* and *Respirando el verano* share striking similarities that invite parallel analyses. A central structuring element in both novels is the house. In *La casa grande* this image functions in opposition to the people of the town, representing, above all, the center of authority and power. The image of the house is evoked from numerous perspectives, from the soldiers encountering it in the first chapter to the children's continuation of the family traditions as its inheritors in the last chapter. The house is a more complex element in *Respirando el verano*. The stories and the lives of Anselmo are intimately related to the *casa* and its heart, the patio. The child Anselmo contemplating the patio is the novel's first image. One of his most moving emotional experiences occurs when he climbs the church tower with Falcón to meditate on his *casa*—its windows, its roof, and the details of its colors. The narrator explains that Anselmo feels a "human concern" prior to this scene (*Respirando el verano*, 33), then observes that Anselmo's feeling has a special meaning, suggesting that he is in the process of discovering the meaning of the concept of *casa*. Celia's life is also inextricably bound to the *casa*. After her arrival at the home from Ovejas in 1871, she leaves only once for two months to be at a hospital in Panama, and "the rest was her house and the patio" (*Respirando el verano*, 131). She develops a symbiotic relationship with the house, which is exactly her age, and it survives the same number of years as she does, falling apart three days after her death. The narrator states that "she and the house became one organ" (*Respirando el verano*, 132). In both Cepeda Samudio and Rojas Herazo, the vitality of life, with its conflicts and hatreds, centers on the *casa*.

Set on the Caribbean coast of Colombia in the early twentieth century, *La casa grande* and *Respirando el verano* evoke a premodern, oral world similar to that of initial parts of *Cien años de soledad*. In both cases the narrative techniques are fundamentally of a Faulknerian modernity, but the fictional world is premodern and oral. (This simultaneous incorporation of the modern and the traditional will be exploited masterfully in *Cien años de soledad*.) Cepeda Samudio stresses orality in two ways. On the one hand, he privileges the spoken word from the first chapter, which is exclusively dialogue. From this chapter forward, reality will be defined to a large extent by what people say. In a world in which written history is an act of exercising political power, what is (subversively) said rather than what is (officially) written becomes essential to an understanding of reality. Cepeda Samudio also uses a patently oral technique: the repetition of key images and themes.

Respirando el verano is set in an essentially traditional and pre-modern oral world. In the fictional world of Rojas Herazo there are readers such as Celia's husband (who constantly rereads *The Iliad*, a text, interestingly enough, based on oral tradition), but many of the characters think and react as members of the primary oral culture of this region of Colombia in the early twentieth century. Characters in *Respirando el verano* are often guided in their actions not by the norms of a writing culture, with its modern science, but rather by inexplicable intuition or impulses. It is an oral culture reasoning that a person in a writing world would identify as irrational.[5] The narrator occasionally assumes a role as a person in an oral culture (a role García Márquez's narrator assumes throughout *Cien años de soledad*); the narrator's description of Celia as one organism with the *casa* is how an oral culture person would view the situation, exhibiting the tendency to conceptualize and verbalize all her knowledge with more or less close reference to the "human lifeworld."[6]

The orality of *La casa grande* and *Respirando el verano* is one aspect of the heterogeneity that typifies the novel as Archive, as defined by González-Echevarría. Both novels represent a heterogeneous synthesis of orality, history, and myth, in addition to other factors. They are constructed around a real historical setting. In *La casa grande*, it is 1928 Ciénaga (even though the town is never named) during the days preceding and following the massacre of the striking banana workers. In *Respirando el verano*, the empirical historical setting is the region of Sucre and Bolívar during the second half of the nineteenth century and the beginning of the twentieth.

González-Echevarría identifies the presence of previous mediating elements in the novel of Archive through which the story is narrated, a type of inner historian and a particular place such as a special room where the Archive is located. In *La casa grande*, the previous mediating element is the decree, the one historical document in the nation's archive, thus drawing the important difference between an official history and a fictional story of human conflict. The only inner historian in *La casa grande* is the figure of the narrator, who has rewritten history by organizing oral history alongside this document. In *Respirando el verano*, there are no real documents but instead an inner historian and a special location for history. The inner historian is Celia, the voice of the past that explains family history to the young Anselmo. Under the influence of Celia, Anselmo begins to sense the secret history of the house, the patio functioning as the special place from which history emanates. The way history and the inner historian are presented in these two novels exemplifies González-Echevarría's observation that the Archive is not so much an accumulation of texts as it is the process whereby texts are written, a process of repeated combinations, of shuffling, and reshuffling ruled by heterogeneity and difference.

The presence of myth in these two heterogeneous texts is associated with orality and the characterization process. In *La casa grande*, Cepeda Samudio creates characters of mythic dimension by repeatedly portraying them as larger than life, a common occurrence in the oral story. Menton has appropriately described *Respirando el verano* as a precursor to *Cien años de soledad*.[7] This observation is well taken; more specifically, García Márquez's previous fiction, along with *La casa grande* and *Respirando el verano*, had its roots in the Caribbean coast's premodern orality and modern Faulknerian techniques and were antecedents to *Cien años de soledad*, the epitome of the Archive novel.

In contrast to *La casa grande* and *Respirando el verano*, Mejía Vallejo's *El día señalado* is conceived strictly as a product of writing culture. The basic structure of this novel—with prologues and dual story lines—belongs to literary culture. This structure and the two narrators' metaphorical method of perceiving the world belong to writing and not oral noetics.

Nevertheless, *El día señalado* does carry a distant relationship with orality—more a case of vague oral effects than assimilation of primary orality or oral residue. As Tomás Carrasquilla (fellow *antioqueño*) had done in his late-nineteenth-century novel *Frutos de mi tierra* (1896), the narrator of *El día señalado* occasionally privileges orality by communicating reality in terms of what is generally said— "lo que dicen." Such procedures, within Antioquia's egalitarian tradition, privilege communication on an oral level, albeit in a minor and relatively insignificant fashion.[8] Authority is momentarily centered on speaking, not writing.

In *El día señalado*, two story lines unfold: one is told by a third-person omniscient narrator concerning a priest in the small town of Tambo, and another by a character who arrives at Tambo to commit an act of revenge. The novel begins with a six-page prologue told by a third-person omniscient narrator that relates the life story of a common boy with a common name (José Miguel Pérez). He experiences a typical childhood—until he sees evidence of La Violencia: mutilated bodies of guerrillas. José Miguel Pérez then becomes a background character mentioned intermittently.

The novel has three parts, each preceded by a prologue. The omniscient narrator relates the story of the priest in a town embroiled in the conflicts of La Violencia; the power structure, associated with the government and soldiers, is in conflict with the rural guerrillas. The first-person account tells of the final stages of this narrator's lifelong search for his father in order to murder him as an act of revenge. The narrator's search is presented in the text as both an obsession and an inevitable process destined to result in an encounter between father and son. The narrator's only emotions throughout the story, in fact, are related to the hatred he feels for his father and his obsession with revenge. The structure reaches a turning point at the end of the second part when the son encounters the father, Chútez, setting the stage for the seemingly inevitable violence of the third part. This story culminates in the son metaphorically killing the father: the son's fighting cock kills Chútez's fighting cock, and the son leaves the town after deciding not to kill his father.

Some readers have pointed out inconsistencies in the two narratives. For example, it has been commented that often there is insufficient difference between the language of the two narrative lines.[9] The reader may conclude that the author has failed to differentiate properly and consistently between the two narrators. On the other hand, the reader may maintain that the narrator-protagonist has a sense for detail, for associations, and for a metaphorical perception of reality usually ascribed to writing culture's novelists and poets. The questions raised by these observations concerning the narrators can be resolved by considering the role of the implied author. This fictional entity employs two narrators who have in common equally traditional and highly authoritarian roles as storytellers. The omniscient narrator assumes the authority from the first paragraph to explain the nature of things; the narrator assumes the authority to be, in effect, a writer. In accordance with the basic plot discussed above, the implied author is indeed a "man"—the patriarchal authority figure. In this sense *El día señalado* has a distant resonance of nostalgia. Beneath the overt trappings of modernity—under the guise of the modern novel's structure—lies a nostalgia for the traditional authority exhibited by nineteenth-century writers such as Tomás Carrasquilla.[10]

Castellanos's *Oficio de tinieblas* and Garro's *Los recuerdos del porvenir*, like *El día señalado*, demonstrate political and cultural violence. These Mexican writers were concerned with women, feminist issues, and political persecution in many of their works. Indeed, they were pioneer feminists of Indo-Afro-Iberoamerica who wrote ambitious modernist novels comparable in narrative technique to the most accomplished fiction of the Boom. Resonances of oral culture, as in *El día señalado*, are also evident in *Oficio de tinieblas*, and both novels can be associated with the novel as Archive. Castellanos was born in the state of Chiapas and grew up near the Chamula Indians, whose conflicts with the landowning elites dated back centuries; both groups are central to *Oficio de tinieblas*. In this novel, she uses the historical uprising in San Cristóbal de las Casas in 1867. Her fictionalized version portrays the struggle of a priestess, or *ilol*, named Catalina Díaz Puiljá, who leads the Chamulas in a rebellion. The novel has a strong historical base in the wars of the *castas de Chiapas* (1869–1871) and the politics of President Lázaro Cárdenas (1934–1940). In addition, one of the characters makes a connection between the Chamula rebellion and an indigenous uprising in Yucatán from 1848 and 1852. The Chiapas rebellion is indirectly associated in *Oficio de tinieblas* with a legend in which a young Chamula woman discovers speaking rocks that convey a divine message.

The *ladinos* attempt to control all aspects of life for the Chamulas, leading to a variety of readings that emphasize domination. The landowners impose a monopoly over the modes of production and subjugate the Indians culturally.[11] Similarly, the figure of the priestess can be seen as that of transgressor of the ladinos' dominant patriarchal order as well as the dominant patriarchal order within her indigenous community. Catalina also can be read as a character in opposition to the Western myth of consecrated maternity that reinforces the role of the woman as the reproductive body of the species. To the contrary, *Oficio de tinieblas* presents maternity as desire, as Catalina's wish that leaves a trace on the collective memory of her people. For Franco, this novel is an ambitious attempt to show the complexity of race, class, and gender. Yet the resolution of these complexities results in a story of female treachery. Castellanos identifies women with other groups marginalized both in older patriarchal structures of the land-owning class and in a Mexico that was being modernized.[12] What mars the novel, according to Franco, is Castellanos's implicit acquiescence in viewing the literal-mindedness of the indigenous population—a legacy of positivism. In *Oficio de tinieblas*, the Chamulas sacrifice a real child (as in Chamula legend/history) because they cannot under-stand the Christian Eucharist as symbolic. Nevertheless, the indige-nous symbolic systems are quite sophisticated, as studies have indi-cated. Given this problem and the novel's pessimistic ending, Franco reads it as "an interesting failure."[13]

In *Oficio de tinieblas*, Castellanos employs many of the techniques of modernist fiction, including the use of multiple points of view and a free indirect style. The novel exudes oral and mythic resonances of *El día señalado*, *Respirando el verano*, and *La casa grande*. *Oficio de tinieblas* opens with the violent rape of an indigenous woman by one of the landowners, conveyed in oral techniques of storytelling. The first chapter is also an imitation of an oral style, replete with the repe-titions typical of this kind of storytelling.

Garro's *Los recuerdos del porvenir* is also a historical novel, set in the small Mexican town of Ixtepec in the 1920s, during the period of the Cristero rebellion that forms the backdrop of the plot. Victo-rious troops of the Mexican Revolution occupy the town and are an opposing force to the traditional nineteenth-century order. Freely ex-ercising the right of invention, Garro fictionalizes a magical world in which people turn into stone, smoke cigarettes without lighting them, and the like. These events have a legend-making and some-times myth-making quality, even though they are not based on the Indian myths of *Oficio de tinieblas* or the supposed magic realism of *Cien años de soledad*. A character who is never fully explained or de-veloped, Felipe Hurtado, is related to some of the magical events, al-though there are other special people, such as Juan Cariño—an eccen-tric who insists on being called "Mr. President."

Los recuerdos del porvenir has seemingly had as many detractors as admirers among scholars and critics. For Brushwood, it is possible to read this novel as an account of the Cristero rebellion and find it satisfactory. Nevertheless, the violence becomes abstract, and the novel's major theme is the failure of love. Brushwood and others have observed that the basic narrative situation created by Garro does not work well: the village of Ixtepec tells its own collective story, but the narrative voice is not convincingly authentic. On the more positive side, Brushwood finds that the personification of Ixtepec results in a telescoping of time from its three aspects into just one, the present.[14] Obviously, Garro was as interested as the Carlos Fuentes of the early 1960s in experimenting with narrative voices in a way that destroyed traditional concepts of time. For Franco, the advantage of the collective protagonist is that it gives voice to all the marginalized elements of Mexico: the old aristocracy, the peasants, women, and the indigenous. Franco also proposes that Garro's appropriation of romance in the first part of the novel satisfies the desire for a happy ending that the second part of the novel disappoints.[15]

Los recuerdos del porvenir is an exceptional novel in several ways. In her reading of it and an early short story by Juan Rulfo, Debra Castillo has observed that each cedes narrative point of view to a "loose woman." The prostitute becomes not only the object of narrative but the agent for narrative self-reflexivity. Thus the fallen woman creates herself in what she tells, and in what she withholds, of the story of herself, and the narrative likewise questions the social and political conditions of textual production in the interstices of her story or her silence.[16]

Like other novels of this period, *Los recuerdos del porvenir* shares qualities of the Archive and demonstrates Garro's obvious interests in oral culture and myth. The narrator explains how some visitors leave the Moncada home, for example, by using an analogy typical of oral cultures: "las visitas huyeron con la velocidad de los insectos" (the guests fled with the speed of insects).[17] A mythic dimension of things is communicated through the presentation of grandiose characters and actions. Juan Cariño, for example, explains his understanding of the consequences of an action by stating: "El hombre se perdería en un idioma desordenado y el mundo caería convertido en cenizas" (Man will be lost in a disordered language, and the world will become converted to ashes; *Los recuerdos del porvenir*, 63). The chorus of female voices becomes the voice of memory in Ixtepec.

Los recuerdos del porvenir emerges as a modernist text comparable in harmonious structure to any of the novels of the Boom and in its stylistic flair to *El día señalado* and *Respirando el verano*. It is formally divided into two parts, the first with fourteen chapters (focusing on Julia) and the second with sixteen chapters (focusing on Isabel). In the beginning, the town is occupied by General Rosas's victorious army. Soldiers establish themselves in the local hotel along with women whom they have kidnapped or seduced. The townsfolk resent

Julia, the general's mistress, as well as Felipe Hurtado. The general attempts to kill Felipe Hurtado, but the latter manages to escape magically, departing with Julia on a white horse into a cloud of darkness. Everything turns in a different direction in the novel's second half. Now General Rosas's army supports the government banning of the Church of Rome. Isabel, who loves her brother and resents being a woman, invests her need for power in General Rosas. As Isabel and several other women betray the Cristero cause, the plot becomes increasingly complex. Isabel and Julia are traitors, and as such, Franco has pointed out, they are outside history.[18]

Relatively ignored in comparison to contemporary novels of the Boom, *Los recuerdos del porvenir* shares several qualities with those novels. This text reveals a writer fully committed to the right of invention along the lines of Fuentes's innovative writings of this period; Garro self-consciously pushes the limits of time and space throughout *Los recuerdos del porvenir* to such an extent that these elements become central themes of the novel. Thus, like Fuentes, Garro is acutely critical of the "progress" of the modern state as conceived and constructed by the postrevolutionary power structure at the same time that she strives (like Fuentes) to surpass the traditional boundaries of time and space. Fuentes's entire fictional work has time as its central theme, and the same can be said of *Los recuerdos del porvenir*. More importantly, Garro uses many of the same strategies later developed by Fuentes to undermine conventional concepts of linear time.

José Emilio Pacheco's *Morirás lejos* is yet another historical novel, but unlike much of this 1960s fiction, it has nothing to do with oral traditions, myth-making, or the novel as Archive. Distant from Faulkner, Castellanos, Garro, and García Márquez, *Morirás lejos* needs to be situated squarely between *Rayuela* and experimental postmodern fiction of the 1970s. Pacheco's novel has historical referents such as the experience of the Jews under attack by the Romans in Israel in the first century A.D. and the Holocaust in Poland during World War II. Pacheco the modernist questions how we know this world of human atrocity by rewriting and reinventing Jewish history in a fragmented form that invites analysis. The degree of certainty with which the reader believes Pacheco's text varies as the novel progresses: all the narrative segments become questionable. In the end, little certainty is possible.

Morirás lejos consists of 101 narrative segments that develop, on one level, as a modernist text that moves from chaos to unity. The apparent chaos lies in the fact that the narration jumps—from one narrative segment to another—in time and space across centuries and oceans, from the first century A.D. to the twentieth, from Israel and Poland to Mexico. Adding to this initial impression of chaos is the presence of a series of inherently ambiguous narrative segments ("Salónica") that systematically negate anything they affirm. These Salónica sections initially portray a character named Eme, who from the window in an apartment building in Mexico City observes an individual named Alguien sitting on a park bench below, reading a newspaper. Once this situation is clarified, however, the narrator begins subverting the operating premises about it to the point that the reader necessarily questions whether Eme really exists, whether Alguien really exists, and whether any of the relevant situations ever existed. Finally, the reader questions in the early stages of the novel what relationships might exist between the destruction of the Jews in Israel and this setting in Mexico City, between the Holocaust in Warsaw and this setting in Mexico City.

After this initial impression of the chaos and disorder so common in modernist texts, the reader begins to discover relationships between the anecdotes set in the Old World and those set in Mexico City. There are parallels, for example, between the *mirada* that Eme directs and the *mirada* from the Torre Antonia down to the Jerusalem that Romans are about to destroy. Later, the reader of this modernist text discovers yet another parallel in the *mirada* that Eme directs down to the Jews he is torturing and destroying in Warsaw.

The postmodern of *Morirás lejos* betrays and subverts the unity suggested in reading this novel as a harmonious, modernist text such as *La casa grande* or *Oficio de tinieblas*. The subversion of the situation of Eme and Alguien does much more than undermine the reader's confidence in the existence of these two supposed characters. By questioning these narrative segments, *Morirás lejos* questions the possibility of writing history, the uses of history, and the legitimacy of historiography.

The boundaries between worlds are blurred and violated in *Morirás lejos* beyond anything suggested in the typical Latin American modernist novel of the 1960s. Pacheco shares the ontological concerns of the postmodern when he blurs the boundaries between the ancient and modern worlds as well as between operations of the Nazis and the "democratic" operation of states such as Mexico. He also blurs the traditional distinction between story and history. Pacheco's novel becomes an ontological text questioning its mode of existence. Does *Morirás lejos* exist as testimony, as historiography, or as fiction? Avoiding the either/or thinking of Western tradition (as Morelli suggests in *Rayuela*), Pacheco's text is a testimonial that subverts the testimonial itself, a historiography that questions historiography itself, and a metafiction that questions the mode of existence of fiction. *Morirás lejos* contains elements that associate it with numerous other modernist works of the 1960s, including the major novels of the Boom. It is such a radically modernist text with so many characteristics of the postmodern, in fact, that it can be read as a transitional work between the high modernism of the Latin American novel of the 1950s and 1960s and some of the more radically experimental postmodern novels published in Indo-Afro-Iberoamerica in the 1970s and 1980s.

The "other" fiction of the 1960s—the relatively unrecognized modernist novels—like the recognized fiction of the Boom, features elements of the past and future of the Latin American novel that many scholars and readers have considered its successes and others have considered its failures. With respect to the past, some of the most accomplished modernist novelists of the 1960s were neo-Faulknerians who attained transcendent regionalism in their work. With respect to the future, some of their experimentation foreshadowed that of postmodern fiction of the 1970s and 1980s. The successes of these less-recognized novelists frequently were on an aesthetic par with the fiction of the Boom. Their faults or "failures," as described by critics as respected as Jean Franco, were basically the same weaknesses signaled by the same critics of the novels of the Boom: they were not entirely and consistently optimistic about radical social change. Nevertheless, these writers, and particularly the women such as Castellanos and Garro, made important aesthetic achievements and critiques of numerous aspects of the dominant classes and the patriarchal order. If they did not thoroughly respond to the old masculinist aesthetic, they made possible more convincing responses that appeared later in the work of highly progressive feminist and postmodern writers.

Like many novels of the Boom, these works exhibit the totalizing impulses of the modernist novelist. This impulse is particularly evident in *Los recuerdos del porvenir* and *Respirando el verano*, in which the authors exploit a broad range of technical possibilities, language registers, and narrative voices to create a "total" narrative universe. Unlike the writers of the Boom, however, Garro and Rojas Herazo did not write the lengthy and ambitious totalizing novel of the late 1960s and early 1970s comparable to García Márquez's *Cien años de soledad*, Vargas Llosa's *Conversación en La Catedral*, or Donoso's *El obsceno pájaro de la noche*.

All six novels discussed above that fell outside the international recognition of the Boom were works of numerous accomplishments. Those of *Los recuerdos del porvenir*, however, are particularly noteworthy. As Castillo points out, part of the contribution of the female perspective dominant in Garro's novel is in giving the reader the complementary female perspective of the experience of war; this novel helps negotiate the gender divide, representing women as subjects of the discourse about war.[19] In addition, Garro's insistence on the right of invention, as well as her totalizing impulses, made *Los recuerdos del porvenir* quite comparable to early novels of the Boom, such as Fuentes's *La muerte de Artemio Cruz* and Vargas Llosa's *La ciudad y los perros*. In the latter part of the twentieth century, Garro's fiction began to receive the recognition it deserves, as has the writing of several of these novelists of the 1960s.

Part V **Toward a Postboom, Feminist, and
Postmodern Novel, 1968–1999**

Eleven **Novelistic and Cultural Contexts in the 1970s and 1980s**

The 1970s and 1980s were characterized by a flourishing of the most heterogeneous and perhaps the most compelling novelistic production seen in any earlier period of the century. The desire to be modern now took a postmodern turn at the same time that the challenge of modernity was intensely embraced by women writers and other marginalized groups, such as writers of gay, lesbian, and testimonial fiction. The novelistic production in this period indicates that the experience of radical discontinuity that Latin American fiction had been attempting to tell since the *vanguardia* years of Torres Bodet and Huidobro was coming to fruition. The appearance of novelists such as the Chilean Isabel Allende, the Puerto Rican Rosario Ferré, and the Brazilian Nélida Piñón ushered in a new era for women writers in Latin America.

Scholars have not reached a consensus about the major directions of Latin American fiction published since the 1960s, nor is there agreement about nomenclature. In the 1970s, it became apparent that the political, aesthetic, and personal bonds of the writers of the Boom were vanishing; some writers and critics began speaking of a "Postboom" of Latin American fiction.[1] By the mid-1980s, it was equally apparent that the quantity and quality of fiction authored by women in Latin America were indicative of a shift from a predominantly masculinist aesthetic to a scenario in which some of Latin America's most notable novelists were women. By the late 1980s, it was also evident that many of Latin America's most innovative writers were participating in a radical and highly innovative version of modernism—a kind of hypermodernism—that some scholars have identified as the postmodern.[2] Experimenting with the postmodern and entering into dialogue with postmodern culture have been yet another end-of-the-century way of exhibiting the century-long desire to be modern.

Politics: Novels of Dictatorship, Exile, and History

The most significant cultural and political context of this period was the rise of repressive military dictatorships in the 1970s and their fall in the late 1980s and the 1990s. The fall of the Somoza regime in Nicaragua was a watershed for the history of Nicaragua. The military coup in 1973 that led to the death of Chile's Salvador Allende, who headed the leftist coalition Unidad Popular, led to the prolonged dictatorship of Augusto Pinochet. His sanguine rule was paralleled by military regimes in Argentina and Brazil in the 1970s. In Argentina, the "Proceso de Reorganización Nacional" (1976–1983) was the euphemistic name the military dictatorships gave to a program that entailed repressing the more progressive sectors of the citizenry. Since the 1980s, the human and cultural meaning of these dictatorships and others is still being accounted for by novelists.

During the 1970s, in fact, enough Latin American writers published novels dealing with military regimes that the "dictator novel" became a common nomenclature. The most celebrated of these novels were Alejo Carpentier's *El recurso del método* (1974), Augusto Roa Bastos's *Yo, el Supremo* (1974), and Gabriel García Márquez's *El otoño del patriarca* (1975);[3] these novelists drew upon the historical record to create fictionalized versions of dictators. Other novels about authoritarian figures were Mario Vargas Llosa's *Conversación en La Catedral* (1969) and Denzil Romero's *La tragedia del generalísimo* (1984), both lengthy and complex works. *Conversación en La Catedral* stands out as one of the most ambitious technical enterprises for Vargas Llosa and for the modernist novel in Latin America; the dictator portrayed here is General Manuel Odría (leader of Peru from 1948 to 1956).

In addition to the four above-mentioned novelists, others published works dealing with either dictators or authority figures. For example, Fuentes's *Terra Nostra* (1975), set primarily in sixteenth-century Spain, can be included here, with the authority figure being Felipe II. Sergio Ramírez's *¿Te dio miedo la sangre?* (1977), moreover, is a complex mosaic of Nicaraguan society under the Somoza dictatorship; it has been described as a "dictator novel without the dictator."[4]

In the 1970s and 1980s, acutely and subtly political fiction appeared that did not fall strictly within the genre of dictator novels. Two very different political novels were Julio Cortázar's *Libro de Manuel* (1973) and Alejandra Pizarnik's *La condesa sangrienta* (1976). In *Libro de Manuel,* Cortázar portrays revolutionaries in a setting of urban guerrilla warfare. This postmodern novel consists of a multiplicity of texts that the protagonist and his friends place together for the next generation—represented by a character named Manuel. Cortázar encourages the reader to think beyond the most immediate political questions to consider broader issues, such as language, sexuality, and modes of interpretation themselves. Erotic play operates in *Libro de Manuel* as an exploration of liberation and a questioning of social norms: the novel portrays eroticism in a variety of facets.[5] The implicit political themes of Pizarnik's *La condesa sangrienta* are more subtle than the surface politics of *Libro de Manuel.* Pizarnik rewrites the story of the real-life Hungarian Countess Erzébet Báthory (died 1614), who tortured and killed more than six hundred young women. Written in metaphoric language that blurs both traditional and modernist concepts of the novel, it is a brief text that consists of eleven vignettes. On the surface, this horrifying text seems divorced from the politics of Argentina. Considered within the context of the military rule over Argentina in the 1970s, however, *La condesa sangrienta* can be read as a meditation on the horror of absolute power.[6] In a political reading of this text, it has been argued convincingly that this novel is a confirmation of the masculinist violence of the patriarchy whose martyrs are betokened by the countess's hundreds of female victims.[7]

Another counterpart to the dictator novels in Latin America was the novel of exile written in Europe or the United States. A first wave of such writers included the Cuban Matías Montes Huidobro (in the United States) and the Chileans Antonio Skármeta (writing in Germany) and Ariel Dorfman (writing in the United States), followed by Guatemalan Arturo Arias and Julia Alvarez from the Dominican Republic (both writing in the United States). The diaspora into exile included writers who found refuge in France, such as Alfredo Bryce Echenique, Luisa Futoransky, Juan José Saer, and Osvaldo Soriano. Spain became the temporary residence for José Donoso, Juan Carlos Onetti, Cristina Peri Rossi, Mario Benedetti, Mempo Giardinelli, Tomás Eloy Martínez, and Pedro Orgambide.[8]

In some cases, the distance of exile produced critique that the writers could not have published in their homelands. In *No habrá más pena ni olvido* (1980), Osvaldo Soriano denounces the massacres under the military dictatorship in Argentina. Tomás Eloy Martínez dramatizes rivalries within the ranks of Peronism in *La novela de Perón* (1985). In *Después de las bombas* (1979) Arturo Arias rewrites the history and experience of the 1954 overthrow by the CIA of the progressive Arbenz government in Guatemala. A modernist text conceived in the mode of many novels of the Boom, *Después de las bombas* tells the story of Máximo Sánchez from childhood to adulthood, with close connections to the *testimonio*.[9] Arias's later novels *Itzam* (1981) and *Jaguar en llamas* (1989) are also closely related to *testimonio*.

Some of the writers were more concerned with the cases of the uprooted individual living abroad, thus taking a more existential than strictly political approach. Daniel Moyano offers an existential focus on exile in *Libro de navío y borrascas* (1983). Reynaldo Arenas's fiction of the 1980s reflected problems associated with the diverse cultural and political issues faced by many Cuban intellectuals living in exile in the United States.

Moyano's existential themes were echoed in Alvaro Mutis's novels concerning the spiritual quest of the protagonist, Gaviero, a sailor, adventurer, and philosopher. The first book of a trilogy, Mutis's *La nieve del Almirante* (1986) contains Gaviero's diary, followed by notes written by persons acquainted with him. These texts, composed of the protagonist's meditations and the thoughts of others about him, offer an examination of Gaviero's spiritual life.

Some novelists developed the novel of exile on a more abstract level than did Mutis, as was the case of Federico Patán in *Ultimo exilio* (1986). The novel portrays a Spaniard's exile in Mexico, but the most significant exile is of psychological space. Luis Arturo Ramos's *Intramuros* (1983) functions in a similar manner, fictionalizing both physical and psychological exile.

Finally, tales of dictatorship and exile can be related to a generalized interest during the 1970s and 1980s in the historical novel.[10] Novelists such as Abel Posse, Rosario Aguilar, Marcos Aguinis, Nélida Piñón, and Fernando del Paso participated in this rewriting of Latin American history. Posse's *Los perros del paraíso* (1983), Aguilar's *El guerrillero* (1976), Aguinis's *La cruz invertida* (1970), Piñón's *A República dos sonhos* (1984), and del Pasos's *Noticias del Imperio* (1987) were just a few of the most prominent historical texts of the 1970s and 1980s. Menton has noted others, among them Edgardo Rodríguez Juliá, César Aira, Juan José Saer, Antonio Benítez Rojo, Márcio Souza, José J. Veiga, Harold Maranhão, and the Martinican Michel Tauriac.[11] In the case of Marcos Aguinis, focus on distant history was a method for discussing contemporary politics metaphorically in Argentina during the dictatorship. In *La cruz invertida*, Aguinis also considers historically based themes, here issues of the Catholic Church. Set in an unnamed Latin American nation, it shows the interaction among the clergy, the oligarchy, the military, communists, and students. Two progressive priests generate the conflict in the novel.

Luisa Valenzuela and José Donoso wrote subtle novels of exile. Valenzuela's *Novela negra con argentinos* (1990) develops a detective story around the presence of two Argentine novelists voluntarily exiled in New York. The text is more a postmodern play on detective novels than a classic rendering of them. Donoso's *El jardín de al lado* (1981) portrays a Chilean writer and his wife exiled in Spain. The two novels share several characteristics including similar imagery, and the theme of both texts is the otherness of exile.[12]

The cultural identity of the Caribbean remained a focus of polemics in the 1970s and 1980s. The ambiguous political status and cultural identity of Puerto Rico was intensely debated among Latin American intellectuals. Novelist and essayist José Luis González contributed significantly to this dialogue with the publication of his influential essay *El país de cuatro pisos* (1980), an analysis of Puerto Rico's culture and society. In a lecture delivered in 1970, Guyanese novelist Wilson Harris promulgated the idea that creative activity should involve "a drama of consciousness which reads back through the shock of place and time for omens of capacity."[13] González, Harris, and Freddy Prestol Castillo agreed that literary activity, indeed, was an engagement with critical thought. In *El Masacre se pasa a pie* (1973), Prestol Castillo novelizes a 1937 massacre of Haitian and Haitian-Dominican families. In this historiographic metafiction, a first-person narrator provides a testimonial account and metacommentary about his own role as witness and as author. This genocide was the outgrowth of historic conflicts between the two Caribbean nations, and the deaths were legitimated by anti-Haitian discourse of the Dominican elite.[14]

Some Brazilian novelists publishing during this period, including Clarice Lispector, Jorge Amado, and Osman Lins, engaged in political, historical, and postmodern exercises comparable to those found among the writers throughout the rest of Indo-Afro-Iberoamerica. Lispector's novels in this period were *Uma apprendizagem ou O livro dos prazeres* (1969), *Agua viva* (1973), and *A hora da estrela* (1977). The first of these three novels involves two individuals' identity search, and Lispector's feminist concerns were increasingly evident. Jorge Amado continued his career as a novelist with *Tereza Batista cansada de guerra* (1972), a rewriting of popular *cordel* ballads. In this playful text, Amado creates an authorial narrator who supposedly knew a legendary heroine personally. Lins published the experimental *Avalovara* (1973).

The Chicano novel—now in dialogue with the Latin American Boom—flourished. During this period, in fact, some of the most compelling Chicano novels of the century appeared. The salient figures included Rolando Hinojosa, Tomás Rivera, Miguel Méndez, and Rudolfo Anaya. The coincidence of the Chicano political movement in the United States and the Boom of the Latin American novel were important factors for these Chicano writers, some of whom have written of their admiration for contemporary Latin American fiction. Among the most notable of these dialogic novels were Rivera's *Y no se lo tragó la tierra* (1971), Anaya's *Bless Me, Ultima* (1972), Méndez's *Peregrinos de Aztlán* (1974), and Hinojosa's *Klail City y sus alrededores* (1975). These writers drew upon their own cultural history as Hispanics in the southwestern United States as well as on Hispanic literary tradition, broadly conceived, to participate in the multicultural dialogue in the United States.[15] The novels written by these authors represented a flowering of the Chicano novel in Spanish.

During the early part of this period, many novelists reaffirmed the political role of the writer. Some of these public intellectuals— Fuentes, Cortázar, and García Márquez—remained most adamant, well into the 1980s, about the political commitment of the Latin American writer. In 1973, Cortázar stated that his "machine gun" for political revolution was literature.[16] Vargas Llosa, Fuentes, and García Márquez had made similar statements in the 1960s.

After the Boom: The Postboom

In the ongoing discussions on the Latin American novel after the Boom, one of the most prominent scholarly exponents of the idea of a Postboom has been Donald Shaw.[17] The novels that Shaw identifies as part of this Postboom represent, in effect, a continuation of the modernist project initiated in Latin America in the 1940s and continued masterfully by the writers of the Boom, particularly García Márquez and Vargas Llosa.[18] Writers such as Antonio Skármeta and Mempo Giardinelli (two of Shaw's Postboom writers) do share generational attitudes that distance them from their immediate predecessors of the Boom. Nevertheless, their fiction is fundamentally a continuation of modernist aesthetics. These writers are by no means traditionalists; indeed, they employ the narrative strategies explored and refined by modernist writers since the 1940s. As such, Skármeta, Giardinelli, Allende, and a host of other Latin American storytellers belong to the tradition of the modernist novel—frequently adding a touch from their local tradition, be it orality, magic realism, or rewriting regional or national history.

The Postboom represents a return to accessibility, more realism, and pop elements that reflect a greater cultural autonomy and the revival of democracy in parts of the continent, according to Shaw.[19] Citing writers such as Skármeta, Shaw proposes that the assumptions made by the Boom writers—whether about literature or society —were to be directly contradicted in the next generation. Making reference to Giardinelli, Shaw emphasizes that the "extreme pessimism" characteristic of the Boom was shifted to a new optimism in the Postboom, although not all scholars agree that the Boom was necessarily so pessimistic.[20] Giardinelli and others have stated that their generation was defeated politically in Latin America and that consequently they lost much of the optimism conveyed by their earlier writing.

Many of the writers associated with the Postboom are politically committed storytellers whose writing can be seen as a post-Macondo phenomenon: they write either with or against the storytelling vitality and magic realist approaches of García Márquez. Writers such as Isabel Allende and Luis Sepúlveda produced a fiction with many overtones and stylistic characteristics from García Márquez's magical fictional worlds.[21] On the other hand, Colombian novelists such as Gustavo Alvarez Gardeazábal in *El bazar de los idiotas* (1974) and Marco Tulio Aguilera Garramuño in *Breve historia de todas las cosas* (1975) have written parodies of *Cien años de soledad*.

Several writers and critics have pointed to the importance of *testimonio* and a closer attachment to empirical reality among Postboom writers. Isabel Allende, for example, believes that her writing breaks from two of the basic tenets of the Boom: she is neither "detached" nor "ironical."[22] Several critics have argued that the Boom writers lacked a radical criticism of society, embracing liberal solutions to mask their acceptance of the status quo. For Shaw, a more radical response to the political reality in Latin America was the Postboom writing of Allende's *De amor y de sombra*, Skármeta's *La insurrección*, and Elena Poniatowska's *La noche de Tlatelolco*. Similarly, Sklodowska has demonstrated the importance of the documentary genre of *testimonio* in Postboom narrative.[23]

In contrast, in studies of Postboom fiction in Mexico, other critics attempt to avoid the reduction of the Mexican novel to the more accessible works only.[24] These scholars take into account the writing of novelists such as Juan García Ponce, Angelina Muñiz, and Humberto Guzmán, whose experiments with fiction are far from accessible. The more accessible writers of Mexican fiction in the 1970s and 1980s who could be associated with a Postboom are Sergio Galindo, Armando Ramírez, Arturo Azuela, Luis Zapata, Vicente Leñero, Luis Spota, and Jorge Ibargüengoitia. Galindo continued his modernist writing into the 1980s, publishing *Terciopelo violeta* in 1985 and *Otilia Rauda* in 1986. In the latter, he uses a backdrop of twentieth-century Mexican history and traditional narrative forms to tell the tale of an attractive and liberated woman, Otilia, and her lover. It is the most attractive story line constructed by Galindo in his career, leaving behind most of the strategies of the small-screen fiction that had been his mainstay for most of his career. Arturo Azuela also published novels with a broad historical scope, beginning with a family story, *El tamaño del infierno* (1973). He followed with the story of a town, *Un tal José Salomé* (1975), and a work about his own generation in the 1960s and 1970s, *Manifestación de silencios* (1979). In *Chin-Chin el teporocho* (1972), Ramírez focuses on everyday life in a working-class neighborhood in Mexico City. Ramírez followed with *Regreso de Chin-Chin el teporocho* (1978), a parody of the popular literature of soap operas and comic books. *La princesa del Palacio de Hierro* (1974) by Sainz was a reaction against the complexities of the fiction of the Boom, and also against the hermetic qualities of the Onda, as new fiction by young writers was identified in Mexico. In this novel, an unnamed female protagonist relates a humorous story of failed relationships, sexual misadventures, and crime.

The most representative writers of the Postboom in Spanish America, according to Shaw, were Isabel Allende, Antonio Skármeta, Luisa Valenzuela, Rosario Ferré, and Gustavo Sainz. Undoubtedly one of the major literary events in the early 1980s, as Shaw has observed, was the publication of Allende's *La casa de los espíritus* in 1982, the same year that García Márquez received the Nobel prize in literature.[25] This novel's overwhelming commercial success, coupled with a generally favorable response among scholars and critics, have made it part of the canon of Postboom writing. An historical novel, it portrays the Chilean oligarchy through magical elements that are easily associated with magic realism. Following the Trueba-del-Valle family through four generations, the novel's context is Chilean society and politics from the beginning of the twentieth century to Pinochet's coup in 1973. Several critics have focused on the women characters in *La casa de los espíritus,* for they are strong and imaginative individuals who resist the patriarchy with heroism; in this characterization of women, Allende challenges the masculinist aesthetic that long pervaded the Latin American novel. For Shaw, what marks this work as a Postboom novel is that the reader can recognize that reality could be generally understood in a chronological sequence of cause and effect, and it is written *as if* the ability to detect historical progress formed part of that understanding. In his discussion of *La casa de los espíritus,* Shaw clarifies as follows: "The whole problem of Postboom writers in Allende's category is precisely to avoid this extreme and to walk an uneasy path between the Barthes—*Tel Quel*—Sarduyian notion that the text can have no exterior referent and the old-fashioned idea that the relationship between signifier and signified is completely unproblematic."[26] Allende followed *La casa de los espíritus* with *De amor y de sombra* (1984) and *Eva Luna* (1987), novels as accessible as her first. *De amor y de sombra* is a continuation of her testimony of political repression in Chile.

Antonio Skármeta's early short fiction, according to Shaw, does not manifest the same optimism and hope to be found in Isabel Allende and other writers of the Postboom. His novel *Soñé que la nieve ardía* (1975), however, can be seen as one of the novels marking a shift from the Boom to the Postboom.[27] This novel deals with politically active working-class individuals in an urban setting. *Ardiente paciencia* (1985) is a love story set during the crucial period in Chile from 1969 to 1973. In this novel and others, including *La insurección* (1982) and *Match Ball* (1989), Skármeta questions middle-class values related to the individualism found in sports and other spheres of bourgeois society. In *No pasó nada* (1980), Skármeta considers the complexities of living in exile as perceived by an adolescent in the family portrayed. His regular use of colloquial language has been associated with the Postboom.[28]

Using Shaw's scheme for the Postboom, one could identify other Latin American novelists (not mentioned by him) as part of the Postboom. Sergio Ramírez and Fanny Buitrago wrote fiction in the 1970s easily associated with this Postboom. Four other Colombian novelists who participated in the Postboom—using Shaw's criteria but likewise not identified by him—were Germán Espinosa, Gustavo Alvarez Gardeazábal, Manuel Mejía Vallejo, and Alvaro Mutis. One of Espinosa's most accomplished novels, *Los cortejos del diablo* (1970), is an historical work set in the colonial period. It portrays Juan de Mañozga, an inquisitor in Cartagena, Colombia, identified by some as the "Torquemada" of the Indies. Espinosa's later novel, *Sinfonía del nuevo mundo* (1990), is an historical novel involving Bolívar, with a quickly moving plot that is apparently directed to a potentially broad reading public.[29]

Like Espinosa, Alvarez Gardeazábal is critical of the Catholic Church in several of his Postboom novels, although his stories generally satirize numerous Colombian institutions and parody modernists who preceded him, such as García Márquez. The most noteworthy of his Postboom novels were *Cóndores no entierran todos los días* (1972), *Dabeiba* (1972), and *El bazar de los idiotas* (1974). All of these novels have the strong story line of Postboom writing. *Cóndores no entierran todos los días* relives the period of La Violencia in Colombia. It is one of the few novels dealing with this civil war not to celebrate the bloody massacres and purely physical aspect of the conflict. In *Dabeiba*, Alvarez Gardeazábal displays his ability to tell stories in relating the life of the inhabitants of the town of Dabeiba over a period of several days. His technical mastery is more evident in this than in his other novels. In his later novels *El titiritero* (1977), *Los míos* (1991), and *Pepe Botellas* (1984), Alvarez Gardeazábal satirizes Colombia's basic institutions and creates situations featuring political power and characters obsessed with power.

Manuel Mejía Vallejo and Alvaro Mutis likewise published novels in the 1970s and 1980s that were modernist in impulse and can be included in the Postboom. Mejía Vallejo's *Aire de tango* (1973) treats an aspect of popular culture in Colombia: the passion for the tango. *Aire de tango* was published, in fact, on June 24, 1973, the thirty-eighth anniversary of the death in Medellín of legendary tango master Carlos

Gardel. In this novel, an unidentified narrator tells anecdotes related to Gardel and an admirer of Gardel in a Medellín neighborhood.

Central American writers who made significant contributions to the Postboom were Carmen Naranjo, Rosario Aguilar, Giaconda Belli, Arturo Arias, and Sergio Ramírez. Naranjo's *Memorias de un hombre palabra* (1968) communicates the fatalism and pessimism that permeate her fiction in general. In her novels *Diario de una multitud* (1974) and *Sobrepunto* (1985), Naranjo expresses similar attitudes while developing the feminist concerns of her later work. Rosario Aguilar's *El guerrillero* made her one of the most noteworthy novelists of Central America. The plot of this work centers on a guerrilla fighter who falls in love with a schoolteacher. Arias's fiction is closely related to *testimonio*, and it shares other characteristics of the Postboom. His novel *Los caminos de Pazil* (1990) has a strong narrative line, relating the struggles of indigenous communities against multinational oil companies. Arias's works escape easy categorization as Postboom, postmodern, or *testimonio*, however. The same can be said of Belli's *La mujer habitada* (1988), about the struggle for women's rights and national liberation in Nicaragua. In *Castigo divino* (1988), Ramírez recreates the history of Nicaragua and Central America in the 1930s.

The most representative writers of the Postboom in Peru were Alfredo Bryce Echenique, Gregorio Martínez, and Isaac Goldemberg. Bryce Echenique's *Un mundo para Julius* (1970) is a story of growing up in upper-middle-class Lima; but more than the typical rite de passage, the novel satirizes this particular social class in a parody of its own language. His other novels are *Tantas veces Pedro* (1981), *La vida exagerada de Martín Romaña* (1981), *El hombre que hablaba de Octavia de Cádiz* (1985), and *La última mudanza de Felipe Carrillo* (1988). Julio Ortega has observed that Echenique's novels are exercises in an aesthetic of hyperbole and performance.[30] Goldemberg's *La vida a plazos de don Jacobo Lerner* (1975) tells the story of not only the disenfranchisement of the protagonist, but of his entire Jewish clan in Peru. It is a novel of the diaspora and cultural conflict.

Some of the most significant Postboom works of the 1970s and 1980s came from writers associated with the Boom itself. Novels such as Vargas Llosa's *Pantaleón y las visitadoras* (1973), Fuentes's *La cabeza de la hidra* (1978), Donoso's *La misteriosa desaparición de la Marquesita de Loria* (1980), and García Márquez's *El amor en los tiempos del cólera* (1985) were these authors' reactions against much of their own work of the 1960s. More specifically, these fictions were a dialogue with the novels of the Boom, for they did not represent a total rejection of the novelists' earlier modernist interests.[31] With *Pantaleón y las visitadoras* and *La tía Julia y el escribidor* (1977), as well as with his fiction of the 1980s, Vargas Llosa returns to some of his demons of the 1960s, obsessions such as the Peruvian military and the role of storytelling in contemporary society. Donoso reacted against his own totalizing impulses with *La misteriosa desaparición de la Marquesita de Loria*, a brief novel in dialogue with erotic and detective fiction.[32]

Some Latin American writers published texts in the period of the Boom yet never were associated with these celebrities. Four such novelists were Salvador Garmendia, Elena Garro, Adriano González León, and Lisandro Chávez Alfaro. Garmendia, who belonged to the Boom generationally but was not a part of the foremost group, also wrote novels that could be associated with the Postboom. His *Memorias de Altagracia* (1974) and *El Capitán Kid* (1983) were a continuation of his interests of the 1960s. Garro continued her novelistic career of the 1960s with the publication of several novels in the 1980s. Like Fuentes, her main theme—indeed, her lifelong obsession—is time. In *Testimonios sobre Mariana* (1980), three voices evoke the life of Mariana, attempting to defeat the loss of memory associated with the passing of time. *La casa junto al río* (1983) is an elaboration of the themes of time and memory; the main character is a woman remembering the past. The relationship between time and the levels of fiction becomes more complex in *Reencuentro de personajes* (1982), as characters from the novels of F. Scott Fitzgerald and Evelyn Waugh appear in the "present" of the "real" Mexico recreated by Garro.

Summarizing, then, the reaction against the writing of the 1960s Boom has been characterized as a Postboom, and the most active writers of this group were Allende, Skármenta, Mejía Vallejo, and Giardinelli, in addition to a host of others who made themselves accessible to a broad readership. They were perhaps more optimistic in vision than the writers of the Boom. The overall panorama of Latin American fiction from the 1970s to the 1990s, however, is far more complex than such generalizations allow the reader to discern. Feminist, gay, and innovative postmodern writing, for example, was quite significant during this period, and it is difficult to make broad and fixed generalizations about the readership, language, or optimism of these frequently marginalized and often postmodern writers.

The Presence of Women Writers

For many readers and critics, the dictator novel, the Postboom, and postmodern fiction were important phenomena in Latin America in the 1970s and 1980s. The most singularly notable cultural shift after the Boom, however, was neither the Postboom nor the postmodern; rather, it was the rise of women writers. Women were quite prominent throughout Latin America and the Caribbean during the 1970s and 1980s. Of course, many women writers participated in Postboom- and postmodern-type literary activity, as well as in the writing of dictator novels, as evidenced in Flor Romero de Nohra's *Los sueños del poder* (1977). The most widely recognized and celebrated woman writer from 1968 to 1990 was Isabel Allende. Several other women, however, were as prolific or more so, even though they did not enjoy the commercial success of Allende. Among the women writers generally taken more seriously than Allende were novelists Elena Poniatowska, Elena Garro, Rosario Ferré, Luisa Valenzuela, Diamela Eltit, Albalucía Angel, Fanny Buitrago, Ana María Shúa, Alicia Borinsky, Julieta Campos, Carmen Naranjo, Cristina Peri Rossi, Alejandra Pizarnik, and Armonía Sommers. These women have been associated with several tendencies in Latin American fiction, from the Postboom and exile writing to feminist and postmodern novels.

In addition, Brazilian writers Clarice Lispector, Helena Parente Cunha, and Nélida Piñón, as well as U.S. Latina novelists Sandra Cisneros, Ana Castillo, and Margarita Cota-Cardenas, entered into a significant dialogue with the Latin American novel. Many of these writers set forth a specifically feminist project: they often viewed women as heirs to earlier traditions and forgers of new ones. Diamela Eltit, Silvia Molloy, Albalucía Angel, and Helena Parente Cunha were well aware of this lineage. Women writers of the 1970s and 1980s were more sophisticated in their use of narrative technique and more affirmative about feminist issues than were writers of previous generations. They tended to use a variety of discourses (journalistic, instructional, legal, and the like) and in the process raised questions about the viability of the very genre of the novel itself. Many of these women wrote for considerable portions of their careers while facing a choice between repression and exile.

Fanny Buitrago was generally less interested in innovation and feminist theory than were Angel, Molloy, and other feminists. Buitrago has published a consistent body of fiction since the 1960s. She writes with interests in oral tradition and modernist aesthetics and, consequently, is easily associated with the Postboom. Her main interests are human relationships, and her characters tend to be isolated, abandoned, and constrained by social morés. Her most complex work was *Cola de zorro* (1970), a family story, but not of the traditional sort. The three major characters in this work—Ana, Emmanuel, and Malinda—are connected by Benito, a man of such special qualities that he is characterized with mythic dimensions. The reader gradually discovers blood relations and other relations that connect the main characters, and the novel is a study of these human relations. Buitrago's novels *Los pañamanes* (1979) and *Los amores de Afrodita* (1983) demonstrate her interest in stories that are accessible to a broad reading public yet avoid the clichés of fiction for mass markets. *Los amores de Afrodita* can be read as a volume of short stories, similar to volumes that appeared throughout Latin America.

The fiction of Elena Poniatowska, Luisa Valenzuela, and Rosario Ferré has not competed in sales with that of writers such as Allende and is not experimental enough to be associated with the postmodern writers. Nevertheless, these three writers do have feminist interests, and their fiction is significant. Poniatowska's early writing was nonfiction, but she has since published several novels. From 1968 to 1990 she published the testimonial books *Hasta no verte Jesús mío* (1969) and *La noche de Tlatelolco* (1971), the collection of stories *De noche vienes* (1979), the epistolary novel *Querido Diego, te abraza Quiela* (1978), and the novel *La "Flor de Lis"* (1988). *Hasta no verte Jesús mío* is an oral history of a washerwoman, Josefina Bórquez, who appears under the fictitious name of Jesusa Palancares. After interviewing Bórquez on a weekly basis for a year, Poniatowska created this fictionalized version of the woman's life. Palancares is a feminist who is defiant of all forms of authority. Her language is a synthesis of popular speech of working-class women of Mexico City, inviting Shaw to categorize this as a Postboom novel. The plot of *La "Flor de Lis"* parallels Poniatowska's own life: the protagonist is from an aristocratic family background, immigrates from France to Mexico City, and eventually comes to understand the social and political realities of her adopted nation. In Poniatowska's work, the documentary spirit is constant, as is her search for social justice in Mexico. She also recognizes the relativity of truths, which links her to postmodern fiction.[33]

Although she shares Poniatowska's interest in *testimonio*, Luisa

Valenzuela has dedicated more of her career strictly to writing fiction. Valenzuela is just as political as Poniatowska, as demonstrated in a body of work focused primarily on politics, language, and women.[34] Her first novel of the 1970s, *El gato eficaz* (1972), deals with a woman narrator's playful—and serious—dialogue with literature. Valenzuela tests the previous limits for women writers with respect to self-censorship and the erotic, frequently incorporating various types of language in her novels. Her novel *El gato eficaz* (1972) also contains these multiple discourses.[35] *Cola de lagartija* (1983) is an overtly political work in which Valenzuela gives the narrator-protagonist her own name. The fictional Luisa Valenzuela of the novel confronts the chaotic process of writing and the increasingly absurd world around her.

Rosario Ferré, Julieta Campos, Sandra Cisneros, Alejandra Pizarnik, Cristina Perri Rossi, Elizabeth Burgos, and Domitila Barrios published heterogeneous works ranging from modernist fiction to *testimonio* narrative. Barrios focuses on her experience as a woman in Bolivia, as Burgos does on women in Guatemala. Burgos is known for her collaboration in Rigoberta Menchú's *testimonio* of political struggles in Guatemala, *Me llamo Rigoberta Menchú y así me nació la conciencia* (1976). Menchú relates the customs of her indigenous people in a small farming community and the loss of family members; the veracity of the book became a polemical issue in the 1990s.[36] Barrios published two books of *literatura testimonial*. Having grown up in a family of miners in Bolivia, she provides an account of her life in *"Si me permiten hablar . . ."* (1976). Her religious experience with a group of Jehovah's Witnesses and her growing political awareness, political commitment, and political activity inform much of this *testimonio*. She also offers an eyewitness description of massacres at the mine. Her book *Aquí, también, Domitila* (1985) is a narrative about a hunger strike to protest the imprisonment of political prisoners.

Many women writers from Venezuela and Latina writers from the United States have been generally unknown beyond their respective national borders. Some scholars, nevertheless, have brought to the forefront the fiction of Venezuelan women writers such as Milagros Matos-Gil, Ana Teresa Torres, and Laura Antillano.[37] Sandra Cisneros, Ana Castillo, and Margarita Cota-Cárdenas have made innovative contributions to the novel as Latina writing in the United States, exploring themes of race and gender. These three writers and several others in the United States criticize racism in Anglo American society, while Castillo's *The Mixquihuala Letters* (1986) explores internalized racism among Latinas. The connections of this novel to Latin America are obvious; Castillo states at its outset that she writes "In memory of the master of the game, Julio Cortázar," thus indicating that it is the author's duty to alert the reader that this is not a book to be read in the usual sequence. Castillo explains that all letters are numbered to aid in following any one of the author's proposed options. Cota-Cárdenas's *Puppet* (1985) is innovative with respect to language, for this work both incorporates multiple languages and is a reflection on language. In this, her writing is comparable to much postmodern fiction published in Latin America in the 1980s. Cisneros's highly successful *The House on Mango Street* (1985) is a series of vignettes about a young girl growing up in a Latino section of Chicago. This is the most celebrated of Cisneros's works on gender and race.

In conclusion, the new feminisms of the 1980s represented a major change of emphasis in the Latin American novel. The critical work of feminist scholars such as Franco, Sommer, Castillo, Guerra, and Castro-Klarén, among others, has situated much of this writing in a Latin American and international context and analyzed the crucial negotiations between this writing and the masculinist aesthetics of much that preceded it.

Queer Discourse and Marginalized Writing

Parallel to the rise of women writers was an increased publication of gay, lesbian, and *testimonio* writing in the 1970s and 1980s. Latin American literature has been historically silent about themes of gender and sexuality. Nevertheless, an increasing number of critics now recognize the presence of queer discourse in the region. A seminal gay novel of Mexican literature was José Ceballos Maldonado's *Después de todo* (1969), a first-person account of the middle-age male protagonist's sexual encounters with teenage boys. The narrative assumes that the reader is not necessarily sympathetic to homoeroticism.[38] David W. Foster has established an inventory of sexual themes by addressing lesbianism and gayness in Latin American literature.[39] He indicates that at the end of the century the multiple discourses of sexuality had become important factors of the Indo-Afro-Iberoamerican novel. The fiction of Silvia Molloy, Luis Zapata, and Fernando Vallejo illustrates the Latin American exploration of the discourses of gender and sexuality.

Significant gay and lesbian novels of this period include Silvia Molloy's *En breve cárcel* (1981), Darcy Penteado's *Nivaldo e Jeronimo* (1981), José Rafael Calva's *Utopía gay* (1983), Luis Zapata's *En jirones* (1985), Oscar Hermes Villordo's *La otra mejilla* (1986), Isaac Chocron's *Toda luna dama* (1988), and Fernando Vallejo's *El fuego secreto* (1986). Chicano/a writers also have produced gay and lesbian texts; in her personal ethnic memoir *Loving in the War Years* (1983), Cherríe Moraga sets forth the idea of a productive Chicana lesbianism. A pioneer gay writer in the Chicano community, John Rechy, wrote of gay relationships.

Luis Zapata and Fernando Vallejo established a place for gay writing in Mexico and Colombia, and they are the most prominent gay writers in their respective homelands. Zapata's novels depict specifically gay characters; his development of gay themes questions and undermines the norms of the heterosexual order. *En jirones* (1985) consists of a notebook *(cuaderno)* that establishes relationships between gay love and writing. It is outstanding as one of the most unabashedly gay books and obviously postmodern texts to appear in Mexico in recent years.

Manuel Puig, Reynaldo Arenas, and Gustavo Alvarez Gardeazábal write on homoerotic themes, though less explicitly than Zapata and Vallejo. In *La traición de Rita Hayworth* (1968), *El beso de la mujer araña* (1976), and *Cae la noche tropical* (1988), Puig explores different stereotypes and concepts of homosexuality. As Foster has suggested, *El beso de la mujer araña* is exceptional for its demonstration of how sexual and political liberation must be viewed as integral parts of the same process.[40] In this novel, Puig explores the power of politics and gender, and the relationship between the two.

Writing identified by scholars of gay and lesbian literature as queer discourse of the 1970s and 1980s served functions similar to that of many feminist and overtly political writers. Queer discourse has contributed as much to the subversion of patriarchal order as many of the feminist and postmodern writers have.

Like many gay and postmodern writers, the authors of *testimonio* tend to move away from totalizing viewpoints to observe the "ubiquity of testimony."[41] The writing of *testimonio* has included practitioners such as Elena Poniatowska, Hernán Valdés, Rigoberta Menchú, Ariel Dorfman, Jacobo Timmerman, Domitila Barrios de

Chungara with Moema Viezzer, Florencia Varas with José Manuel Vargara, Violeta Parra, and Angela Zago. Linda Craft has observed the nontotalizing and *testimonio* impulse in much Central American fiction.[42]

The Postmodern Novel

As of the late 1960s, it became increasingly evident among critics that the radically heterogeneous literary phenomenon in Latin America corresponded in many ways to what was being called postmodern fiction in the West. The term Postboom has been useful to distinguish some tendencies of fiction published after the 1960s Boom. However, as the heterogeneity of this writing became more evident, the term Postboom has been increasingly limited as a rubric for the rich variety of literary phenomena produced since the early 1970s. By the 1980s, it became more appropriate to describe some of the new novels—although certainly not all of them—published since the late 1960s and early 1970s with a term that captured exactly what it was: postmodern fiction. Thus, there has been a growing acceptance of the idea of a postmodern novel in Latin America. If the writers identified with the Postboom tended to follow modernist aesthetics, postmodern writers have demonstrated other interests. These interests have been particularly evident since 1968, with the novels of Manuel Puig, Severo Sarduy, Ricardo Piglia, Diamela Eltit, and others. And as we have seen, some postmodern writers such as Reynaldo Arenas and Silvia Molloy can be easily associated with Postboom gay or lesbian writing.

Umberto Eco claims that the postmodern is born at the moment when the world has no fixed center and power is not something unitary that exists outside of us. This moment occurred in Latin American literature with the rise of Borges, who became a seminal figure for many European theorists and Latin American postmodern novelists in the 1960s and 1970s, even though the now-classic Borges fiction they most admired was published in the 1940s. The Argentine's two seminal books were *El jardín de los senderos que se bifurcan* (1941) and *Ficciones* (1944). More specifically, Borges's "La biblioteca de Babel" and "Pierre Ménard, autor del Quijote" are foundational texts for postmodern fiction in Latin America. In them, the boundary between fiction and essay is blurred, opening the way for the fictionalized theoretical prose of Severo Sarduy, Ricardo Piglia, José Balza, and several others. Borges's fiction operates in a fashion similar to what Hutcheon notes in the fiction of North American and European postmodern writers: the narrator's discourse is paradoxically postmodern, for it both inscribes a context and then contests its boundaries.

After Borges, two of the most notable contributions to the later publication of Latin American postmodern fiction were Cortázar's *Rayuela* (1963) and João Guimarães Rosa's *Grande Sertão: Veredas*. Cortázar's work in itself was not a fully elaborated postmodern work, but its chapters at the end featuring Morelli were a radical proposal for postmodern fiction. In the late 1960s and early 1970s, the postmodern novel began to appear in Latin America, usually under the sign of either Borges or Cortázar, and it was constituted by such experimental fictions as Cabrera Infante's *Tres tristes tigres* (1967), Néstor Sánchez's *Siberia Blues* (1967), and Manuel Puig's *La traición de Rita Hayworth* (1968). Other key novels for early Latin American postmodern fiction were José Emilio Pacheco's *Morirás lejos* (1967), Alberto Duque López's *Mateo el flautista* (1968), José Donoso's *El obsceno pájaro de la noche* (1970), and Severo Sarduy's *Cobra* (1972). *Cobra*, in fact, has become a seminal text for postmodern writing in Latin America.

The Postboom, to a large extent, can be read as a post-*Cien años de soledad* phenomenon; the postmodern novel in Latin America can be read as a post-*Rayuela* event. The wild experimentation of *Rayuela*, as well as Morelli's call for an "anti-novel," opened the door to a postmodern fiction that has frequently been a dialogue with *Rayuela*. Another important factor to the rise of the postmodern since *Rayuela* was the first generalized presence of Joyce in Latin American fiction in the 1960s. As Gerald Martin has delineated, Joyce's entry into the general consciousness of the Latin American writer comes late and is not really noticeable until the appearance of works such as *Rayuela* and Cabrera Infante's *Tres tristes tigres* (1967).[43] In addition, it should be pointed out that Cortázar's popularization of the ludic in Latin American fiction was accompanied by a broad-based entrance of the ludic in modern fiction. As Motte has demonstrated, the ludic is essential to such internationally recognized writers as Breton, Nabokov, Perec, Calvino, and Eco;[44] these writers were not only translated, but quite well known among Latin American novelists of the 1960s.

Other radical and innovative novelists soon appeared on the Latin American literary scene, including Diamela Eltit, Ricardo Piglia, Luis

Rafael Sánchez, Héctor Libertella, Salvador Elizondo, Carmen Boullosa, Ignacio Solares, José Balza, and R. H. Moreno-Durán. In their
early writing, Libertella and Eltit were particularly interested in the
type of linguistic innovations utilized by Sarduy. Seen in their totality,
these postmodern writers and their cohorts offer radically diverse
kinds of postmodernisms—perhaps a postmodern phenomenon in
itself: if *Culture* (with a capital C and singular) becomes cultures
in postmodernity, as Hutcheon has suggested, then the provision-
ality and heterogeneity of postmodern cultures in Latin America is
even more extreme than in the United States.[45] Many of these Latin
American postmodern writers—like their First World counterparts—
are interested in heterogeneous discourses of theory and fiction. Consequently, the essays of Severo Sarduy, Tununa Mercado, and José
Balza read like fiction and vice versa; Eltit's early fiction appropriated the theoretical discourses of Derrida, Baudrillard, Deleuze, and
others. Balza has preferred not to distinguish between the essays and
the fiction of his "exercises," and Tununa Mercado has published texts
of fiction/essays.

Several scholars have noted the postmodern tendency to bridge the
gap between what was formerly considered "elite" and "popular" art.[46]
For theorists such as Hutcheon, postmodernism's relationship with
contemporary mass culture is not just one of implication but also one
of critique. This argument is perhaps stronger in the Latin American
case because the historical and political bases have been consistently
present.

The appearance of several radically innovative novels in 1968 was
one clear indicator of a cultural shift among some writers in the direction of the postmodern novel. These works of 1968 were Cortázar's
62: modelo para armar, Puig's *La traición de Rita Hayworth,* Jorge
Guzmán's *Job-Boj,* Alberto Duque López's *Mateo el flautista,* José
Agustín's *Inventando que sueño,* and Salvador Elizondo's *El hipogeo
secreto.* These six novels and many to follow in the 1970s and 1980s
were as obviously indebted to Cortázar's *Rayuela* as Castillo's *Mix-
quiahuala Letters.* Duque López's *Mateo el flautista* is dedicated to a
character in *Rayuela,* and it is difficult to imagine the creation of such
playful experiments as *Inventando que sueño* without *Rayuela* as a
precedent.

These novels place into practice, in different ways, Morelli's radical proposals in *Rayuela* for the "anti-novel," the description of which
is quite similar to many of the theoretical propositions developed a

decade later by Hassan, Hutcheon, and other theorists of the postmodern novel. The most direct connection between Morelli's proposal and these novels is Cortázar's own *62: modelo para armar*, which is an outgrowth of Morelli's propositions in chapter 62 of *Rayuela*. In chapter 62, Morelli sets forth the possibility of constructing a novel on the basis of random notes and observations. In *62: modelo para armar*, the characters are caught up in a pattern of random events in four places: London, Paris, Vienna, and "the City." Another of Morelli's many critiques involves the concept of "character," in essence, the same question many postmodern novelists set forth about the possibility of a unified subject.

The fiction of Manuel Puig in general, and *La traición de Rita Hayworth* (1968) in particular, were a watershed for the postmodern novel in Latin America. In *La traición de Rita Hayworth*, Puig established a postmodern reader with an active and unstable role to play, for there is no controlling narrator to organize the anecdotal material related by a multiplicity of voices. In telling the story of the young boy Toto, the main referent is not Argentina, but Hollywood film. His later novels, such as *The Buenos Aires Affair* (1973) and *El beso de la mujer araña* (1976) question gender-based behavior, genre-bound thinking, and concepts of authority and truth.[47]

Two experimental postmodern novels published in Mexico were José Agustín's *Inventando que sueño* and Salvador Elizondo's *El hipogeo secreto*. The former consists of a set of stories that can be read as separate pieces or as a novel. It functions like an album of rock music containing several songs, and rock music is one of the predominant themes of the book. *El hipogeo secreto* is an even more experimental metafiction, with overtones of Wittgenstein's philosophy.

Fuentes's *Terra Nostra* is a Borgesian postmodern text that rediscovers the heterogeneity of Latin American culture and the radical heterogeneity of postmodern culture in Indo-Afro-Iberoamerica. Set in sixteenth-century Spain, *Terra Nostra* has been described by Brian McHale as an anthology of postmodern themes and devices.[48] In addition to the particulars of Latin American history, Fuentes is concerned with how history, culture, and identity are constructed and then understood.

Sergio Pitol's novelistic production, almost as vast and encyclopedic as Fuentes's, shares the modernist and postmodern impulses of his Mexican compatriot. His early endeavor *El tañido de una flauta* (1972), establishes a fictionalized dialogue with other literatures, arts, and film, interwoven around three related plot lines. Pitol continues his Bakhtinian dialogue in *Juegos florales* (1982), *El desfile de amor* (1984), and *Domar a la divina garza* (1988). *Domar a la divina garza* includes a fictionalized metacommentary on texts of Nikolai Gogol, Italo Calvino, and Dante Alighieri. Pitol's work has not only many of the encyclopedic literary impulses of Fuentes's *Terra Nostra*, but also shares metafictional and historical qualities of the fiction of Fernando del Paso and of Ricardo Piglia's *Respiración artificial*.[49]

After the hyperexperimentation of the late 1960s that culminated in the fiction of Pacheco, Fuentes, Agustín, and Elizondo, postmodern fiction in Mexico after 1968 was less hermetic and more accessible. Nevertheless, postmodern attitudes of the 1960s became more acute. In addition to the work of such recognized writers as Fuentes, the later postmodern writers in Mexico included Luis Arturo Ramos, María Luisa Puga, Brianda Domecq, Carmen Boullosa, and Ignacio Solares. Ramos's early writing, particularly his short fiction, had clear affinities with Cortázar. His novel *Este era un gato* (1987) tells of a retired U.S. Marine captain who had participated in the 1914 invasion of Veracruz. Like much postmodern historiographic metafiction, this novel does not fall into either "presentism" (denial of the past) or nostalgia in its relation to the past.

Carmen Boullosa and Ignacio Solares also have contributed to the Mexican postmodern novel. Solares established well-defined interests in both history and invention in his novels *Puerta al cielo* (1976), *Anónimo* (1979), *El árbol del deseo* (1980), *La fórmula de la inmortalidad* (1982), *Serafín* (1985), *Casas de encantamiento* (1988), and *Madero, el otro* (1989). Boullosa's first novel, *Mejor desaparece* (1987), contains the subjective *mirada*, the gaze, of Fuentes's and Ramos's fiction. Like Ramos and Solares, Boullosa consistently places storytelling ahead of her interests in innovation per se.

In the 1970s and 1980s, postmodern fiction in the Southern Cone nations and the Andean region was prominently exemplified by writers such as Piglia, Eltit, Borinsky, Libertella, Mercado, Adoum, Angel, Moreno-Durán, Darío Jaramillo, and Balza. Borinsky's *Mina cruel* (1989) is one of her early *novelas de espectáculo* (as she has identified her comic and absurd fiction). In its dialogue with Macedonio Fernández and Manuel Puig, the comic absurd in *Mina cruel* consists of surfaces that are a mix of kitsch and camp. Without any of the moralizing of much fiction of exile, this novel includes a backdrop of repression, bare survival, and exile. Tununa Mercado's highly experimental *Canon de alcoba* (1988) is one of her first theoretical fictions on the experience of exile and writing. Her treatment of exile goes beyond the exhausted themes of nostalgia and alienation. Libertella's postmodern writing often blurs the traditional boundaries between essay and fiction; two of his volumes that read more like essayistic than fictional exercises are his most engaging contributions. Libertella questions the viability of both the Spanish language and writing in a subtle and subversive fashion in *El paseo internacional del perverso* (1990), a short novel that averts its status as a novel and as any fixed language. It also avoids any fixed subject, for the main character, an itinerant person who travels around the world, never takes on any fixed identity.

The postmodern innovators to appear in Colombia in the 1970s were Andrés Caicedo, Umberto Valverde, Albalucía Angel, Marco Tulio Aguilera Garramuño, Rodrigo Parra Sandoval, and R. H. Moreno-Durán. In the 1980s, Darío Jaramillo published his first postmodern novel, *La muerte de Alec* (1983), a self-conscious meditation on the functions of literature. Moreno-Durán published a hermetic trilogy titled *Fémina Suite* in the late 1970s and early 1980s, followed by *Los felinos del Canciller* (1985). Important subjects of this later novel are language and writing. The characters are diplomats by profession, but their passion is philology. Moreno-Durán creates humorous parallels between language and diplomacy.

One of the most productive writers of the Venezuelan postmodern is José Balza, who has published numerous volumes of fiction, including several books of variations and combinations that he, like Moreno-Durán, calls his "exercises." His texts, including *Setecientas palmeras plantadas en el mismo lugar* (1974), *D* (1987), *Percusión* (1982), and *Medianoche en video: 1/5* (1988), often blur the line between fictional and essayistic discourses. In *Medianoche en video: 1/5*, Balza relates a history of the modernization of Venezuela as told through the development of radio and television. Postmodern fiction in Venezuela has also been produced by Alejandro Rossi, Francisco Massiani, Humberto Mata, Carlos Noguera, and Angel Gustavo Infante.

The postmodern writers of Uruguay who have followed the paths of Hernández, Borges, and Cortázar include Híber Conteris, Armonía Sommers, Cristina Peri Rossi, Teresa Porzekanski, and Napoleón Baccino Ponce de León. Conteris wrote *El diez por ciento de la vida* (1986) while incarcerated as a political prisoner. This novel can be read as a detective tale; like the fiction of Eltit, however, it can also be deciphered as a postmodern allegory of resistance.

With respect to the postmodern in Brazil, Ignácio de Loyola Brandão and Roberto Drummond were two of the most experimental. De Loyola Brandão's novel *Zéro* (1974) invites comparisons with Cortázar's *Libro de Manuel* and Piglia's *Respiración artificial*; the relationship between a police interrogator and his captive is devised as a complex puzzle to be deciphered only by the most discerning postmodern reader. De Loyola Brandão's *Não verás país nenhum* (1982) stands out as a futuristic novel in which the author openly recognizes his literary masters, one being Kurt Vonnegut. With frequent black humor, de Loyola Brandão communicates a sense of exhaustion in Brazilian society. In *Sangue de Coca-Cola* (1983), Drummond appropriates the popular culture of *carnaval* in some ways similar to Luis Rafael Sánchez's *La guaracha del Macho Camacho*. Underlying the beat of this popular music, however, is a rewriting of the recent history of Brazil under military dictatorships.

Central America has not generally been a locus of postmodern writing. In spite of that, the Costa Ricans Carmen Naranjo and Samuel Rovinski, the Guatemalan Mario Roberto Morales, and the Honduran Roberto Quezada have published novels with postmodern tendencies. Morales's *Los demonios salvajes* (1978) and Naranjo's *Diario de una multitud* (1986) were early manifestations of these trends.

The most noteworthy figures of postmodern fiction in Ecuador during the 1970s and 1980s were Jorge Enrique Adoum, Iván Eguez, and Abdón Ubidia. One of the most experimental novels to be published in Ecuador was Adoum's *Entre Marx y una mujer desnuda* (1976), which, like *Terra Nostra*, engages an array of postmodern themes and devices. A lengthy meditation on the novel and the nation, the subject of this work fluctuates, but it begins with a self-reflexive metacommentary on how novels begin. Eguez has published several volumes of fiction since the 1970s and has written two novels with postmodern tendencies, *La Linares* (1976) and *Pájaro de memoria (1984)*.

Some critics have suggested that the heterogeneous and disjunctive Caribbean has always been a postmodern culture. Novels such as Severo Sarduy's *Cobra* and Luis Rafael Sánchez's *La guaracha del Macho Camacho* support such a proposition.[50] The writing of Sarduy contributes significantly to the Caribbean postmodern, and it has had considerable impact on the Latin American postmodern in general. Written in the hermetic mode of Lezama Lima, *Cobra* (1972) is Sarduy's novelistic reflection on language and writing. In it, language is not just a means of communication, but a meditation on the very function of language. The novel's title refers to a poem by Octavio Paz from *Conjunciones y disyunciones* that dramatizes the generation of language. The association of words in this poem creates more words, a process parallel to much of *Cobra*, which was one of the early Latin American texts to blur the line between fictional and theoretical discourse; this novel refers freely to Derrida and Lacan. Works such as *Maitreya* (1978) and *Colibrí* (1983) represent a continuation of Sarduy's postmodern project. Sarduy returns to the very roots of Latin American culture, deconstructing its most basic elements, beginning with language. A culture as inherently postmodern as Cuba's has produced several other postmodern writers, including Senel Paz and René Vásquez Díaz.

In contrast to Sarduy, the writing of Luis Rafael Sánchez has little relationship with literary theory, for it is based primarily in popular culture. *La guaracha del Macho Camacho* refers to the Puerto Rican music that permeates the text, the *guaracha*. The novel's title is that of a popular song; Sánchez takes a refrain from it as his epigraph and includes its lyrics in an appendix. In his one-paragraph preface, he writes that the story is about the success of this song as well as the miserable and splendid extremes of life. The fragmented text is filled with the popular music, mass culture, and the heterogeneous cultural reality of everyday life in Puerto Rico, highlighted by an enormous traffic jam and appearances by Puerto Rican television star Iris Chacón. As in the fiction of Sarduy, space and characters are conceived in a fashion opposed to modernist procedures. Sánchez's *La importancia de llamarse Daniel Santos* (1988) is a more overtly postmodern text about a popular singer of the 1940s and 1950s, the Puerto Rican Daniel Santos. The author figure, who is identified in the text as a gay writer named Luis Rafael Sánchez, travels from Puerto Rico to several Latin American cities where the singer had performed, in search of the complete story of Santos.

The work of Edgardo Rodríguez Juliá also escapes genre definition. His first heterogeneous text, *Las tribulaciones de Jonás* (1981), is a testimonial account of the renowned Puerto Rican political figure Luis Muñoz Marín. *El entierro de Cortijo* (1983) centers on the wake for a popular band leader, an experience that was especially significant for

Puerto Ricans of African descent. Alonso has pointed out that Rodríguez Juliá does not attempt to impose coherence on the conflicting
and contradictory gestures in these two texts; there is no overarching
interpretive scheme.[51] *La noche oscura del Niño Avilés* (1984), offers
the active postmodern reader a series of historical and fictional documents to decipher.

Benítez Rojo has described the Caribbean as a culture of "per-
formers,"[52] and the postmodern fictions of Sarduy, Sánchez, and
Rodríguez Juliá are indeed performances. Benítez Rojo's reference to
the "aquatic" quality of Caribbean culture also recalls the aquatic
quality of the ever-transforming texts of Sarduy and Sánchez. The
heterogeneous, aquatic, and double-coded nature of the unresolved
contradictions in these Caribbean texts places it among the premier
examples of postmodern fiction in Latin America.

The overall heterogeneity—the radical modernity—of
the Latin American novel of the 1970s and 1980s far surpassed the
innovations in writing that had yet been witnessed in the century.
The novel of dictators and of exile, along with the Postboom, gay,
feminist, and postmodern writing, meant both refined modernism
and a hypermodernism with theoretical and cultural interests that
exceeded those of their predecessors of the *vanguardia*. Women and
explicitly political novelists wrote within the general framework of
these modernist and postmodern modes, producing fiction dealing
with issues of feminism, gender, sexuality, and politics. Gay and lesbian writing was more visible and explicit than ever before. Heterogeneous cultural areas, such as the Caribbean, also surfaced as forceful cultural entities. And heterogeneous genres such as the *testimonio*
blurred the boundaries of narrative.

Feminist writing had become central to Latin American fiction by
the late 1980s. As Naomi Lindstrom has explained, the difficult problem of adapting European and North American feminism to Latin
America has been the theoretical work of feminist critics such as
Debra Castillo, Sara Castro-Klarén, Lucía Guerra-Cunningham, and
Gabriela Mora.[53] In addition, Jean Franco, Francine Masiello, and
Doris Sommer have made valuable contributions to this effort. Feminist writing, as well as that of gay novelists such as Manuel Puig, signaled the end of a masculinist aesthetic as the predominant mode in

Latin America; this shift was a process increasingly evident since the early 1960s.

As writers of the 1970s and 1980s entered into dialogue with the powerful cultural experience of the Boom, the results took two broad directions. On the one hand, writers of a fundamentally modernist impulse—following the footsteps of Faulkner, Vargas Llosa, and García Márquez—continued telling stories in an accessible fashion that attracted a broad readership in Latin America and abroad. These writers (some of whom critics associated with the Postboom) of modernist interests included Isabel Allende, Elena Garro, Antonio Skármeta, and the Vargas Llosa and García Márquez of the 1970s and 1980s.

On the other hand, writers of more postmodern interests—following the footsteps of Borges, Cortázar, and the later Donoso—constructed fictions that were generally less accessible, more experimental, and of interest to a more limited readership of academics, writers, and intellectuals. These postmodern writers also tended to share an admiration for Joyce, Roland Barthes, and Severo Sarduy. One could read Eltit, Pizarnik, and others as postmodern feminists. Yet certainly there is no definitive line that divides modernist from postmodern writing. Fuentes, Puig, Molloy, and many other novelists, in fact, exhibit characteristics associated with both tendencies. Fuentes, Vargas Llosa, Garro, Pitol, and del Paso share totalizing impulses typical of high modernist writing, while in some of their works in this period they exhibit postmodern tendencies.

Twelve **Rereading the Spanish American Novel of the 1970s and 1980s**

The desire to be modern was fully realized in the novel by the 1970s and 1980s in the Spanish-speaking Americas. The resultant fiction of this period—be it of a Postboom, feminist, postmodern, gay, or *testimonio* character—was internationally recognized, translated more than ever, and patently heterogeneous. Novels representative of postmodern and feminist tendencies in Spanish American fiction include Carlos Fuentes's *Terra Nostra* (1975), Ricardo Piglia's *Respiración artificial* (1979), Sylvia Molloy's *En breve cárcel* (1981), Albalucía Angel's *Las andariegas* (1984), and Diamela Eltit's *Por la patria* (1986). Works that show a reaction against the complexity and totalizing impulses of the novels of the Boom include Gustavo Alvarez Gardeazábal's *El bazar de los idiotas* (1974), Gustavo Sainz's *La princesa del Palacio de Hierro* (1974), Vargas Llosa's *La tía Julia y el escribidor* (1977), and Rosario Ferré's *Maldito amor* (1986). The appearance of *El bazar de los idiotas*, *La princesa del Palacio de Hierro*, and *La tía Julia y el escribidor* in the 1970s likewise was an unequivocal indicator of this shift. Indeed, these three works share an accessibility and humor that had not been common practice among the most prominent novelists of the 1960s. The exception was *Tres tristes tigres*, an important predecessor to these three humorous novels. *La tía Julia y el escribidor* became an immediate bestseller in Latin America; Alvarez Gardeazábal and Sainz sold their novels well in Colombia and Mexico, respectively.

El bazar de los idiotas was a dialogue with the fiction of the Boom and, more specifically, a parody of *Cien años de soledad*. Seen in retrospect, it was also a forerunner of the fiction of Isabel Allende. It relates a bizarre story focusing on a pair of miracle-producing adolescents in Tuluá, a small town near Cali, Colombia. The humor and magical quality of some of the events of the novel recall *Cien años de soledad*; in this case, two masturbating idiots become heroes in Tuluá and Colombia. The two idiots become heroes when they discover that, despite their mental deficiencies and inability to cope with life in conventional terms, through masturbation they can miraculously cure illnesses. As their fame grows in the process of their becoming heroes, so does the economy of the surrounding area, which becomes a tourist center. A significant aspect of their becoming heroes involves the people they cure—a gallery of types ranging from a paralyzed ex-beauty queen to a homosexual suffering from "sickness of the soul" after losing his lover. The idiots attain hero status when their feats achieve such fame that national and foreign experts converge upon Tuluá. On the last page of the novel, however, everything ends: they die, assassinated by their bastard half brother.

When the narrator's focus in *El bazar de los idiotas* moves near to that of the perception of the characters, the effect is ironic. At other times this use of language reflects more the pettiness of the inhabitants of Tuluá. Similarly, the narrator inverts the normal terms of language, using a commercial language to describe the workings and the language of the Church to describe the activities of the idiots. In reference to the Church, for example, the members are called "clients." The language employed in reference to the idiots tends to be ecclesiastical. This use of language by Alvarez Gardeazábal is comparable to that in the fiction of Piglia and Eltit.

Alvarez Gardeazábal, like García Márquez, occasionally privileges orality over writing. In many instances, premodern oral noetics are superior to writing culture's technology. In *El bazar de los idiotas*, modern technology is totally ineffective: when Andrés is bitten, the local specialists and the Japanese experts fail to cure him; when Insesita is paralyzed, neither national doctors nor specialists from Boston can do anything for her. The irrationality of the idiots' methodology humorously underlines modern technology's failures.

Also like García Márquez, Alvarez Gardeazábal uses procedures intimately associated with oral storytelling. The narrator assumes the role of the writer who has access to anecdotes which the (oral-culture) citizenry of Tuluá have forgotten. This narrator's apparently total access to Tuluá's story includes both oral and written versions. Indeed, much of what he narrates has oral roots—what has been said *(dizque)* and perhaps repeated over the years. The narrator's seemingly complete access to orality and full exploitation of it both reveals the author's totalizing impulse and constitutes a successful exploitation of Latin America's cultural heterogeneity.

El bazar de los idiotas is critical of many of Colombia's traditional institutions and social conventions. At the same time, it playfully parodies at least two texts of the Boom: Vargas Llosa's *La casa verde* and, above all, García Márquez's *Cien años de soledad.*

Gustavo Sainz does not refer as directly to the novels of the Boom as does *El bazar de los idiotas,* but *La princesa del Palacio de Hierro* should be read as a reaction not only to the narrative complexity of Boom novels, but also to the complex narratives published by Mexican writers of the postmodern and irreverent Onda—José Agustín and Sainz. By the early 1970s, the Mexican novel had become extremely experimental and hermetic.[1] *La princesa del Palacio de Hierro* derives its humor from different sources than does *El bazar de los idiotas;* now the narrator functions within the fictional world. Sainz's novel is a lengthy first-person narrative—a monologue by a woman that could well be one side of a rambling telephone conversation. An employee of a department store (the "Palacio de Hierro" of Mexico), she narrates her life to an unidentified friend. Her story begins with her adolescence and covers several years; her life is banal yet paradoxically never boring and consists of a series of relationships that inevitably fail. The special quality of the experiences that inform the novel is her particular way of developing her relationships and her mode of expression that was surprisingly uninhibited for a female character in a Mexican novel of the mid-1970s. In this sense, *La princesa del Palacio de Hierro* anticipates some feminist fiction of the 1980s and 1990s (such as Susan Torres Molina's *Dueña y señora*), in which the discursive levels of women are opened even more radically.[2]

A key to the humor in *La princesa del Palacio de Hierro* is the presence of a fictitious character whose presence is felt although she never appears as a character per se and is not identified throughout the novel's 345 pages. This entity is the "tú" to whom the protagonist directs her monologue from the first lines. The presence of this *tú* is key for the novel's humor, as seen in this passage: "A veces nos reuníamos para hablar de nuestros problemas. Y cuando estábamos juntas empezábamos a hablar de todas las cosas que habían pasado, los cambios de maridos, los orgasmos felices, los abandonos y cosas así" (Sometimes we'd get together to talk about our problems. And when we were together we began to talk about everything that had happened, the changing of spouses, the great orgasms, the abandonments, and things like that).[3] The reader notes a loss of the basic intimacy of the conversation; this principle, the violation of the code of intimacy between the princess and her fictitious reader by part of the real reader, is the basis of the humor in the novel.

The main strategy to fictionalize the reader in *La princesa del Palacio de Hierro*, however, relates to the intellectual and analytical content of this novel. The reader is superior to the characters observed and fundamentally an intellectual. A strategy employed to fictionalize this intellectual (and superior) reader is the inclusion of a series of quotations of the poetry of Oliverio Girondo at the end of each of the princess's twenty-one monologues. They have the effect of distancing the reader, and they make the somewhat frivolous anecdotes a focus of analysis.

In the process of reading *La princesa del Palacio de Hierro*, the reader also becomes aware that Sainz, like Alvarez Gardeazábal and Vargas Llosa, communicates critical attitudes about basic national institutions. The institution in *La princesa del Palacio de Hierro* is language, placing Sainz close to the interests of Eltit and Piglia. The flow of the princess's verbalization is an expression of her inability to understand her past or herself. She speaks in concentric circles without being able to hit a mark, find a center, or perhaps reach a kind of self-awareness. Her metaphors express the banality of a life consisting of repetitive cycles that recreate themselves in a series of substitutions but which, in reality, never change.

When Vargas Llosa published *La tía Julia y el escribidor* in 1977, he had already reacted against the complexities of the Boom and explored humor with his novel *Pantaleón y las visitadoras* (1973). In *La tía Julia y el escribidor*, as in *El bazar de los idiotas* and *La princesa del Palacio de Hierro*, the reader encounters a humorous entertainment. In this semi-autobiographical novel, Vargas Llosa relates the double story of a young Mario marrying his older aunt and the ongoing stories of radio soap operas in 1950s Perú. *La tía Julia y el escribidor* presents four persons who are writers. The first, Pedro Camacho, appears in chapters narrated by Marito. Camacho can be described more precisely as a "scribbler," to use the term of Roland Barthes. The second writer is Marito, the young narrator of the odd-numbered chapters. The third writer present in the novel can be identified as Pedro Camacho as narrator, who appears implicitly as such in the even-numbered chapters (text of the nine soap operas).

It is important to make the fundamental distinction between an author (in this case the *person* Pedro Camacho) and a narrator (the fictional entity present in any narrative). The fourth writer is Mario Vargas Llosa himself, the author of several novels and, a notable factor here, of numerous critical and theoretical texts. These four writers are related; the relationships among them are the basis for the dynamic interaction among the "writers" of the novel. Marito learns about the art of writing; one of the themes of the novel is this art, and the relationships among the writers give the reader a prolonged experience of the act of writing itself. In this experience the reader contributes to the creative process, incorporating "theoretical" writings; and it becomes evident that the novel proposes a corollary to the problem of writing: reading. The reader is invited to resolve technical problems of reading, and the reader concurrently encounters the act of reading as a theme in itself.[4]

Marito's career as a writer deals directly with a complementary problem: the reader. The young novelist discovers that his first obstacle to the attainment of literary success depends less on literary merit than on the reaction of his readers. He uses Aunt Julia as a reader, for example, and discovers for the first time the discrepancy between the author's perception of his literary creation and that of the reader. When he reads her "The Humiliation of the Cross," he notes that precisely what she criticizes are the imaginative elements. This anecdote is important, for it is an early lesson in the realization that in the communication of fiction a new entity exists: the reader.

La tía Julia y el escribidor begins with an epigraph from a novel by the Mexican novelist Salvador Elizondo: "I write. I write that I am writing. Mentally I see myself writing that I am writing and I can also see myself seeing that I am writing." (Elizondo's solipsistic observations continue for several more lines.) Such a commentary reflects a common attitude of writers of Indo-Afro-Iberoamerica in the 1970s. Vargas Llosa's novel can be seen as part of a general trend toward self-conscious, postmodern fiction. This is Vargas Llosa's first novel about writing. Nevertheless, it has features that distinguish it from much metafiction. The dynamics of reading and writing make this novel more entertaining, like Sainz's *La princesa del Palacio de Hierro*, than much self-conscious fiction, which is often characterized as dry "writers' writing."

Ferré's *Maldito amor*, like *El bazar de los idiotas* and *La tía Julia y el escribidor*, interacts with popular culture; in this case, the very title is that of a popular, late-nineteenth-century love song in Puerto Rico. The volume *Maldito amor* contains a novel and three short stories whose themes are interrelated.[5] The novel is the story of several generations of the de la Valle family in Puerto Rico. The setting is the family ranch near the village of Guamaní. The eventual ruin of their sugarcane business destroys the family. The main theme of the novel has a feminine focus: it involves the search for personal identity of the women of the de la Valle family and extends to a search for social identity in Puerto Rican society at large.[6] Much of this identity search relates to various bloodlines that have descended from Spain, Africa, and the Americas and that different characters represent.

The novels of Alvarez Gardeazábal, Vargas Llosa, and Sainz offer the possibility of subtle political readings. In *Maldito amor*, however, a more obvious political search is evident. Here the characters represent various positions with respect to the appropriate relationship with the United States. Ferré uses several female and male narrative voices to articulate these positions in terms of identity and politics. The novel begins with an unidentified voice that narrates the history of the region of Guamaní; this opening describes the ideal world that pervaded before North American mainland interests dominated the island. Later in the text, the reader realizes that this voice belongs to Hermenegildo, the narrator and historian of the de la Valle family. As Lee Skinner has demonstrated, however, Hermenegildo's attempts to construct a coherent, totalizing historical discourse centering around the heroic figure of de la Valle and to inscribe nostalgias into that historical project are shattered from within the novel's text.[7] Thus, this decentered fiction takes a certain postmodern turn away from the "total" novel.

Fuentes's *Terra Nostra* obviously exhibits numerous totalizing impulses, thus distinguishing it from *La princesa del Palacio de Hierro* and *Maldito amor*; Fuentes's lengthy novel represents an attempt to rewrite Latin American cultural history in a comprehensive manner that has led to its characterization, mentioned earlier, as a postmodern anthology. As a postmodern text, *Terra Nostra* articulates the twelfth-century proclamation that "Nothing is true, everything is permitted." Attributed to Hasa-Sabbah in the year 1164, this statement is particularly appropriate because Fuentes, too, frequently returns to the Middle Ages in his act of recovering history and knowledge.

Like much postmodern fiction, *Terra Nostra* is strongly historical and political. Fuentes's awareness of historical discourse and, above all, his questioning of the very assumptions of Western historiography align *Terra Nostra* with the postmodern. It is Fuentes's rewriting of the medieval, renaissance, and neoclassical architecture of El Escorial. His tendency toward double-coding is evident, for example, in his characters. Many of them at the same time are and are not specific historical characters; authority figures are and are not historical Spanish kings and queens. Most of the novel's major figures have double codes rather than any fixed, singular identity. These multiple identities in constant transformation call into question the very concept of psychic unity and the individual subject.

Ricardo Piglia's *Respiración artificial* and Diamela Eltit's *El cuarto mundo* are comparable to Fuentes's work with respect to historical truth. Piglia joins Fuentes and Eltit in the search for the historical origins of language and culture of the Americas. Eltit's investigation into the "mother language" in *Por la patria* has as its equivalent in Piglia a questioning of the "father language" in *Respiración artificial*.

Piglia opens *Respiración artificial* with the question "¿Hay una historia?" and then keeps the reader intrigued throughout the novel, even though the action is minimal. This novel can be read as a meditation on Argentine and Latin American cultural and political history. Rather than re-creating historical space and time, Piglia delves into the question of how national histories are constructed and institutionalized. Like Eltit, Piglia is thus concerned with the concept of *patria* and its origins. *Respiración artificial* returns to the roots of Argentine nationhood in the nineteenth century, as national history and family history are fused in this novel. A character named Tardewski (a Pole living in Argentina) is the Argentine intellectual par excellence: a European situated on the periphery (in the province of Entre Ríos) speculating about European culture as it interacts with Argentine literature.

Piglia proposes a mediated version of historical truth, according to Daniel Balderson.[8] All understanding, historical and other, is considerably mediated in this novel. A multiplicity of voices narrates, and there is no narrative authority. The primary narrator in part I, Renzi, is only a provisional narrator at best, and a substantial portion of part 2 consists of letters from his friends and others. The mediation takes more subtle technical forms, too, when Renzi narrates what others have written or told him. In part 2, Tardewski narrates, but most of his narration is actually a quotation of another, or a quotation of a quotation, thus recalling similar procedures employed by Sainz. This constant mediation in part 2 forces the reader to engage in an ongoing and intense process of evaluation of the sources of possible truths in the story.

Piglia's dedication of the novel resonates with multiple meanings: it is to "Elías and Rubén who helped me to come to know the truth of history." After the experience of *Respiración artificial*, it is difficult to imagine knowing any significant truths about Argentine history. Truths are, in the end, unspeakable. On the other hand, the reader can speculate that "coming to know the truth of history" could well mean coming to know the truth of history as impossible to know. More than discovering Argentina's true past, the reader observes how truths are constructed in the Argentine cultural and political environment.

Respiración artificial, like Fuentes's *Terra Nostra* and Eltit's *Por la patria*, also sets forth the issue of *patria* and language, particularly in long discussions on Argentine literature (most of which appear in the second half of the book). Characters are highly critical of turn-of-the-century poet Leopoldo Lugones, a literary icon who has been institutionalized in Argentina. Lugones is criticized as the National Poet with the most "pure language" and thus can be associated, implicitly, with the "sanitization" process of the Proceso de Reorganización Nacional. Roberto Arlt, in contrast, is much admired by the characters in *Respiración artificial* (as he is extratextually by Piglia) and represents the opposite of Lugones's purity—Arlt's language can be characterized as often crude, clumsy, even vulgar. By criticizing Lugones and praising Arlt, Piglia critiques the very foundations of the traditional Argentine concept of *patria*. The key modern characters in *Respiración artificial*, tellingly enough, feel very limited and imprisoned by their mother tongue or unable to communicate in it.

Several situations in *Respiración artificial* lead one to read them as metaphors for the writer's circumstance under a repressive regime, as was the Argentine military dictatorship of the late 1970s. This novel is a protest against the military regime in Argentina, but it is a subtle criticism that also places into question how language and writing can function and survive under such regimes.

La princesa del Palacio de Hierro, Terra Nostra, and *Respiración ar-*

tificial are experiments with fiction, but Diamela Eltit's *Por la patria* is one of the most radical aesthetic and political experiments of the 1970s and 1980s. Ortega has observed that in this novel "the communitarian is the feminine subjective space of the subversive."[9] Eltit relates a story of contemporary Chile, alluding to the political repression of the Pinochet regime but always returning to the historical origins of language, repression, and resistance. Going back to medieval epic wars, she inevitably associates these historical conflicts with the contemporary situation. Thus, Eltit's postmodern is patently historical and political. By exploring the origins of the mother language and incorporating numerous historical and colloquial languages into *Por la patria*, Eltit is concerned with the relationship originally explored by Foucault between language and power, also the subject of much of the writing of Piglia and Fuentes.

Por la patria, like Eltit's previous novel *Lumpérica*, reveals a sense for origins in Latin, the "mother" of the Romance language family that is present in both these novels. The discursive contexts change in the different fragments of *Por la patria*, evoking a connection with the heritage in Latin and resonances of medieval Spanish and Italian. These historical languages coexist, in unresolved contradiction, with a modern masculine discourse subverted by other contemporary discourses—colloquial Chilean Spanish and feminine discourse.

Molloy's *En breve cárcel* and Angel's *Las andariegas* share many of Eltit's and Piglia's concerns. *En breve cárcel* is the story of an Argentine woman who returns to an apartment in New England where she had once had an affair with another woman and where she writes a memoir about this experience. From the initial pages in the novel, it becomes evident that the process of writing is also a process of constructing this relationship and of rewriting and remembering, acts that suggest a new beginning. She struggles with her expression, and her self-conscious rereading of her writing makes this novel comparable to much postmodern fiction. The narrator-protagonist is also engaged in an identity search related to her writing—what Foster has described as the topos of the "prison-house of love."[10]

In this novel, Molloy avoids the use of the word "lesbian" in the text, thus continually destabilizing the notion of a fixed or essential identity. Consequently, the novel's process of coming into being is paralleled by the protagonist's coming into being. The provisional and continuously disputed ontological status of this protagonist is one of the novel's postmodern characteristics. The narrator-protagonist continually destabilizes other boundaries, as does Eltit, and this process is typical of much postmodern fiction.

It gradually becomes evident that the protagonist's relationship with her father underlies her later relations with women and with the text that she is constructing. Nevertheless, her relationship with her mother is important in the formation of the feminine subject. It is this relationship between the mother and the daughter, as well as the relationship between her sisters and their lovers, that are major influences on the process of constructing *En breve cárcel.*

Las andariegas is Albalucía Angel's most explicitly feminist and most radical experiment in fiction yet. Like *En breve cárcel,* it represents a search for an *écriture feminine* as well as an evocation of a woman's sense of courage. *Las andariegas* is a postmodern project in the sense that it is a self-conscious attempt to fictionalize poststructuralist feminist theory. It begins with two epigraphs, a statement by the author that sets forth the feminist project, and then a third epigraph. The first epigraph is from *Les Guérrilleres* by Monique Wittig and refers to women breaking the existing order and to their need for strength and courage. The second epigraph is from *Las nuevas cartas portugesas* by Maria Isabel Barreno, Maria Teresa Horta, and Maria Velho da Costa and refers to women as firm and committed warriors. These two epigraphs are explained by the author's page-long statement, the third prefatory section to appear before the narrative. Angel relates that her reading of Wittig's *Les Guérrilleres* inspired her to undertake this project with women warriors who advance "from nowhere to history." She uses images from stories of her childhood as a guide, transforming them into fables and cryptic visions. The final product of her search, according to Angel, is the hope for a better future than women have held throughout time. The third epigraph is from the mythology of a Colombian indigenous group, the Kogui, and emphasizes the role of the woman figure in creation.

The innovative language and experimental techniques of *Las andariegas* are important aspects of its *écriture feminine.* Much of the narrative consists of brief phrases, often with unconventional punctuation. Rather than developing a consistent plot, these phrases often contain an image. The use of linguistic imagery is supported by visual images—a set of twelve drawings of women. Angel also experiments with the physical space of language in the text in a manner similar to the techniques of concrete poetry. The four pages of this type consist of a variety of circular and semicircular arrangements of the names of women famous in history. These four pages universalize the story of the constantly traveling women. *Las andariegas* ends with a type of epilogue of another quotation from Monique Wittig, comprising four brief sentences that call for precisely the undertaking that is the essence of this novel: a new language, a new beginning, a new history for women. This new beginning, in turn, relates to the *re*writing and new beginning suggested in Molloy's *En breve cárcel*.

In this period after the Boom, many writers turned toward more accessible texts, frequently offering readers literary versions of everyday popular culture. When they used humor, these writers, including Vargas Llosa and Alvarez Gardeazábal, were accused by some of being superficial or socially irresponsible. Nevertheless, these two writers as well as Sainz and others were as critical as those who used more sober tones to articulate their stances toward such venerated institutions of Latin American culture and society as the Spanish language. As a reaction to redemocratization under capitalism, writers such as Eltit and Angel veered from the center to the margins, and their writing tended to focus on marginality and the periphery as themes. All of these writers began to explore new ways to engage readers in literature. Many female and male writers of this period wrote texts that made it difficult—perhaps impossible—to continue to speak of a dominant masculinist aesthetic in Latin American literature. Feminists such as Molloy and Angel, in fact, were not only critical of traditional gender roles, but proposed new beginnings for the women of all Latin America.

Thirteen   **Modern, Postmodern, and
Transnational: The Latin American
Novel in the 1990s**

The postmodern and transnational interests of the
Latin American writer were evident in the 1990s, a period when the
Latin American novel was a heterogeneous cultural manifestation of
modernist, postmodern, post-postmodern, feminist, and gay fiction.
These fives modes overlap in many ways, frequently sharing a commitment to subverting the predominant discourses of authority and
power. Novelists still writing in a primarily modernist vein were associated in Latin America with what was called the Boom and the
Postboom. Among these, in the view of many readers and critics,
were Carlos Fuentes, Mario Vargas Llosa, Rosario Ferré, César Aira,
Mempo Giardinelli, Isabel Allende, and Antonio Skármeta.

Laura Esquivel became one of the best-selling writers of the decade
with her first novel, *Como agua para chocolate* (1990); in its English
translation, *Like Water for Chocolate,* this novel had considerable
repercussions throughout the Americas in the 1990s. Writers such as
Diamela Eltit, Alicia Borinsky, and Ricardo Piglia, with a more radical aesthetic and political agenda that some critics have identified
as postmodern, published in the 1990s, as did a new generation of
post-postmodern writers that included such novelists as the Mexicans
David Toscana, Juan Villoro, and Jorge Volpi, the Chilean Alberto Fuguet, and the Bolivian Edmundo Paz Soldán.[1] Feminist, gay, and lesbian writers, who became quite visible in the 1980s—and some of
whom can easily be associated with the modernist and postmodern
novel—continued writing in the 1990s. By the 1990s, Elena Poniatow-

ska, who had been known primarily as a journalist and author of *testimonio*, became established as a prominent feminist novelist with the publication of her *Tinísima* (1992).

Latin American writers and their readers observed the economic and cultural globalization of the 1990s. The most important cultural context of the increasingly transnational 1990s was the aftermath of the fall of the Berlin Wall, the implementation of the North American Free Trade Agreement (NAFTA), and accords that were made on a lesser scale throughout the Americas. Globalization was an important phenomenon of the 1990s, and many Latin American intellectuals, including novelists and cultural critics such as Néstor García Canclini, were critical of this change. With the end of the Cold War and its bipolar agenda, Latin American leaders and intellectuals had to rethink and reconfigure the old lines of left versus right and the attendant ideological boundaries.

NAFTA and globalization meant a new relationship between the United States and the other nations of the Americas, particularly Mexico. The uprising in Chiapas in 1993 served as a reminder to the Mexican government that the new economic order was not successfully incorporating all segments of Mexican society. The ongoing delegitimization of the PRI culminated in its loss of credibility among the majority of the populace in Mexico by the end of the 1990s.[2] Throughout the decade, the nation mulled over the memory of Vargas Llosa's public declaration in the early 1990s that Mexico's PRI was *la dictadura perfecta*. Colombia's endless crises led to de facto civil war by the late 1990s, with the country's terrain divided among the government, leftist groups, and drug lords. Several Colombian novelists wrote fiction related to this crisis and the drug culture; Fernando Vallejo's *La virgen de los sicarios* (1994), set in the periphery of Medellín, was one of the most widely read.

One significant cultural factor in the 1990s globalization has been the effect of multinational publishing companies on the novelistic production of Latin America. The expansion of these multinational publishing firms has shrunk the space for new writers and innovative fiction. Two young writers, the Chileans Alberto Fuguet and Sergio Gómez, responded to this situation with a volume of fiction titled *McOndo* (1996),[3] which they deem an anti-magic realist set of fictions.

In the 1990s, several Latin American nations were still paying the political and social and economic costs of the dictatorships of the 1970s and 1980s, particularly in Chile and Argentina. In Decem-

ber 1999, leftist and conservative candidates for the presidency of
Chile engaged in a heated campaign with considerable residue from
the legacies of Allende and Pinochet. In the 1999 elections, social-
ist Ricardo Lagos and rightist Joaquín Lavín fought to a virtual draw,
causing a runoff election in early 2000. Lagos led a center-left coalition that was a reaction to the free-market-type economic programs
institutionalized in Chile during the dictatorship. This election also
demonstrated the disillusionment with the political establishment
in Chile: hundreds of thousands of usually civic-minded Chileans refused to vote or cast blank ballots. Similarly, novelists in Chile and
throughout Latin America were disinterested in assuming the political role of the public intellectual. Some of these writers, such as Diamela Eltit and Alicia Borinsky, took the position that the publication
of fictional texts did not authorize them to make public political pro-
nouncements; Eltit considered the subtle cultural resistance of her
fiction to be their only desired political statement.

In Argentina, many citizens were still pursuing answers to the dis-
appearance of adults and children during the "dirty war" of the 1970s
and 1980s under the military dictatorships of the Proceso de Reorganización Nacional (1976–1983). Writers continued to reflect on issues
of exile in books such as the Argentine Tununa Mercado's *En estado
de memoria* (1992). In general, the redemocratization under capitalism created a new series of crises and responses among novelists in
Latin America. For some of these repatriated novelists, the counter-
site of exile became a new imaginary condition to be reflected upon,
as in the fiction of Mercado and Borinsky.

The transnational 1990s witnessed the ongoing breakdown and
blurring of cultural borders. The figures of Rosario Ferré, Alicia Borinsky, Luis Arturo Ramos, and David Toscana are telling in describing these shifting borders. The Puerto Rican Ferré wrote all her early
work in Spanish; in the 1990s, she began to write in English for the
U.S. readership and then self-translated into Spanish. Borinsky is a
writer of Argentine birth residing in the United States since the late
1960s who has made a career as a scholar of Latin American literature, first at Johns Hopkins University and later at Boston University. She has published fiction in Spanish in Argentina and in English
in the United States. Interestingly, Borinsky received a "Latino" literature prize in 1996, awarded by the Latin American Writers Center. Luis Arturo Ramos spent most of his career writing in his native
state of Veracruz in Mexico, but in the 1990s lived in El Paso, Texas,

making him culturally a border writer. David Toscana lives in Monterrey, Mexico, distant from the cultural centers of Mexico City and the United States. His career as a writer in Monterrey does not depend on local support, however, but rather on his use of the Internet and the moderate success that his novel *Estación Tula* (1995) has attained in English translation as *Tula Station* (2000). These four writers (and many others throughout the Americas) blur the increasingly subjective and fragile borders of what have traditionally been called "Latin American," "Latino," and "Hispanic" writers.

The U.S.–Mexican border was intensely discussed and analyzed in the 1990s. The spaces of Mexican immigrants, as Chicana Rosaura Sánchez pointed out in 1993, like that of exile, become a counter-site of sorts, an imaginary heterotopia of displacement in opposition to the real sites of work and home.[4] Chicano novelists such as Helena María Viramontes, Rolando Hinojosa, and Miguel Méndez often communicate a sense of being displaced between two locations and belonging to neither. For example, in *Mother Tongue* (1994) by Chicana Demetria Martínez, the search for identity in Anglo society is an experience of living in-betweenness.

Another cultural border of increasing significance was the metaphorical borderland on the Eastern corridor of the United States that is shared with Caribbean writers. Thus, another counter-site was in the Northeastern region of the United States, where writers such as Gianini Braschi, Oscar Hijuelos, and Julia Alvarez wrote in a variety of discourses and languages. Central American novelists such as Sergio Ramírez, Arturo Arias Rodrigo Rey Rosa, Juan Escoto, Gloria Guardia, and Mario Roberto Morales attempted to write beyond the borders of their culturally marginalized nations. Certainly Ramírez and Arias have been the most successful in being recognized beyond the border of Central America. Braschi's *Yo-Yo Boing* (1999) is an allegorical border novel that deals with the cultural and linguistic borders between the Caribbean culture of the Spanish language and Anglo culture. More important, it is a gender essay in the sense that it questions the genre border between the "novel" and the "essay" at the same time that its topic is the status and reality of women in modern society.

The modernist novelists associated with the Boom and Postboom continued publishing totalizing works such as *Los años con Laura Díaz* (1999) by Carlos Fuentes, *Los cuadernos de don Rigoberto* (1997) by Mario Vargas Llosa, *Tinísima* (1992) by Elena Poniatowska, *Hija de la fortuna* (1999) by Isabel Allende, *La boda del poeta* (1999) by Antonio Skármeta, and *Santo Oficio de la memoria* (1991) by Mempo Giardinelli. At the same time, ethnic discourses were paramount, as Chicano novelists such as Sandra Cisneros, Rolando Hinojosa, and Rudolfo Anaya continued publishing in the 1990s. The Chileans Marco Antonio de la Parra and Marcela Serrano, the Peruvian Alfredo Bryce Echenique, the Brazilian João Ubaldo Ribeiro, and the Argentines César Aira and Marcos Aguinis participated in the 1990s continuation of the Postboom, as did the Mexicans Enrique Serna, Vicente Leñero, and Héctor Aguilar Camín and the Nicaraguan Sergio Ramírez.

Fuentes, Poniatowska, Serna, Giardinelli, Héctor Aguilar Camín, César Aira, and Juan José Saer wrote historical novels of vast dimensions, although their attitudes about the potential of being historical voices varied. Fuentes's *Los años con Laura Díaz* is another of Fuentes's vast historical novels, seemingly covering the entire twentieth century in its scope. Also ambitious was Poniatowska's *Tinísima*, an account of the life of Tina Modotti as well as history of early-twentieth-century Mexico. Enrique Serna moves back to the nineteenth century to provide a version of the life of one of Mexico's anti-heroes, Santa Ana. Serna's interest in historical accuracy and legitimacy is far superior to Fuentes's, as is evident in the historical guidelines and documentation he provides at the end of *El seductor de la patria*. Mempo Giardinelli published a lengthy and totalizing rewriting of Argentine history, *Santo Oficio de la memoria*, which tells the story of the Domenicelle family. Giardinelli's alter ego, Pedro, returns from exile in Mexico and is one of the four principal narrators of this novel. The work explores connections between exile, immigration, history, and literature. Giardinelli privileges the role of the woman, giving major roles to La Nona (a first-generation Italian immigrant) and Franca (a woman writer in search of identity). Franca's role relates this book to the gender essay of Braschi. Consistent with Giardinelli's previous novels and vision as a writer, he incorporates contemporary conflicts and critique in this historical work. Skármeta's historical vision takes the reader to pre–World War I Europe in *La boda del poeta*, a tale of a love affair. Aguilar Camín's *El resplandor de la madera* (1999) deals with the nineteenth-century exploitation of the jungle in Yucatán for the production of lumber. Less concerned with historical veracity and documentation, and winking at both Cortázar and postmodern fiction, Aguilar Camín offers the reader the possibility of different readings. In this novel, one story line tells of a cacique, while another relates the history of a small town.

Rosario Ferré and César Aira wrote less ambitious historical novels. In Ferré's *Vecindarios excéntricos* (1998), a female narrator tells not only the story of two families, but the social history of Puerto Rico. Aira's *La liebra* (1991) is set in nineteenth-century Argentina, where a British naturalist, a relative of Darwin, engages in a search for a rare type of hare. This search places him in contact with recognizable people and places in Argentina. Aira's *La mendiga* (1998) lacks historical ambition; it is the story of two exceptional women, one impoverished and the other an actress.

Although Fuentes and Giardinelli wrote historical novels, not all of the Boom and Postboom works, of course, were historical. Many of these writers, such as the Chileans Marcela Serrano and Marco Antonio de la Parra, the Brazilians João Ubaldo Ribeiro and Moacyr Scliar, and the Cuban Pedro Juan Gutiérrez, wrote of situations that were local and contemporary. In *Antigua vida mía* (1995), Serrano relates the feminine experience throughout generations, as narrated by a woman. De la Parra's *Cuerpos prohibidos* (1991) is a young man's story, told by himself and set in a specific neighborhood in Santiago. It is a novel of voyeurism and eroticism with a nineteenth century-type plot, and the generational language is both attractive and entertaining. Gutiérrez's *El rey de la Habana* (1999) is set in the Havana of 1990s poverty, with a testimonial-type account of minimal survival, focusing on the life of the Rey, who lives as a beggar, a thief, a taxi driver, and a professional don Juan. But Gutiérrez explores other levels of human survival beyond the material, questioning the spiritual poverty of the characters, as well as the role of memory in the entire process.

Much of the recent fiction of Fuentes and Giardinelli exhibits some postmodern tendencies, and the same can be said of Vicente Leñero, María Luisa Mendoza, and Gonzalo Celorio. Leñero's *La vida que se va* (1999) is a family story of personal relationships that presents different explanations and truths with no final authority. It is the narration of a reporter's encounter with the grandmother of a deceased colleague. The journalist writes the grandmother's tale, and the game of chess becomes the central metaphor for the narrative's complexities. Mendoza relates an anecdote of human relations in *Fuimos mucha gente* (1999) and fictionalizes some of the postmodern destinies found in Ramos and Piglia. Celorio's *Amor propio* (1991) tells the story of three characters in a three-part work covering the period from 1965 to 1980. In this early work, too, Celorio's main theme is the progressive degeneration of the individual and the nation, a matter evident in *Y retiemble en sus centros la tierra* (1999). His text *El viaje sedentario* (1994) is a set of memoirs, fictions, and reflections only vaguely related to either the genre of the essay or the novel. In some ways, it can be associated with Braschi's gender essay, even though gender itself is not Celorio's primary interest.

Some of the most innovative fiction of the 1990s was published not by the writers of the Boom but by those with postmodern interests. In Mexico, for example, the "Serie Rayuela Internacional," coordinated by Hernán Lara Zavala, represented an effort to publish experimental writers throughout Latin America, and this series included writers such as Tununa Mercado, Diamela Eltit, and the young Mexican Margarita Mansilla. This series was one of several important efforts to support fiction that falls outside the commercial mainstream.

Postmodern novelists of the 1970s and 1980s, such as Diamela Eltit, Ricardo Piglia, Alicia Borinsky, Tununa Mercado, Darío Jaramillo, and R. H. Moreno-Durán, continued their postmodern projects well into the 1990s. Each of them and several of their postmodern cohorts, such as José Balza and Gustavo Sainz, published noteworthy novels. The 1990s offered a wide variety of postmodern and feminist trends as found in novels such as Eltit's *Los vigilantes* (1994) and *Los trabajadores de la muerte* (1998), Piglia's *La ciudad ausente* (1992) and *Plata quemada* (1997), Luis Arturo Ramos's *La casa del ahorcado* (1993), Darío Jaramillo's *Cartas cruzadas* (1995), Solares's *El sitio* (1995), and Alicia Borinsky's *Cine continuado* (1997).

Eltit, Mercado, and Borinsky wrote engaging and sometimes purposely irritating works that resist easy or entertaining reading; at the same time, they are works that play a political role in the cultural sphere. Relatively unconcerned with either accessibility or having a large readership, Eltit, Mercado, and Borinsky challenge the reader. Their novels tend to leave the reader lacking sufficient information to construct a complete story, and thus they question the authority of the Boom novelist to create the total novel. Resisting the new redemocratization under capitalism, these writers often looked to the periphery or the margins for destabilization of the meaning produced by the center. Consequently, writers with these interests often included marginalized characters in their novels. In Chile, this radical stance was theorized in the late 1980s and early 1990s by Eltit and a group of her cohorts—artists such as Juan Dávila, Eugenio Dittborn, and Paz Errázuriz and the cultural critic Nelly Richard.

Eltit's fiction often needs to be read by the active postmodern reader as political allegory, and she has spoken about the "scenes of power" as well as the ideology of the body in extratextual interviews and in her books of fiction. In the 1990s, she published *Vaca sagrada* (1991), *Los vigilantes* (1994), and *Los dictadores de la muerte* (1998). Like her earlier fiction, these are political allegories that resist literal interpretation and address unspeakable themes related to gender and the body, such as incest and rape. *Los vigilantes* has been read as a national allegory unfolding within an Oedipal triangle; it also addresses issues of political writing.[5] *Los dictadores de la muerte* can be read as a political allegory that re-elaborates Eltit's themes of power and the body, with the father figure once again prominent. Here, the daughter figure is engaged in a symbolic search for the father in a trip from Santiago to Concepción.

Alicia Borinsky pursued her novelistic career in both Argentina (where she is read as an Argentine writer) and in the United States (where she is read in English translation as a "Latina" writer). She calls her books *Sueños del seductor abandonado* (1995) and *Cine continuado* (1997) *novelas de espectáculo;* they relate more to show and spectacle than to the expectations of much modernist fiction. To paraphrase what she herself has observed in Cortázar, Borinsky (echoing Morelli of *Rayuela* and Macedonio Fernández) wants to dismantle the notion of causality as an adequate tool for explaining behavior; she undermines the unity of character with strong selves.[6] This dismantling and undermining is a radical literary project; her characters are often in a process of transformation, as they were in Severo Sarduy's *Cobra*. Thus, the characters of *Cine continuado* have little fixed identity, and there is little causality in the series of fragments that constitute this novel. In addition, there is no consistent pattern that could appear in virtually any order without significantly changing the experience of her novel, thus suggesting the arbitrary nature of identity. Writing after and against Sarduy and Donoso, Borinsky's ludic approaches to the topoi of postmodern literature and poststructualist theory place her in a rarefied group of postmodern writers. By turning the postmodern kitsch of Puig into raucous spectacle, she parodies the theory and practice of much postmodern fiction.

Piglia's *Plata quemada*, in contrast, does not deal at all with theory; it is in the basic genre of detective fiction, telling the intricate story of a crime that the newspapers of Buenos Aires reported in 1965. Given the participation of politicians in the crime, *Plata quemada* offers a political level of reading.

In Mexico, Carmen Boullosa, Ignacio Solares, Gustavo Sainz, Angelina Muñíz-Huberman, Ethel Krauze, Brianda Domecq, Aline Petterson, Silvia Molina, Margo Glantz, Luisa Josefina Hernández, María Luisa Mendoza, Federico Patán, Luis Arturo Ramos, and Bárbara Jacobs continued their postmodern writing of the 1980s. Boullosa's *La milagrosa* (1993), *Cielos de la tierra* (1997), and *Treinta años* (1999) were noteworthy contributions in the 1990s. In *La milagrosa*, Boullosa tells the story of a faith healer. The novel is symptomatic of a nation and a fiction that are irrational; paradoxically, it also involves a search for understanding of things beyond the rational. *Cielos de la tierra* is a postmodern work in which language becomes the only sustaining force not only of memory but of reality itself.

Both *La milagrosa* and Ignacio Solares's *El gran elector* (1993) are implicit critiques of politics in postmodern Mexico. They represent the crisis of authority in Mexican society, the crisis of a world with little transcendence and truth. Both novels contain a multiplicity of discourses—popular, political, ecclesiastical—in unresolved contradiction. Their concerns are predominantly ontological in a world with characters suffering identity crises.

Gustavo Sainz continued his experimental writing with *A la salud de la serpiente* (1991) and *La novela virtual* (1998). The former is a novel of more than eight hundred pages, but in accordance with Sainz's ongoing interest in experimentation, the work consists of one sentence, centered on the Tlatelolco massacre and related events that took place in Mexico City in 1968. This novel also deals with the political and cultural movements of 1968. On a different level of reading, *A la salud de la serpiente* is a dialogue with the intellectuals and writers who surrounded Sainz when he was living the experience of the 1960s. In its totality—as a story of the young rebels and as a literary dialogue—this work is a postmodern questioning of power relations. *La novela virtual* and *Quiero escribir pero me sale espuma* (1997) are a continuation of Sainz's hyper-experimental and self-conscious fiction.

In general, the fiction of Jacobs and Muñiz-Huberman has not been as experimental as Sainz's. Nevertheless, Jacobs's novel *Adiós humanidad* (1999) is a self-conscious and ludic approach to telling a family story in an autobiographic mode but with focus on a character named Cool Charlie. Jacobs offers the active postmodern reader a series of sections on "Technique" and a "Glossary." Her referents are a wide variety of writers and artists from William Blake to Edvard Munch. Muñiz-Huberman's *Dulcinea encantada* (1992), like the work of Jacobs, Ramos, and Patán, blurs the boundaries between interior and exterior reality as well as between fantasy and empirical reality. It is a metafiction that offers the possibility of multiple levels of intertextual reading.

Colombians Darío Jaramillo, Rodrigo Parra Sandoval, and R. H. Moreno-Durán continued their postmodern projects well into the 1990s. Jaramillo's *Cartas cruzadas* (1995) is an epistolary novel that communicates much of the urban experience of living in postmodern Colombia as well as the author's special relationship with writing and culture. More specifically, *Cartas cruzadas* relates a story of human relations in the 1970s, when cocaine culture was on the rise in the region of Antioquia. More important, Jaramillo's novel suggests that fiction affects and has superiority over empirical reality. In both this novel and *Novela con fantasma* (1996), Jaramillo writes with a minimalist approach to language with self-conscious commentary and understatement as a rhetorical strategy. Jaramillo's fiction is critical in the most subtle ways, but Parra Sandoval and Moreno-Durán authored postmodern novels that overtly debunk such sacred Colombian institutions as its academic and cultural traditions. Parra Sandoval's *Tarzán y el filósofo desnudo* (1996) is a satirical academic novel, and Moreno-Durán's *El caballero de la invicta* (1993) fictionalizes urban decay and cultural decadence.

Numerous new writers of the 1990s advanced a postmodern literary and political agenda into the 1990s, but their condition of relative marginality and lack of a broad readership minimalized their recognition. Some of these writers are the Argentines Clara Obligado and Rodrigo Fresán, the Guatemalan Rodrigo Rey Rosa, and the Brazilians Ana Miranda and Lya Luft. Living in Spain, Obligado is distant from potential readers and critics in both Latin America and the United States. Her first novel, *La hija de Marx* (1996), is a transgressive exploration of homoerotics as well as heterosexual erotics, set in the historical context of the nineteenth-century Europe of Karl Marx's daughter. Rey Rosa was born in Guatemala but spent years living and writing in New York and Morocco. His novels *Cárcel de árboles* (1991), *El cojo bueno* (1996), *Que me maten si* (1997), and *La orilla africana* (1999) are an impressive body of fiction that constructs a tenuous relationship between the interior and exterior worlds of the characters. In *La orilla africana*, the two main characters, Hamsa and Angel Tejedor, are only tangentially related in a text with the stylistic minimalism of Darío Jaramillo.

In the 1990s, various groupings of young novelists declared their independence from the predominant modes of the multinational literary industry. Some of these new novelists were young enough to be the third generation in Latin America to declare its aesthetic and political independence from the Boom. Many of these writers were also adamant about distancing themselves from the ways of "magic realism" and the commercialism of novelists such as Isabel Allende.

These declarations included the publication of the volume titled *McOndo* in Chile and, in the late 1990s, the statements of the self-declared *generación del crack* in Mexico, which included writers Ignacio Padilla and Jorge Volpi. There was some overlapping among writers of the two groups, and they repeated the three-decade tradition of declaring the death of the Boom and of magic-realist writing.

A generation of post-postmodern novelists born from the mid-1950s to the late 1960s shared a set of experiences and attitudes that distinguishes them from other writers of the decade. Novelists David Toscana (Mexico, born in 1961), Jorge Volpi (Mexico, born in 1968), Juan Villoro (Mexico, born 1956), Philip Potdevín (Colombia, born 1955), Edmundo Paz Soldán (Bolivia, born 1967), Alberto Fuguet (Chile, born 1964), and Rodrigo Fresán (Argentina, born 1963), among others, wrote texts that were in many ways indistinguishable from much of the postmodern fiction written in the 1980s and 1990s by novelists of other generations. Indeed, some of these young, post-postmodern writers were less interested in technical experimentation than the most radical innovators among their postmodern predecessors.

Having been born since the mid-1950s, these post-postmodern novelists share the common experience of being the first generation of Latin American writers to have been reared on television. National television was first available in Colombia in 1955 and was broadcast throughout Latin America from the late 1950s to the early 1960s. Toscana, Potdevín, Fuguet, and others have emphasized the centrality of television to their cultural experience. The young Colombian Octavio Escobar Giraldo (author of *El último diario de Tony Flowers*), in fact, claims that the television experience determined his cultural formation as a writer far more than the reading of canonical modernist literary texts.[7] This experience represents a paradigm shift from all of their predecessors—whether modernist, Postboom, or postmodern—who have generally been avid readers of Proust, Joyce, Faulkner, Dos Passos, and many of the other canonical modernists of the West. The postmodern writers of the Piglia and Eltit generation also tend to share not only the political experience of 1968 but also the common cultural experience of the international group of ludic writers that included Eco, Nabokov, Calvino, and Perec. In contrast, this generation of post-postmodern writers is generally more distant from Borges and Cortázar than any group of writers this century, although some of these novelists do still read Borges with interest.[8]

The paradigm shift of the young post-postmodern writers, however, should not be construed to mean that they write in a literary vacuum. Their cultural interests range from television and film to the writings of Vargas Llosa, Fuentes, Paul Auster, and William Gass. In the 1990s, these young novelists read the translations of foreign writers that appeared with the Spanish publishing company Anagrama, which included Auster. One of their main transnational connections with international culture has been the Internet; they are the first generation to use the Internet for communication and the word processor for writing from the beginning of their literary careers. Colombian writer Juan B. Gutiérrez, in fact, has published his novel *Condiciones extremas* (1998) on the Internet.

The eclectic literary interests and cultural baggage of these young writers still includes Borges in some cases. In 1999, Rodrigo Fresán authored a fictionalized version of an encounter with Borges titled "El día en que casi mato a Borges."[9] David Toscana also read Borges but considers the Argentine a mere model for form and style; Onetti is a writer with whom he feels a closer affinity.[10]

The two most active Chilean writers of this generation have been Antonio Ostornol and Alberto Fuguet. In his third novel, *Los años de la serpiente* (1991), Ostornol challenges the postmodern reader with a variety of languages and texts that only vaguely constitute something like a novel. Fuguet's *Mala onda* (1991) is a fictionalized testimonial of postmodern Chile under Pinochet's regime, written in the hip, young language of Chile's alienated youth of the dictatorship. His novels *Tinta roja* (1996) and *Por favor, redobinar* (1998) are a continuation of Fuguet's urban chronicles, which, like the fiction of Ostornol and Potdevín, only vaguely belong to the genre of the novel.

Among these new novelists of the 1990s, the Mexican Jorge Volpi and the Colombian Philip Potdevín published lengthy novels that exhibit some of the totalizing impulses of the writing of the Boom, some postmodern aspects, and no small amount of interest in the commercial market. Their common literary tradition, as Mexican and Colombian writers, is more the writing of Umberto Eco (particularly *In the Name of the Rose*) than the fiction of any contemporary Latin American writer. Volpi's *En busca de Klingsor* (1999) is set in Hitler's Germany and is a novel of suspense, with a fast-moving plot. At the same time that the thick plot develops, Volpi elaborates theories on science and the novel as a genre. Potdevín's *Metatrón* (1999) offers as much scientific and historical erudition as *En busca de Klingsor*, but less plot, although it does relate a complex intellectual and spiritual search.

Toscana, Fresán, and Paz Soldán construct fiction with a clear story line. Toscana's two novels of the 1990s, *Estación Tula* (1995) and *Santa María del Circo* (1998) are quite traditional and linear in many ways, giving the reader an initial impression of a conventional plot. His *Estación Tula*, however, is a multilayered exercise in unresolved contradictions in the process of telling part of the history of a rural town, Tula, and human relations in it. With vague echoes of Cervantes, Fuentes, and García Márquez, Toscana offers fiction that also interacts with film and television in ways that reiterate Escobar Giraldo's statements about the importance of television for this generation. Like Darío Jaramillo and Luis Arturo Ramos, Toscana creates situations in his text that suggest that fiction not only affects empirical reality but seems to determine some aspects of everyday reality. Fresán's *Esperanto* (1995) fictionalizes elements of postmodern culture: the protagonist is a thirty-five-year-old musician who has the public image of a James Dean.

Many of the writers of the late 1990s wrote accessible texts with an easily recognizable story line. Toscana, Giraldo, and Fresán are all writers of this type. A few novelists—certainly a small minority by the end of the 1990s—continued along the lines of a highly experimental vein. The young Mexican Margarita Mansilla, for example, published *Karenina express* (1995), which includes the story of a writer's interest in Tolstoi's *Ana Karenina*. Colombia's Héctor Abad Faciolince, Hugo Chaparro Valderrama, and Juan B. Gutiérrez published experimental novels. Abad Faciolince's *Asunto de un hidalgo disoluto* (1994) is a self-conscious and narcissistic story of a seventy-two-year-old man who narrates the vicissitudes of his life from his adolescence, using the model of the Spanish picaresque novel. Chaparro Valderrama's *El capítulo de Ferneli* (1992) is one of the most wildly innovative fictions published in Colombia for more than two decades; it has origins in detective fiction, horror movies, Cortázar, Sue Grafton, and Raymond Chandler. Gutiérrez's *Condiciones extremas* is a hyperfiction that integrates text and image in such a way that the organizing principle is time, and the themes are technology, power, racism, and pollution.

Other innovators of this generation are the Cubans Senel Paz and René Vasquez Díaz, the Colombian Santiago Gamboa, the Ecuadorian Leonardo Valencia, the Peruvian Jaime Bayly, and the Chilean Lina Meruane. Bayly's *Yo amo a mi mami* (1999) is a story of an adolescent's rite de passage. Meruane has published a set of brief narrative texts titled *Las infantas* (1998) that can be read as a novel.

Queer discourse of the 1990s was typically dedicated to the subversion of the patriarchal order.[11] Gay and lesbian writers have contributed to a variety of heterogeneous cultural configurations that have shaped recent postmodern Latin American fiction. Gay and lesbian writers Luis Zapata, José Rafael Calva, Luis Arturo Ojedas, and Sara Levy have established a cultural space previously unknown in Mexico. The journal *Debate feminista* and the magazine *Fem* promoted the new sexual politics of gay and lesbian writing in Mexico, and Nelly Richard's journal *Revista de crítica cultural* opened new space for heterogeneous writing in Chile. Autobiographical essays such as Jaime Manrique's *Eminent Maricones* (1993) and Reynaldo Arenas's memoir *Antes que anochezca: autobiografía* (1992) present issues related to modern and postmodern writing as well as queer discourse in Latin America. Both of these works can be related to the gender essay of Braschi. The writings of Manrique, Arenas, Silvia Molloy, Fernando Vallejo, and a host of other writers have reaffirmed the end to the masculinist aesthetic of earlier in the century. Chicana Terri de la Peña's schematic lesbian novel, *Margins* (1992), affirms a lesbian continuum in Hispanic culture that can also be observed in the writings of Cherríe Moraga.[12]

With the globalization of the 1990s and the transnational cultural interaction of this period, the desire to be modern is evident in ways significantly different from the totalizing projects of the Boom, as well as from many of the writers of the Postboom. Young writers of the post-postmodern, including the authors of the first cybertexts, are redefining what it means to be modern and "literary."

In the 1960s, Cortázar and the writers of the Boom called for a radical modernization of the Latin American novel. They were the aesthetic and political revolutionaries of their times, and their voices were heard not only in Latin America but throughout the Hispanic world, including the U.S. Southwest, as well as the French- and English-speaking Caribbean. Among the Chicano writers, the diversity of cultural identities produced a frequent intersection of competing discourses of gender, ethnicity, and class.[13] The fiction of Chicano writers Sandra Cisneros, John Rechy, and Tomás Villaseñor and the Haitian Edwidge Danticat attest to this intersection in the 1990s; this new fiction also made evident the blurred cultural borders of the transnational 1990s. By the end of the century, in fact, transnational writing was one of the most active and productive modes of the youngest group of novelists.

The continued importance of the historical novel relates directly to the growing production of *testimonio*: readers encountered fiction and quasifictional accounts of real events with an interest in learning about historical and empirical reality, just as they did at the beginning of the century. Some of the historical novels, such as Serna's *El seductor de la patria*, contain the ample documentation needed to assure the reader of the historical veracity of the fiction. The unstable borders of the *testimonio* and historical fiction were tested once again when a polemic arose around the veracity of certain details in Rigoberta Menchu's testimonial account of the war in Guatemala.[14]

By the end of the century, the desire to be modern was played out in a variety of increasingly heterogeneous ways. Borges's reaffirmation of the right of invention in the 1940s had been a seminal contribution to this growing heterogeneity. The 1960s Boom represented a turning point in this process, for the right of invention became a fait accompli in all regions of Indo-Afro-Iberoamerica. By the 1960s, the predominantly masculinist aesthetic had begun to wane, and by the 1980s, women writers were at the forefront of the multiple aesthetic and political agendas of Latin American writing. In the 1990s, postpostmodern, feminist, and queer writing, as well as other heterogeneous discourses, challenged the more commercialized and popular versions of traditional and modernist fiction of the Americas as well as dominant cultural and political discourses of authority.

Notes

Preface

1. Octavio Paz, "Prólogo," in *Poesía en movimiento: México, 1915–1966* (Mexico City: Siglo XXI, 1966).
2. Studies on postmodern fiction in Latin America include Santiago Colás, *Postmodernity in Latin America: The Argentine Paradigm* (Durham, N.C.: Duke University Press, 1994); Antonio Benítez Rojo, *La isla que se repite: El Caribe y la perspectiva posmoderna* (Hanover, N.H.: Ediciones del Norte, 1989); Rosalía V. Cornejo-Parriego, *La escritura posmoderna del poder* (Madrid: Editorial Fundamentos, 1993). In my volume *The Postmodern Novel in Latin America* (New York: St. Martin's, 1996), I emphasize the political implications and themes of innovative fiction in Latin America.

Chapter 1

1. Francine Masiello and Doris Sommer, among other scholars, have done important research to identify and study the work of women writing in the early twentieth century. See in particular Masiello's *Between Civilization and Barbarism: Women, Nation, and Literary Culture in Modern Argentina* (Lincoln: University of Nebraska Press, 1992), and Sommer's *Foundational Fictions: The National Romances of Latin America* (Berkeley: University of California Press, 1991).
2. See John S. Brushwood, *The Spanish American Novel: A Twentieth-Century Survey* (Austin: University of Texas Press, 1975), chapter 1.
3. Cathy L. Jrade, *Modernismo, Modernity, and the Development of Spanish American Literature* (Austin: University of Texas Press, 1998), 4.
4. Masiello, *Between Civilization and Barbarism,* 116.
5. Masiello, *Between Civilization and Barbarism.*

6. David W. Foster, *Gay and Lesbian Themes in Latin American Writing* (Austin: University of Texas Press, 1991), 11.

7. Among those who have written of a "realist-naturalist" novel in Latin America see, for example, Brushwood, *Spanish American Novel*, chapter 1.

8. Beatriz Sarlo cited in Carlos Alonso, *The Burden of Modernity: The Rhetoric of Cultural Discourse in Spanish America* (Oxford: Oxford University Press, 1998), 115.

9. Aníbal González, "Modernist Prose," in *Twentieth Century*, vol. 2 of *The Cambridge History of Latin American Literature*, ed. Roberto González-Echevarría and Enrique Pupo-Walker (New York: Cambridge University Press, 1966), 69.

10. Naomi Lindstrom, "Argentina," in *Handbook of Latin American Literature*, 2d ed., ed. David W. Foster (New York: Garland Publishing, 1992), 16.

11. Aníbal González, "Modernist Prose," 110.

12. Ibid., 106.

13. Brushwood, *Spanish American Novel*, 37.

14. John S. Brushwood, *Mexico in Its Novel: A Nation's Search for Identity* (Austin: University of Texas Press, 1966), 171.

15. Francine Masiello discusses at length the prostitute as literary object in *Between Civilization and Barbarism*, chapter 4.

16. Ibid., 136.

17. I have discussed the novels and ideology of Soledad Acosta de Samper at more length in *The Colombian Novel, 1847–1987* (Austin: University of Texas Press, 1991), 33–35.

18. Debra Castillo makes reference to the "masculinist aesthetic" of early-twentieth-century writing in *Easy Women: Sex and Gender in Modern Mexican Fiction* (Minneapolis: University of Minnesota Press, 1998), chapter 2, "Meat Shop Memories: Gamboa."

19. Jrade, *Modernismo*, 137.

20. Masiello, *Between Civilization and Barbarism*, 89.

21. For discussion of *Santa* and a masculinist aesthetic see Castillo, *Easy Women*, chapter 2.

Chapter 2

1. The writers' struggle as described in chapter 2 was basically a male project in the early twentieth century, although several women writers who really belonged to the nineteenth century, such as Soledad Acosta de Samper, continued publishing well into the twentieth.

2. David W. Foster, Debra Castillo, and Francine Masiello have made this forceful argument. See Foster, *Gay and Lesbian Themes*; Castillo, *Easy Women*; and Masiello, *Between Civilization and Barbarism*.

3. Brushwood, *Spanish American Novel*, 6.

4. Manuel Díaz Rodríguez, *Sangre patricia* (1902; reprint, Caracas: Ediciones Nueva Cádiz, 1950), 7. All subsequent quotations are from this edition. Author's translations throughout except as otherwise noted.

5. Andrew P. Debicki, "Díaz Rodríguez's *Sangre patricia:* A 'Point of View' Novel," *Hispania* 53, no. 1 (March 1970): 59–66.

6. Recognizing the place of humans in the animal kingdom was a common device in Latin American fiction of this period, as Debra Castillo has observed in Federico Gamboa's *Santa;* see Castillo, *Easy Women,* chapter 2.

7. Jorge Ruffinelli, *El primer Mariano Azuela* (Xalapa: Universidad Veracruzana, 1982), 72.

8. Ibid., 66.

9. Mariano Azuela, *Los de abajo* (1916; reprint, Mexico City: Fondo de Cultura Económica, 1970), 47. All subsequent quotations are from this edition.

10. José Emilio Pacheco, prologue to *Diario de Federico Gamboa (1892–1939),* by Federico Gamboa. (Mexico City: Siglo Veintiuno Editores, 1977), 22.

11. Castillo, *Easy Women,* 53.

12. Federico Gamboa, *Santa,* in *Novelas de Federico Gamboa* (Mexico City: Fondo de Cultura Económica, 1965), 736. All subsequent quotations are from this edition.

13. Brushwood, *Mexico in Its Novel,* 151.

14. Castillo, *Easy Women,* chapter 2.

15. Ibid., 41.

16. Pocaterra mentions Efraím and María, the main characters of Isaacs's *María;* José Rafael Pocaterra, *Política feminista* (Caracas: Tipografía Cultura, 1913), 76. Subsequent quotations are from this edition.

17. See Beatriz Sarlo's article on *miradas,* "El imperio de los sentimientos: Ficciones de circulación periódica en la Argentina (1917–1925)," *Hispamérica* 39 (1984): 3–17.

18. Debra Castillo, in *Easy Women,* chapter 2, discusses a similar issue of commodity value in *Santa.*

19. Walter Ong has studied the explicit and implicit complicity between reader and writer in "The Writer's Audience Is Always a Fiction," *Publications of the Modern Language Association* 90, no. 1 (January 1975): 9–21. Castillo has studied the issue of complicity and the reader as voyeur in *Santa* in *Easy Women,* chapter 2.

20. Manuel Gálvez, *El mal metafísico,* 3d ed. (Buenos Aires: Espasa-Calpe, 1962), 65. All quotations are from this edition.

21. For a study of ideology, grammar, and the Regeneration in Colombia see Gilberto Gómez Ocampo, *Entre "María" y "La vorágine": La literatura colombiana finisecular (1886–1903)* (Bogotá: Ediciones Fondo Cafetero, 1998).

22. See Castillo's discussion of sales of this erotic book in *Easy Women,* chapter 2.

23. The editorial history of *Santa* is reviewed in Gamboa, *Novelas de Federico Gamboa.*

24. Gamboa, *Diario,* 29.

25. Ibid.

Chapter 3

1. Several scholars have questioned the validity of the centrality of *lo nacional* as a critical theme. In *La vibración del presente* (Mexico City: Fondo de Cultura Económica, 1987), Noé Jitrik is quite critical of the lengthy debates on *lo nacional* and refers to them as a "peste" (plague).

2. Naomi Lindstrom and several other scholars place *Don Segundo Sombra* in the *vanguardia;* Lindstrom, *Twentieth-Century Spanish American Fiction* (Austin: University of Texas Press, 1994), 73–74.

3. See Roberto González-Echevarría, *Alejo Carpentier: The Pilgrim at Home* (Ithaca: Cornell University Press, 1977), 52.

4. Ibid., 56.

5. Puerto Rico was the exception, for its interests in the avant-garde were more of local than European origin. See Noé Jitrik, *Vertiginosas textualidades* (Mexico City: Universidad Autónoma de México, 1999), 193–226.

6. Gerald Martin has provided an informed and thorough overview of the presence of Joyce in Latin American fiction in *Journeys through the Labyrinth: Latin American Writers in the Twentieth Century* (London: Verso, 1989).

7. Masiello, *Between Civilization and Barbarism*, 140–142.

8. María Bustos Fernández, *Vanguardia y renovación en la narrativa latinoamericana* (Madrid: Editorial Pliegos, 1996), 69.

9. See Merlin Forster and K. David Jackson, compilers, *Vanguardism in Latin American Literature: An Annotated Bibliographical Guide*, 133.

10. Jitrik, *La vibración*, 198.

11. Vicky Unruh, *Latin American Vanguards: The Art of Contentious Encounters* (Berkeley: University of California Press, 1994), 2.

12. Masiello, *Between Civilization and Barbarism*, 146–147.

13. Brushwood, *Spanish American Novel*, 103–104.

14. César Uribe Piedrahita, *Toá* (Bogotá: Instituto Colombiano de Cultura, 1979), 130.

15. Anna Housková, "Tipo de novela mundonovista," *Revista de Crítica Literaria* 13, no. 26 (1987): 69.

16. Brushwood, *Spanish American Novel*, 103.

17. Benito Lynch, *La evasión* (Barcelona: Editorial Cervantes, 1918), 11.

18. When I use the terms "oral culture" and "orality" in this study, I refer to oral tradition as delineated by Walter Ong in *Orality and Literacy: The Technologizing of the Word* (London: Methuen, 1982).

19. Brushwood makes brief comparisons between Aguilera Malta and García Márquez in *Spanish American Novel*, 99.

20. Ibid., 111.

21. Elzbieta Sklodowska, *Todo ojos, todo oídos: control e insubordinación en la novela hispanoamericana* (1895–1935) (Amsterdam: Editions Rodopi, 1997), 163–182.

22. Frank Dauster, *Xavier Villaurrutia* (Boston: Twayne Publishers, 1971), 40.

23. Carol Clark D'Lugo, *The Fragmented Novel in Mexico: The Politics of Form* (Austin: University of Texas Press, 1997), 35.

24. Arturo Torres Rioseco cited in Brushwood, *Spanish American Novel*, 81.

25. Gustavo Pérez Firmat, *Idle Fictions: The Hispanic Vanguard Novel, 1926–1934* (Durham, N.C.: Duke University Press, 1982), 139.

26. The ongoing research on the *vanguardia* has produced an ever-growing list of novels of *vanguardia*. See the work of Verani, Forster, Bustos Fernández, and others.

Chapter 4

1. See Lindstrom's discussion of *Don Segundo Sombra* in *Twentieth-Century Spanish American Fiction*, 73–75.

2. Sommer has studied these *criollista* novels as important texts for nation building in *Foundational Fictions*.

3. Carlos Alonso, *The Spanish American Regional Novel* (Cambridge: Cambridge University Press, 1990), epilogue, 163.

4. See Sommer, *Foundational Fictions*, chapter 1.

5. In making this statement, Sommer seems to overlook the historical work of writers such as Fuentes and García Márquez who have written historical novels and addressed the issue of the *otra historia* that they relate. In *Foundational Fictions*, Sommer states: "But since the 1960s, since Latin America's post-Borgesian Boom in narrative and France's self-critical ebullience in philosophy and literary studies, we have tended to fix on the ways that literature undoes its own projects" (10).

6. Ricardo Guiraldes, *Don Segundo Sombra* (1926; reprint, Barcelona: Losada, 1968), 11. All subsequent quotations are from this edition.

7. Alonso, *Spanish American Regional Novel*, 79–108.

8. In general, scholars have been hypercritical about these *criollista* classics. Doris Sommer, Carlos Alonso, and Seymour Menton have offered a more balanced and generous reading of these novels.

9. Brushwood, *Spanish American Novel*, 46.

10. Alonso, *Spanish American Regional Novel*, 107.

11. The point about Guiraldes's elitism is well taken. Nevertheless, a response to those critics who have made this point is his interest in oral tradition, which is a democratizing factor in the novel.

12. Rómulo Gallegos, *Doña Bárbara* (1929; reprint, with prologue and notes by Mariano Picón Salas, Mexico City: Editorial Orión, 1971). All subsequent quotations are from this edition.

13. Sharon Magnarelli, *The Lost Rib: Female Characters in the Spanish-American Novel* (Cranbury, N.J.: Associated University Presses, 1985), 44.

14. Mariano Picón Salas, "A veinte años de *Doña Bárbara*," in Gallegos, *Doña Bárbara*, 7–19.

15. Sommer, *Foundational Fictions*, 274.

16. Ibid., 275.

17. Ibid., 289.

18. Ibid., 284.

19. Ibid., 283.

20. Emir Rodríguez Monegal popularized the term "total novel" in *El Boom de la novela latinoamericana* (Caracas: Editorial Tiempo Nuevo, 1972).

21. Robin William Fiddian, "James Joyce and Spanish-American Fiction: A Study of the Origins and Transmissions of Literary Influence," *Bulletin of Hispanic Studies* 66 (1989): 23–39.

22. Ibid. For Fiddian, "total" novels are typically Joycean.

23. See Kessel Schwartz, *New History of Spanish American Fiction* (Coral Gables, Fla.: University of Miami Press, 1972), 1:259.

24. For Carrasquilla's negative comments on Rivera see Eduardo Neale-Silva, *Horizonte humano. Vida de José Eustasio Rivera* (Madison: University of Wisconsin Press, 1960). Brushwood is among harsh critics of the protagonist; see his *Spanish American Novel*, 42–45.

25. Randolph Pope, "*La vorágine*," in *The Analysis of Literary Texts: Current Trends in Methodology*, ed. Randolph Pope (Ypsilanti, Mich.: Bilingual Press, 1980), 256–257; and Magnarelli, *Lost Rib*, 38.

26. Jean Franco and Otto Olivera, among others, have called Cova a "romantic poet." See Franco, *The Modern Culture of Latin America: Society and the Artist* (New York: F. A. Praeger, 1967), and Otto Olivera, "El romanticismo de José Eustasio Rivera," *Symposium* 14 (1960): 7–25.

27. Magnarelli, *Lost Rib*, 38.

28. See for example Brushwood, *Spanish American Novel*, 53–55, and Bull, "Nature and Anthropomorphism in *La vorágine*," *Romantic Review* 39 (December 1948): 307–318.

29. José Eustasio Rivera, *La vorágine* (1924; reprint, Buenos Aires: Losada, 1970), 35. Subsequent references are from this edition.

30. Magnarelli, *Lost Rib*, 42.

31. For a history of the editions of *María* see Donald McGrady, *Jorge Isaacs* (New York: Twayne Publishers, 1972).

32. Neale-Silva, *Horizonte humano*; for an overview of *La vorágine*'s reception see chapters 15 and 16.

33. Ibid., 297; in the original edition of Neale-Silva's study, a photo is included of Arturo Cova as it appeared in an edition of *La vorágine*.

34. Jonathan Tittler, *Narrative Irony in the Contemporary Spanish American Novel* (Ithaca: Cornell University Press, 1984), 190.

35. Schwartz, *New History*.

36. Teresa de la Parra, *Las memorias de Mamá Blanca* (1929; reprint, Caracas: Monte Avila, 1989), 90. All quotations are from this edition.

37. Sommer, *Foundational Fictions*, 292.

38. Ibid., 293.

39. I have discussed the orality in the fiction of Carpentier, García Márquez, and Vargas Llosa in *The Modern Latin American Novel* (New York: Twayne Publishers, 1998).

Chapter 5

1. Scholars and writers who have made this connection between the fiction of *vanguardia* and postmodern fiction include Unruh, Bustos Fernández, Piglia, and Eltit.

2. David Daiches, "What Was the Modern Novel?" *Critical Inquiry* 1, no. 4 (June 1975): 813–820.

3. In *Enciclopedia de la literatura argentina*, ed. Pedro Orgambide and Robert Yahni (Buenos Aires: Editorial Sudamérica, 1970), 477.

4. The two-volume edition of the novels of Jaime Torres Bodet is *Narrativa completa* (Mexico City: Editorial Offset, 1985). With respect to the scholarly recognition of Jaime Torres Bodet see Beth Miller, editor, *Ensayos contemporáneos sobre Jaime Torres Bodet* (Mexico City: Universidad Nacional Autónoma de México, 1976).

5. Recent readings of *Proserpina rescatada* include those in Pérez Firmat, *Idle Fictions*, Bustos Fernández, *Vanguardia y renovación*, and D'Lugo, *Fragmented Novel*.

6. D'Lugo, *Fragmented Novel*, 37.

7. Ibid., 38.

8. Jaime Torres Bodet, *Proserpina rescatada*, in Torres Bodet, *Narrativa completa*, 1:232. All subsequent quotations in text, cited with page numbers, are from this edition.

9. Pérez Firmat, *Idle Fictions*, 98–99.

10. Bustos Fernández, *Vanguardia y renovación*, 27.

11. D'Lugo, *Fragmented Novel*, 40.

12. In *Proserpina rescatada*, Torres Bodet follows the technical strategies generally associated with modernist fiction (fragmentation, innovative use of time and space, and the like). Nevertheless, I inquired of a group of graduate students at the University of California, Riverside, who are well versed in postmodern fiction whether they would associate *Proserpina rescatada* (which we had just read in a graduate seminar) more closely with Agustín Yáñez's high modernist text *Al filo del agua* (1947) or Salvador Elizondo's experimental and postmodern *Farabeuf* (1965). Interestingly, the majority of these students were adamant in affirming that they would associate *Proserpina* more closely with *Farabeuf* than with *Al filo del agua*. I consider this student reaction yet another indicator, albeit subjective, of the connection between the fiction of *vanguardia* and postmodern fiction in Latin America.

13. Brian McHale has explained that the emphasis on the ontological rather than the epistemological is typical of postmodern fiction; see McHale, *Postmodernist Fiction* (New York: Methuen, 1987).

14. Vicente Huidobro, *Mío Cid Campeador* (Madrid: Ibero-Americana de Publicaciones, 1929), 22. All subsequent quotations are from this edition.

15. Before the postmodern novel of the 1970s and 1980s, important predecessors who used language as a subject of fiction were Borges, Cortázar, and Cabrera Infante.

16. When I speak of the "ambition" of the novelists of the Boom, I refer spe-

cifically to the length of the novels as a factor in these ambitious modernist projects.

17. Hugo J. Verani, editor, *Las vanguardias literarias en hispanoamérica* (Mexico City: Fondo de Cultura Económica, 1986), 52.

18. Pérez Firmat, *Idle Fictions*, 82.

19. Torres Bodet, *Margarita de niebla*, in Torres Bodet, *Narrativa completa*, 29.

20. Pérez Firmat, *Idle Fictions*, 83.

21. McHale discusses the importance of the ontological in *Postmodernist Fiction*.

22. Merlin Forster, in Beth Miller, editor, *Ensayos contemporáneos*, 71.

23. Bustos Fernández, *Vanguardia e renovación*, 72.

24. Martín Adán, *La casa de cartón* (1928; reprint, Lima: Librería Editorial Juan Mejía Baca, 1971), 38.

25. José Carlos Mariátegui, in preface to Adán, *La casa de cartón*, 93.

26. Borges in preface to Adolfo Bioy Casares, *La invención de Morel* (1940; reprint, Buenos Aires: Emecé Editores, 1986), 12. Quotations are from this edition.

27. I discuss the crisis of truth in the postmodern novel of the 1970s and 1980s in my *Postmodern Novel.*

28. Lucía Guerra-Cunningham, *La narrativa de María Luisa Bombal* (Madrid: Playor, 1980), 73.

29. Ibid., 70–71.

30. Borinsky, *Theoretical Fables: The Pedagogical Dream in Contemporary Latin American Literature* (Philadelphia: University of Pennsylvania Press, 1993), 113.

31. Unruh, *Latin American Vanguards*, 169.

Chapter 6

1. Brushwood introduced the idea of Borges reaffirming the "right of invention"; see Brushwood, *Spanish American Novel*, chapters 11 and 12.

2. Césaire quoted in Michael J. Dash, *The Other America: Caribbean Literature in a New World Context* (Charlottesville: University Press of Virginia, 1998), 64.

3. Dash, *The Other America*, 62.

4. Simon Gikandi discusses the modernism of *Cahier* in *Writing in Limbo* (Ithaca: Cornell University Press, 1992), 5.

5. Ibid., 22.

6. Eduoard Glissant, *Caribbean Discourse: Selected Essays*, trans. Michael J. Dash (Charlottesville: University Press of Virginia, 1989), 91.

7. Gikandi, *Writing in Limbo*, 16.

8. See González-Echevarría, *Alejo Carpentier*, and Michael Dash, *The Other America.*

9. Dash, in *The Other America*, has drawn this comparison between Alexis and Carpentier.

10. González-Echevarría quoted in Dash, *The Other America*, 89.

11. Daiches, "What Was the Modern Novel?"

12. Many of the Latin American nations experienced a more localized version of the paradigm shift described as the general pattern in Latin America. In Colombia, for example, the publication of three modernist (and overtly Faulknerian) texts signaled this shift: García Márquez's *La hojarasca* (1955), Héctor Rojas Herazo's *Respirando el verano* (1962), and Alvaro Cepeda Samudio's *La casa grande* (1962). David Viñas's *Cayó sobre su rostro* (1955) served a similar function in Argentina.

13. See Brushwood, *Spanish American Novel*, especially chapters 12 and 13.

14. In numerous interviews and essays, García Márquez has spoken highly of *Pedro Páramo*. In a personal interview in Cartagena in March 1994, García Márquez described *Pedro Páramo* as the novel he wished he had written.

15. Yolanda Forero-Villegas has studied the rise of modernist fiction in Colombia in *Un eslabón perdido: La novela colombiana de los años cuarenta (1941–1949)*.

16. For a further discussion of the *bogotazo* and the period of La Violencia see Orlando Fals Borda, Germán Guzmán Campos, and Eduardo Umaña Luna, *La violencia en Colombia* (Bogotá: Carlos Valencia Editores, 1980).

17. For further study of these strategies in Onetti's novels see Josefina Ludmer, *Onetti: Los procesos de construcción del relato* (Buenos Aires: Editorial Sudamericana, 1977), and Djelal Kadir, *Juan Carlos Onetti* (Boston: Twayne Publishers, 1977).

18. Bustos Fernández, "Ana Isabel, detrás de la reja: identidad y procesos de subjetivación en *Ana Isabel, una niña decente*," in *Escritura y desafío*, ed. Edith Dimo and Amarilis Hidalgo de Jesús (Caracas: Monte Avila Editores, 1995).

19. Jean Franco, *An Introduction to Spanish American Literature* (Cambridge: Cambridge University Press, 1994), 252.

20. José David Saldívar, *The Dialectics of Our America* (Durham, N.C.: Duke University Press, 1991), 50.

21. González-Echevarría cited in Dash, *The Other America*, 77.

22. See Richard Callan, *Miguel Angel Asturias* (Boston: Twayne Publishers, 1970), 54.

23. See Alonso, *Burden of Modernity*.

24. González-Echevarría has pointed out that the most appropriate description of the "marvelous real" in *El reino de este mundo* is actually the "fantastic"; González-Echevarría, *Alejo Carpentier*, 98.

25. Ibid., 18.

26. See Ramón Saldívar, *Chicano Narrative: The Dialectics of Difference* (Madison: University of Wisconsin Press, 1990) 69.

27. For further study of the Afro–Latin American novel see Richard Jackson, *Black Writers and Latin America* (Washington, D.C.: Howard University Press, 1998), and Marvin A. Lewis, *Treading the Ebony Path: Ideology and Violence in Contemporary Afro-Colombian Prose Fiction* (Columbia: University of Missouri Press, 1987).

28. For ample studies of magic realism see Seymour Menton, *Magic Realism Discovered, 1918–1981* (Philadelphia: Art Alliance Press, 1983); Lois Parkinson Zamora and Wendy B. Faris, editors, *Magical Realism: Theory, History, Community* (Durham, N.C.: Duke University Press, 1995). I would propose that much of what is identified as magic realism in the Spanish American novel is actually typical expression of oral culture in literature; see Ong, *Orality and Literacy*, and Raymond Leslie Williams, *The Colombian Novel, 1847–1987* (Austin: University of Texas Press, 1991), chapter 4.

Chapter 7

1. Brushwood has pointed out the importance of these four writers in the reaffirmation of the right of invention in the 1940s in *Spanish American Novel*, chapter 12.

2. García Canclini quoted in Alonso, *Burden of Modernity*, 3–4.

3. There has been a consistency in Latin America in the resistance to modernity, even among scholars and critics. Torres Rioseco's reaction to innovative literature of the 1920s can be compared to a similarly negative later critique of postmodern culture among critics such as García Canclini and Nelson Osorio.

4. I discuss Fuentes's situation in Mexico in the mid-1940s in Raymond Leslie Williams, *The Writings of Carlos Fuentes* (Austin: University of Texas Press, 1997), part 1.

5. Lindstrom, *Twentieth-Century Spanish American Fiction*, 100.

6. Joseph Sommers, *After the Storm* (Albuquerque: University of New Mexico Press, 1968), 42.

7. I refer to formal qualities of the oral tale as defined by Walter Ong, among them "copiousness"; see Ong, *Orality and Literacy*, chapter 2.

8. Agustín Yáñez, *Al filo del agua* (1947; reprint, Mexico City: Editorial Porrúa, 1969), 354. All quotations are from this edition.

9. Brushwood, *Spanish American Novel*, 165.

10. Ibid., 166

11. Ibid., 167.

12. Ibid., chapters 12 and 13.

13. Yvette Jiménez de Báez, *Juan Rulfo, del páramo a la esperanza: Una lectura crítica de su obra* (Mexico City: Fondo de Cultura Económica, 1990), 197.

14. Terry J. Peavler, *El texto en llamas: El arte narrativo de Juan Rulfo* (New York: Peter Lang, 1988). Peavler writes that the novel has sixty-six to seventy segments, depending on the edition; the 1981 edition of the Fondo de Cultura Económica has seventy.

15. Peavler, *El texto en llamas*, 46–47.

16. Ibid., 63.

17. Ibid., 84.

18. Lindstrom, *Twentieth-Century Latin American Fiction*, 155.

19. Brushwood, *Mexico in Its Novel*, 31

20. Juan Rulfo, *Pedro Páramo* (1955; reprint, Mexico City: Fondo de Cultura, 1981), 9.

21. Jiménez de Báez, *Juan Rulfo,* 268.

22. D'Lugo, *Fragmented Novel,* 70.

23. Ibid., 79–80.

24. Brushwood, *Spanish American Novel,* 168.

25. Lindstrom, *Twentieth-Century Spanish American Fiction,* 106.

26. Brushwood, *The Spanish American Novel,* 168.

27. D'Lugo offers more connections with Paz in *Fragmented Novel,* 97.

28. See chapter 12 of this study for more discussion of the ontological element in postmodern fiction. The concept is from McHale, *Postmodernist Fiction.*

29. Cortázar quoted in Mario Goloboff, *Julio Cortázar: La biografía* (Barcelona: Seix Barral, 1998), 88.

30. García Canclini and Alonso emphasize the problems of modernity and modernization in Latin America. These problems obviously exist and are historically based. Nevertheless, the present study also indicates that writers from each generation of the twentieth century embraced modernity.

Chapter 8

1. José Donoso discusses the development of the political positions of the writers of the Boom in his *Historia personal del Boom* (Barcelona: Anagrama, 1972).

2. See C. L. R. James's argument in *The Black Jacobins: Toussaint L'Ouverture and the Santo Domingo Revolution* (New York: Vintage, 1963).

3. Dash, *The Other America,* 44–45.

4. Wilson Harris, *Tradition, Writing, and Society: Critical Essays* (London: New Beacon, 1967), 30.

5. Raymond D. Souza, *Guillermo Cabrera Infante: Two Islands, Many Worlds* (Austin: University of Texas Press, 1996), 93

6. Raymond D. Souza, *The Poetic Fiction of José Lezama Lima* (Columbia: University of Missouri Press, 1983), 21–37.

7. Selwynn R. Cudjoe, editor, *Caribbean Women Writers* (Wellesley, Mass.: Calaloux Publications, 1990), 42.

8. Bobby Chamberlain sets forth the reading as political allegory in *Jorge Amado* (Boston: Twayne Publishers), 61–64.

9. Brushwood, *Spanish American Novel,* chapters 15–16.

10. McHale, *Postmodernist Fiction,* 11.

11. Other noteworthy novels of the period 1962–1967 include *Bomarzo* (1962) by Manuel Mujica Lainez, *Manuel Pacho* (1962) by Eduardo Caballero Calderón, *El siglo de las luces* (1962) by Alejo Carpentier, *Acto y ceniza* (1963) by Manuel Peyrou, *La situación* (1963) by Lisandro Otero, *Gestos* (1963) by Severo Sarduy, *Los burgueses* (1964) by Silvina Bullrich, *Toda la luz a mediodía* by Mauricio Wácquez, *El peso de la noche* (1965) by Jorge Edwards, and *Alrededor de la jaula* by Haroldo Conti.

Chapter 9

1. Fiddian uses these three elements as typical of the total novel; see Fiddian, "James Joyce."

2. Fuentes discusses his cycle "La Edad del Tiempo" at length in an interview published at the end of Williams, *Writings of Carlos Fuentes*.

3. Wendy Faris, *Carlos Fuentes* (New York: Frederick Ungar Publishing, 1983), 55–56.

4. Ibid., 58.

5. In his studies of the Postboom, Shaw argues that the writers of the Boom were "pessimistic." See Donald Shaw, *The Post-Boom in Spanish Fiction* (Albany: State University of New York Press, 1998), and *Antonio Skármeta and the Post-Boom* (Hanover, N.H.: Ediciones del Norte, 1994).

6. McHale, *Postmodernist Fiction*, 15.

7. Ong, *Orality and Literacy.*

8. Gabriel García Márquez, *Cien años de soledad,* trans. Gregory Rabassa under the title *One Hundred Years of Solitude* (New York: Harper and Row, 1970), 27.

9. Roberto González-Echevarría develops the concept of Archive in *Myth and Archive: A Theory of Latin American Narrative* (Durham: Duke University Press, 1990).

10. Lucille Kerr, *Reclaiming the Author: Figures and Fictions from Spanish America* (Durham: Duke University Press, 1992), 27.

Chapter 10

1. For critical studies on Cepeda Zamudio and Rojas Herazo see Brushwood, *Spanish American Novel;* Seymour Menton, *La novela colombiana: planetas y satélites* (Bogotá: Plaza y Janés, 1977); and Williams, *Colombian Novel.*

2. See Williams, *Colombian Novel,* chapter 1.

3. Franz Stanzel makes the distinction between the narrating self and the experiencing self in *Narrative Situations in the Novel* (Bloomington: Indiana University Press, 1971).

4. Héctor Rojas Herazo, *Respirando el verano* (Bogotá: Ediciones Faro, 1962), 66. Subsequent quotations in text are from this edition.

5. Ong states that oral and writing noetics are so profoundly different that the way a writing culture person thinks may seem ridiculous or senseless to an individual in an oral culture, and vice-versa. Oral cultures use situational rather than abstract noetic processes; this manner of thinking is prevalent among characters in *Respirando el verano.* See Ong, *Orality and Literacy,* 51.

6. Ibid., 42–43; Ong discusses the conceptualization of things "close to the human lifeworld."

7. Seymour Menton, "*Respirando el verano,* fuente colombiana de *Cien años de soledad,*" originally published in *Revista Iberoamericana* 41, no. 91 (April–June 1975): 203–217.

8. See Williams, *Colombian Novel*, chapter 5.

9. Menton, *La novela colombiana*, 217-246.

10. Manuel Mejía Vallejo spoke often of his admiration for Carrasquilla. For example, see his essay "Don Tomás Carrasquilla y Kurt Levy," in Mejía Vallejo, *Hojas de papel* (Bogotá: Universidad Nacional, 1985).

11. See Beth Miller, "Historia y ficción en *Oficio de tinieblas* de Castellanos: Un enfoque Gramsciano," in *De la crónica a la nueva narrativa mexicana: Coloquio sobre literatura mexicana*, ed. Merlin H. Forster and Julio Ortega (Mexico City: Editorial Oasis, 1986), 407-422.

12. Franco, *Plotting Women*, 139.

13. Ibid., 141.

14. Brushwood, *Spanish American Novel*, 258.

15. Franco, *Plotting Women*, 134-135.

16. Castillo, *Easy Women*, 63.

17. Elena Garro, *Los recuerdos del porvenir* (Mexico City: Editorial Joaquín Mortiz, 1963), 28. Quotations are from this edition. Ong would identify this passage as "close to human lifeworld."

18. Franco, *Plotting Women*, 138.

19. Castillo, *Easy Women*, 82.

Chapter 11

1. See Shaw, *Post-Boom*, and Philip Swanson, *The New Novel in Latin America: Politics and Popular Culture after the Boom* (Manchester, England: Manchester University Press, 1995). In these two studies, Shaw and Swanson cite numerous other writers and scholars who have commented on the Postboom; Shaw cites novelists Antonio Skármeta and Mempo Giardinelli at length.

2. Book-length studies on the postmodern novel in Latin America include Benítez Rojo, *La isla que se repite*; John Beverly and José Oviedo, editors, *The Postmodernism Debate in Latin America: A Special Issue of Boundary 2* 20, no. 3 (fall 1993); Colás, *Postmodernity in Latin America*; Cornejo-Parriego, *La escritura posmoderna*; Salvador C. Fernández, *Gustavo Sainz: Postmodernism in the Mexican Novel* (New York: Peter Lang, 1999); George Yúdice, Jean Franco, and Juan Flores, editors, *On Edge, the Crisis of Contemporary Latin American Culture* (Minneapolis: University of Minnesota Press, 1992); Roberto González-Echevarría, *La ruta de Severo Sarduy* (Hanover, N.H.: Ediciones del Norte, 1987); Nelly Richard, *La estratificación de los márgenes* (Santiago, Chile: Francisco Zegers, 1989); Lauro Zavala, *La precisión de la incertidumbre: posmodernidad, vida cotidiana y escritura* (Toluca, Mexico: Universidad Autónoma del Estado de México, 1999).

3. Among the numerous studies on these dictator novels see Angel Rama, *Los dictadores latinoamericanos* (Mexico City: Fondo de Cultura Económica, 1976).

4. Linda J. Craft, *Novels of Testimony and Resistance from Central America* (Gainesville: University Press of Florida, 1997), 59.

5. Tittler, *Narrative Irony*, chapter 6.

6. David W. Foster, "Of Power and Virgins: Alejandra Pizarnik's *La condesa sangrienta*," in *Structures of Power: Essays on Twentieth-Century Spanish-American Fiction*, ed. Terry J. Peavler and Peter Standish (Albany: State University of New York Press, 1996), 146.

7. Ibid., 148.

8. Among the numerous studies of the exile of these writers see Jean Franco, *Critical Passions: Selected Essays* (Durham: Duke University Press, 1999), 60–61; Mempo Giardinelli, "Dictaduras y el artista en el exilio," *Discurso Literario* 3 (1985): 41–49; and Shaw, *Post-Boom*.

9. Craft, *Novels of Testimony*, 134–149.

10. With respect to the historical novel in Latin America see in particular Seymour Menton, *Latin America's New Historical Novel* (Austin: University of Texas Press, 1993), and Raymond D. Souza's *La historia en la novela hispanoamericana moderna* (Bogotá: Tercer Mundo Editores, 1988).

11. Menton studies these authors in *Latin America's New Historical Novel*.

12. Sharon Magnarelli compares the two novels in "Images of Exile/Exiled Images: the Cases of Luisa Valenzuela and José Donoso," *Revista de Estudios Hispánicos* 31, no. 1 (January 1997): 61–76.

13. Wilson Harris, *History, Fable, and Myth in the Caribbean and Guianas* (Georgetown: Ministry of Information and Culture, 1970), 82.

14. Fernando Valerio-Holguín, "Primitive Borders: Cultural Identity and Ethnic Cleansing in the Dominican Republic," in *Primitivism and Identity in Latin America*, ed. Erik Camayd-Frixas and José Eduardo González (Tucson: University of Arizona Press, 2000), 81.

15. Studies on these Chicano novelists include Ramón Saldívar, *Chicano Narrative*; José David Saldívar, *The Rolando Hinojosa Reader: Essays Historical and Critical*; and César A. González-T., editor, *Rudolfo A. Anaya: Focus on Criticism*.

16. Julio Cortázar quoted in Goloboff, *Julio Cortázar*, 228.

17. See Shaw, *Post-Boom*, and Swanson, *New Novel*.

18. In terms of narrative technique, the writers of the Boom continued using the basic strategies associated with the modernist novel.

19. Shaw, *Post-Boom*, 3–24.

20. Ibid., 10. Shaw describes the writers of the Boom as pessimistic, though it could be argued—depending on which texts of the Boom one reads— that they were neither consistently pessimistic nor optimistic. Certainly some factors in the writings of Fuentes, Vargas Llosa, Cortázar, and García Márquez made them pessimistic. Nonetheless, an ongoing faith in the future of humanity suggests some optimism. Considering a broader range of fiction than Shaw includes, I do not concur with Shaw that the writers of the Post-boom are necessarily more optimistic than the writers of the Boom. It likewise would be difficult, given the numerous texts at hand, to generalize that the writers of the Postboom are necessarily more pessimistic.

21. See Menton, *Magic Realism Rediscovered*, and Parkinson Zamora and Faris, editors, *Magical Realism*.

22. Allende cited in Shaw, *Post-Boom*, 11.

23. Elzbieta Sklodowska, *Testimonio hispanoamericano: Historia, teoría, poética* (New York: Peter Lang, 1992), chapters 1 and 2.

24. Recent studies by Brushwood, Kay S. García, and Cynthia Steele include Mexican novels that would fit into Shaw's description of the Postboom. See Brushwood, *La novela mexicana, 1967-1982* (Mexico City: Enlace/ Grijalbo, 1985); García, *New Perspectives from Mexican Women Writers* (Albuquerque: University of New Mexico Press, 1994); and Steele, *Politics, Gender, and the Mexican Novel, 1968-1988* (Austin: University of Texas Press, 1992).

25. Shaw, *Post-Boom*, 53.

26. Ibid., 57.

27. Ibid., 76.

28. Ibid., 79. Shaw proposes that the use of colloquial language is typical of the Postboom. The preponderance of colloquial language in Spanish American fiction before, during, and after the Boom makes it difficult to accept this proposal as a defining characteristic of one particular group of writers.

29. Menton, *Latin America's New Historical Novel*, 123.

30. Julio Ortega, *El hilo del habla: la narrativa de Alfredo Bryce Echenique* (Guadalajara: Universidad Guadalajara, 1994), chapter 1.

31. With respect to narrative technique and the formal aspects of their work, most of the Postboom writers employed the narrative strategies typical of modernist fiction, even though some of them did not engage in such ambitious, lengthy, and complex works as had the writers of the Boom in the 1960s.

32. Swanson, *New Novel*, 95-96.

33. Sklodowska makes this point with respect to Poniatowska's *La noche de Tlatelolco*; see Sklowdowska, *Testimonio hispanoamericano*, 159.

34. Magnarelli, "Luisa Valenzuela," in *Spanish American Women Writers: A Bio-Bibliographical Source Book*, ed. Sharon Magnarelli and Diane Marting (Westport, Conn.: Greenwood Press, 1990), 533.

35. Ibid., 537.

36. The polemics associated with Rigoberta Menchú involved accusations that her story was not historically accurate. See David Stoll, *Rigoberta Menchú and the Story of All Poor Guatemalans* (Boulder, Colo.: Westview Press, 1999).

37. For further discussion of these women writers in Venezuela see Julio Ortega, *El principio radical de lo nuevo: Postmodernidad, identidad y novela en América Latina* (Mexico City: Fondo de Cultura Económica, 1997), and Amarilis Hidalgo de Jesús, *La novela moderna en Venezuela* (New York: Peter Lang, 1995).

38. Foster, *Gay and Lesbian Themes*, 104.

39. See Foster's *Gay and Lesbian Themes* and his *Sexual Textualities: Essays on Queering Latin American Writing* (Austin: University of Texas Press, 1997).

40. Foster, *Sexual Textualities*, 15.

41. Sklodowska, *Testimonio hispanoamericano*, 64.

42. Craft, *Novels of Testimony*.

43. Martin, *Journeys through the Labyrinth*.

44. Warren Motte has analyzed this international group of ludic writers in *Playtexts: Ludics in Contemporary Literature* (Lincoln: University of Nebraska Press, 1995).

45. Linda Hutcheon, *A Poetics of Postmodernism: History, Theory, Fiction* (New York: Routledge, 1988).

46. Shaw also considers the use of "popular" art a characteristic of the Postboom. Given the widespread presence of popular culture in contemporary Latin American literature, however, it is not entirely clear if the presence of popular culture should be used as a defining characteristic of either a Postboom or the postmodern.

47. Lucille Kerr, *Suspended Fictions: Reading Novels by Manuel Puig* (Urbana: University of Illinois Press, 1987), 244.

48. McHale, *Postmodernist Fiction*, 15.

49. Salas Elorza has discussed Pitol as a postmodern writer in *La narrativa dialógica de Sergio Pitol* (Cranston, R.I.: Ediciones Inti, 1999).

50. In *La isla que se repite*, Benítez Rojo has discussed the inherent postmodernity of Caribbean culture.

51. Alonso, "*La guaracha del Macho Camacho:* The Novel as Dirge," *Modern Language Notes* 100, no. 2 (March 1985): 350.

52. Benítez Rojo, *La isla que se repite*.

53. Naomi Lindstrom, *The Social Conscience of Latin American Writing* (Austin: University of Texas Press, 1998), 141–142.

Chapter 12

1. Brushwood has noted the experimentation in the Mexican novel of the late 1960s and early 1970s in *La novela mexicana*.

2. See Foster, *Gay and Lesbian Themes*.

3. Gustavo Sainz, *La princesa del Palacio de Hierro* (Mexico City: Joaquín Mortiz, 1974), 180.

4. I have studied the readers and writers in *La tía Julia y el escribidor* at more length in Raymond Leslie Williams, *Mario Vargas Llosa* (New York: Ungar, 1986).

5. Suzanne S. Hintz, *Rosario Ferré: A Search for Identity* (New York: Peter Lang, 1995), 47.

6. Ibid., 49.

7. See Lee Skinner, "Pandora's Log: Charting the Evolving Literary Project of Rosario Ferré," *Revista de Estudios Hispánicos* 29 (1995): 461–476.

8. Daniel Balderson, "Latent Meanings in Ricardo Piglia's *Respiración Artificial* and Luis Gusman's *El corazón de junio*," *Revista Canadiense de Estudios Hispánicos* 12, no. 2 (winter 1988): 212.

9. Julio Ortega, "Diamela Eltit y el Imaginario de la Virtualidad," in Julio Ortega, *El discurso de la abundancia* (Caracas: Monte Avila, 1992), 53.

10. Foster, *Gay and Lesbian Themes*, 111.

Chapter 13

1. In this chapter, I am referring to postmodern writers born after 1954 as "post-postmodern writers" to distinguish them from the previous generation of postmodern writers.

2. In July 2000, after the period covered in this study, the delegitimization of the PRI was evident in the election of PAN candidate Vicente Fox as president of Mexico.

3. Alberto Fuguet and Sergio Gómez, editors, *McOndo* (Barcelona: Mondadori, 1996).

4. Rosaura Sánchez, "Discourses of Gender, Ethnicity and Class in Chicano Literature," in *Feminisms: An Anthology of Literary Theory and Criticism*, edited by Robyn R. Warhol and Diane Price Herndl (New Brunswick, N.J.: Rutgers University Press, 1997), 1021.

5. Idelber Avelar, *The Untimely Present: Postdictatorial Latin American Fiction and the Task of Mourning* (Durham, N.C.: Duke University Press, 1999), 179.

6. Borinsky, *Theoretical Fables*, 56.

7. Escobar Giraldo described this aspect of his cultural formation to me in a personal interview in Bogotá in 1995.

8. David Toscana, interview with the author, Riverside, Calif., March 10, 2000.

9. See this story in Pablo Brescia and Lauro Zavala, editors, *Borges múltiple: Cuentos y ensayos de cuentistas* (Mexico City: Universidad Nacional Autónoma de México, 1999).

10. Toscana, interview.

11. Foster, *Sexual Textualities*.

12. Ibid., 7.

13. Sánchez, "Discourses of Gender," 1021.

14. The polemic around the veracity of Rigoberta Menchu's *Me llamo Rigoberta Menchú y así me nació la conciencia* arose when David Stoll published *Rigoberta Menchú and the Story of All Poor Guatemalans*. In response to Stoll, Arturo Arias edited *The Rigoberta Menchú Controversy* (Minneapolis: University of Minnesota Press, 2001).

Bibliography

Adán, Martín. *La casa de cartón.* 1928. Reprint, Lima: Editorial Juan Mejía Baca, 1971.

Agosín, Marjorie, Elena Gascón-Vera, and Joy Renjilian-Burgy, eds. *María Luisa Bombal: Apreciaciones críticas.* Tempe, Ariz.: Bilingual Press/ Editorial Bilingue, 1987.

Alegría, Fernando. *Nueva historia de la novela hispanoamericana.* Hanover, N.H.: Ediciones del Norte, 1986.

Alonso, Carlos. *The Burden of Modernity: The Rhetoric of Cultural Discourse in Spanish America.* Oxford: Oxford University Press, 1998.

———. "*La guaracha del Macho Camacho:* The Novel as Dirge," *Modern Language Notes* 100, no. 2 (March 1985): 348–360.

———. *The Spanish American Regional Novel.* Cambridge: Cambridge University Press, 1990.

Arias, Arturo, ed. *The Rigoberto Menchú Controversy.* Minneapolis: University of Minnesota Press, 2001.

Avelar, Idelber. *The Untimely Present: Postdictatorial Latin American Fiction and the Task of Mourning.* Durham, N.C.: Duke University Press, 1999.

Azuela, Mariano. *Los de abajo.* 1916. Reprint, Mexico City: Fondo de Cultura Económica, 1970.

Balderson, Daniel. "Latent Meanings in Ricardo Piglia's *Respiración Artificial* and Luis Gusman's *En el corazón de junio,*" *Revista Canadiense de Estudios Hispánicos* 12, no. 2 (winter 1988): 207–219.

Bellini, Guiseppe Bellini. *Historia de la literatura hispanoamericana.* Madrid: Editorial Castalia, 1985.

Benítez Rojo, Antonio. *La isla que se repite: El Caribe y la perspectiva posmoderna.* Hanover, N.H.: Ediciones del Norte, 1989.

Beverly, John and José Oviedo, eds. *The Postmodernism Debate in Latin America. A Special Issue of Boundary 2* 20, no. 3 (fall 1993).

Bioy Casares, Adolfo. *La invención de Morel.* Buenos Aires: Emecé Editores, 1940.

Blanco Arnejo, María D. *La novela lúdica experimental de Julio Cortázar.* Madrid: Editorial Pliegos, 1996.

Bombal, María Luisa. *La última niebla.* 1927. Reprint, Santiago: Editorial Nascimento, 1941.

Borges, Jorge Luis. Prologue to *La invención de Morel,* by Adolfo Bioy Casares. Buenos Aires: Emecé Editores, 1940.

Borinsky, Alicia. *Theoretical Fables: The Pedagogical Dream in Contemporary Latin American Literature.* Philadelphia: University of Pennsylvania Press, 1993.

Brescia, Pablo, and Lauro Zavala, eds. *Borges múltiple: cuentos y ensayos de cuentistas.* Mexico City: Universidad Nacional Autónoma de México, 1999.

Bruce-Novoa, Juan. "The U.S.-Mexican Border in Chicano Testimonial Writing: A Topological Approach to Four Hundred and Fifty Years of Writing the Border." *Discourse* 18, no. 1 (fall–winter 1995–1996).

Brushwood, John S. *La novela mexicana (1967–1982).* Mexico City: Enlace/ Grijalbo, 1985.

————. *Mexico in Its Novel: A Nation's Search for Identity.* Austin: University of Texas Press, 1966.

————. *The Spanish American Novel: A Twentieth-Century Survey.* Austin: University of Texas Press, 1975.

Bull, William. "Nature and Anthropomorphism in *La vorágine.*" *Romantic Review* 39 (December 1948): 307–318.

Burgos, Fernando, ed. *Prosa hispánica de vanguardia.* Madrid: Discuro/ Orígenes, 1986.

Bustos Fernández, María. *Vanguardia y renovación en la narrativa latinoamericana.* Madrid: Editorial Pliegos, 1996.

Callan, Richard. "The Archetype of Psychic Renewal in *La vorágine.*" *Hispania* 54, no. 3 (September 1971): 470–476.

————. *Miguel Angel Asturias.* Boston: Twayne Publishers, 1970.

Camayd-Freixas, Erik, and José Eduardo González, eds. *Primitivism and Identity in Latin America.* Tucson: University of Arizona Press, 2000.

Castillo, Debra. *Easy Women: Sex and Gender in Modern Mexican Fiction.* Minneapolis: University of Minnesota Press, 1998.

————. *Talking Back: Toward a Latin American Feminist Criticism.* Ithaca: Cornell University Press, 1992.

Chamberlain, Bobby. *Jorge Amado.* Boston: Twayne Publishers, 1984.

Chanady, Amaryll, ed. *Latin American Identity and Constructions of Difference.* Minneapolis: University of Minnesota Press, 1994.

Colás, Santiago. *Postmodernity in Latin America: The Argentine Paradigm.* Durham, N.C.: Duke University Press, 1994.

Cornejo-Parriego, Rosalía. *La escritura posmoderna del poder.* Madrid: Editorial Fundamentos, 1993.

Cortázar, Julio. "Adán Buenosayres, de Leopoldo Marechal." *Realidad, Revistas de Ideas* (Buenos Aires), no. 14 (March–April 1949): 232.

Craft, Linda J. *Novels of Testimony and Resistance from Central America.* Gainesville: University Press of Florida, 1997.

Cudjoe, Selwynn R., ed. *Caribbean Women Writers.* Wellesley, Mass.: Calaloux Publications, 1990.

Cymermann, Claude. "La literatura hispanoamericana y el exilio." *Revista Iberoamericana,* no. 164-165 (July–December 1993): 523–550.

Daiches, David. "What Was the Modern Novel?" *Critical Inquiry* 1, no. 4 (June 1975): 813–820.

Dash, Michael J. *The Other America: Caribbean Literature in a New World Context.* Charlottesville: University Press of Virginia, 1998.

Dauster, Frank. *Xavier Villaurrutia.* Boston: Twayne Publishers, 1971.

de Beer, Gabriella. *Contemporary Mexican Women Writers.* Austin: University of Texas Press, 1997.

Debicki, Andrew P. "Díaz Rodríguez's *Sangre patricia:* A 'Point of View' Novel." *Hispania* 53, no. 1 (March 1970): 59–66.

de Costa, René. *Huidobro: Los oficios de un poeta.* Mexico City: Tierra Firme, 1984.

de la Parra, Teresa. *Las memorias de Mamá Blanca.* 1929. Reprint, Caracas: Monte Avila Editores, 1989.

DiAntonio, Robert E. *Brazilian Fiction: Aspects of Evolution of the Contemporary Narrative.* Fayetteville: University of Arkansas Press, 1989.

Díaz Rodríguez, Manuel. *Idolos rotos.* Madrid: Editorial América, 1920.

———. *Sangre patricia.* 1902. Reprint, Caracas: Ediciones Nueva Cádiz, 1950.

Dimo, Edith, and Amarilis Hidalgo de Jesús, eds. *Escritura y desafío.* Caracas: Monte Avila, 1995.

D'Lugo, Carol Clark. *The Fragmented Novel in Mexico: The Politics of Form.* Austin: University of Texas Press, 1997.

Donoso, José. *Historia personal del Boom.* Barcelona: Anagrama, 1972. Reprint, Barcelona: Seix Barral, 1983.

Droscher, Barbara, and Carlos Rincón, eds. *Acercamientos a Carmen Boullosa.* Berlin: Edition Tranvía/Verlag Walter Frey, 1999.

Elizondo, Salvador. "Dos libros de Torres Bodet: *La casa* y *Los días.*" In *Ensayos sobre Jaime Torres Bodet,* ed. Beth Miller, 13-17. Mexico City: Universidad Nacional Autónoma de México, 1976.

———. *Farabeuf.* (Mexico City: Joaquín Mortiz, 1965).

Fals Borda, Orlando, Germán Guzmán Campos, and Eduardo Umaña Luna. *La violencia en Colombia.* Bogotá: Carlos Valencia Editores, 1980.

Faris, Wendy B. *Carlos Fuentes.* New York: Frederick Ungar Publishing, 1983.

Fernández, Salvador. *Gustavo Sainz: Postmodernism in the Mexican Novel.* New York: Peter Lang, 1999.

Fiddian, Robin William. "James Joyce and Spanish-American Fiction: A Study of the Origins and Transmissions of Literary Influence." *Bulletin of Hispanic Studies* 66 (1989): 23–39.

Forero-Villegas, Yolanda. *Un eslabón perdido: la novela colombiana de los años cuarenta (1941-1949) primer proyecto moderno en Colombia.* Bogotá: Editorial Kelly, 1994.

Forster, Merlin, and K. David Jackson, comps. *Vanguardism in Latin American Literature: An Annotated Bibliographical Guide.* Westport, Conn.: Greenwood Press, 1990.

Forster, Merlin H., and Julio Ortega, eds. *De la crónica a la nueva narrativa mexicana: Coloquio sobre literatura mexicana.* Mexico City: Editorial Oasis, 1986.

Foster, David W. *Gay and Lesbian Themes in Latin American Writing.* Austin: University of Texas Press, 1991.

———. "Of Power and Virgins: Alejandra Pizarnik's *La condesa sangrienta.*" In *Structure of Power: Essays on Twentieth-Century Spanish-American Fiction,* ed. Terry J. Peavler and Peter Stardich. Albany: State University of New York Press, 1996.

———. *Sexual Textualities: Essays on Queering Latin American Writing.* Austin: University of Texas Press, 1997.

———, ed. *Handbook of Latin American Literature.* Second Edition. New York: Garland Publishing, 1992.

Franco, Jean. *Critical Passions: Selected Essays,* ed. Mary Louise Pratt and Kathleen Newman. Durham, N.C.: Duke University Press, 1999.

———. *An Introduction to Spanish-American Literature.* Cambridge: Cambridge University Press, 1994.

———. *The Modern Culture of Latin America: Society and the Artist.* New York: F. A. Praeger, 1967.

———. *Plotting Women: Gender and Representation in Mexico.* New York: Columbia University Press, 1989.

Fuentes, Carlos. *Agua quemada.* Mexico City: Fondo de Cultura Económica, 1981.

———. *Cambio de piel.* Mexico City: Joaquín Mortiz, 1967.

———. *La muerte de Artemio Cruz.* Mexico City: Fondo de Cultura Económica, 1962.

———. *La región mas transparente.* Mexico City: Fondo de Cultura Económica, 1958.

———. *Terra Nostra.* Mexico City: Joaquín Mortiz, 1975.

———. *Zona sagrada.* Mexico City: Siglo XXI, 1967.

Fuguet, Alberto, and Sergio Gómez, eds. *McOndo.* Barcelona: Mondadori, 1996.

Gallegos, Rómulo. *Doña Bárbara.* 1929. Reprint, Mexico City: Editorial Orión, 1971.

Gálvez, Manuel. *El mal metafísico.* Buenos Aires: Espasa-Calpe Argentina, 1962.

Gamboa, Federico. *Diario de Federico Gamboa (1892–1939).* Comp. José Emilio Pacheco. Mexico City: Siglo Veintiuno Editores, 1977.

———. *Novelas de Federico Gamboa.* Mexico City: Fondo de Cultura Económica, 1965.

García, Kay S. *New Perspectives from Mexican Women Writers.* Albuquerque: University of New Mexico Press, 1994.

García Corales, Guillermo. *Relaciones de poder y carnavalización en la novela chilena contemporánea.* Santiago: Ediciones Asterión, 1995.

García Márquez, Gabriel. *Cien años de soledad.* Buenos Aires: Editorial Sudamericana, 1967. Trans. Gregory Rabassa under the title *One Hundred Years of Solitude.* New York: Harper and Row, 1970.

———. *Crónica de una muerte anunciada.* Bogotá: Editorial Oveja Negra, 1981.

———. *El amor en los tiempos de cólera.* Barcelona: Bruguera: 1985.

———. *El general en su laberinto.* Bogotá: Editorial Oveja Negra, 1989.

———. *La hojarasca.* Bogotá: Ediciones Sipa, 1955.

———. *La mala hora.* Madrid: Talleres de Gráficas Luis Pérez, 1962.

Garro, Elena. *Los recuerdos del porvenir.* Mexico City: Joaquín Mortiz, 1963.

Giardinelli, Mempo. "Dictaduras y el artista en el exilio." *Discurso literario* 3 (1985): 41–49.

Gikandi, Simon. *Writing in Limbo.* Ithaca: Cornell University Press, 1992.

Glantz, Margo. *Repeticiones: ensayos sobre literatura mexicana.* Xalapa: Universidad Veracruz, 1979.

Glissant, Eduoard. *Caribbean Discourse: Selected Essays.* Trans. Michael J. Dash. Charlottesville: University Press of Virginia, 1989.

Goic, Cedomil. *La novela chilena.* Santiago: Editorial Universitaria, 1971.

Goloboff, Mario. *Julio Cortázar: La biografía.* Barcelona: Seix Barral, 1998.

Gómez Ocampo, Gilberto. *Entre "María" y "La vorágine": la literatura colombiana finisecular (1886-1903).* Bogotá: Ediciones Fondo Cafetero, 1998.

González, Aníbal. *La novela modernista hispanoamericana.* Madrid: Editorial Gredos, 1987.

———. "Modernist Prose." In *Twentieth Century.* Vol. 2 of *The Cambridge History of Latin American Literature,* ed. Roberto González-Echevarría and Enrique Pupo Walker. New York: Cambridge University Press, 1996.

González-Echevarría, Roberto. *Alejo Carpentier: The Pilgrim at Home.* Ithaca, N.Y.: Cornell University Press, 1977.

———. *La ruta de Severo Sarduy.* Hanover, N.H.: Ediciones del Norte, 1987.

———. *Myth and Archive: A Theory of Latin American Narrative.* Durham, N.C.: Duke University Press, 1990.

———. *The Voice of the Masters: Writing and Authority in Modern Latin American Literature.* Austin: University of Texas Press, 1985.

González-Echevarría, Roberto, and Enrique Pupo Walker, eds. *The Cambridge History of Latin American Literature.* New York: Cambridge University Press, 1996.

Graça Aranha, José Pereira de. *Canaã.* Rio de Janeiro: Edições de Ouro, 1902.

Guerra-Cunningham, Lucía. *La narrativa de María Luisa Bombal.* Madrid: Playor, 1980.

Guiraldes, Ricardo. *Don Segundo Sombra.* 1926. Reprint, Buenos Aires: Losada, 1966.

Harris, Wilson. *History, Fable, and Myth in the Caribbean and Guianas.* Georgetown: Ministry of Information and Culture, 1970.

———. *Tradition, Writing, and Society.* London: New Beacon, 1967.

Herrera-Sobek, María. *Chicana Literary and Artistic Expressions.* Santa Barbara, Calif.: Center for Chicano Studies, 2000.

Hidalgo de Jesús, Amarilis. *La novela moderna en Venezuela*. New York: Peter Lang, 1995.

Hintz, Suzanne S. *Rosario Ferré: A Search for Identity*. New York: Peter Lang, 1995.

Housková, Anna. "Tipo de novela mundonovista." *Revista de Crítica Literaria* 13, no. 26 (1987): 67–85.

Huidobro, Vicente. *Mío Cid Campeador*. Madrid: Ibero-Americana de Publicaciones, 1929.

Hutcheon, Linda. *A Poetics of Postmodernism: History, Theory, Fiction*. New York: Routledge, 1988.

———. *The Politics of Postmodernism*. New York: Routledge, 1989.

Jackson, Richard. *Black Writers and Latin America*. Washington, D.C.: Howard University Press, 1998.

James, C. L. R. *The Black Jacobins: Toussaint L'Ouverture and the Santo Domingo Revolution*. New York: Vintage, 1963.

Jiménez de Báez, Yvette. *Juan Rulfo, del Páramo a la esperanza: Una lectura crítica de su obra*. Mexico City: Fondo de Cultura Económica, 1990.

Jitrik, Noé. *La vibración del presente*. Mexico City: Fondo de Cultura Económica, 1987.

———. *Vertiginosas textualidades*. Mexico City: Universidad Nacional Autónoma de México, 1999.

Jrade, Cathy L. *Modernismo, Modernity, and the Development of Spanish American Literature*. Austin: University of Texas Press, 1998.

Kadir, Djelal. *Juan Carlos Onetti*. Boston: Twayne Publishers, 1977.

———. *The Other Writing: Postcolonial Essays in Latin America's Writing Culture*. West Lafayette, Ind.: Purdue University Press, 1993.

Kerr, Lucille. *Reclaiming the Author: Figures and Fictions from Spanish America*. Durham, N.C.: Duke University Press, 1992.

———. *Suspended Fictions: Reading Novels by Manuel Puig*. Urbana: University of Illinois Press, 1987.

Larreta, Enrique. *La gloria de don Ramiro*. 1908. Reprint, Madrid: Espasa Calpe, 1960.

Lewis, Marvin A. *Treading the Ebony Path: Ideology and Violence in Contemporary Afro-Colombian Prose Fiction*. Columbia: University of Missouri Press, 1987.

Lindstrom, Naomi. "Argentina." In *The Handbook of Latin American Literature*, 2d ed., ed. David W. Foster. New York: Garland Publishing Company, 1992.

———. *Macedonio Fernández*. Lincoln, Neb.: Society of Spanish and Spanish-American Studies, 1981.

———. *The Social Conscience of Latin American Writing*. Austin: University of Texas Press, 1998.

———. *Twentieth-Century Spanish American Fiction*. Austin: University of Texas Press, 1994.

———. *Women's Voice in Latin American Literature*. Boulder: Lynne Rienner Publishers, 1989.

Ludmer, Josefina. *Onetti: los procesos de construcción del relato.* Buenos Aires: Editorial Sudamericana, 1977.

Lynch, Benito. *La evasión.* Barcelona: Editorial Cervantes, 1918.

Magnarelli, Sharon. "Images of Exile/Exile(d) Images: The Cases of Luisa Valenzuela and José Donoso." *Revista de Estudios Hispánicos* 31, no. 1 (January 1997): 61–76.

———. *The Lost Rib: Female Characters in the Spanish-American Novel.* Cranbury, N.J.: Associated University Presses, 1985.

———. "Luisa Valenzuela." In *Spanish-American Women Writers: A Bio-Bibliographical Source Book,* ed. Diane E. Marting, 532–545. Westport, Conn.: Greenwood Press, 1990.

Martin, Gerald. *Journeys through the Labyrinth: Latin American Fiction in the Twentieth Century.* London: Verso, 1989.

Marting, Diane E., ed. *Spanish-American Women Writers: A Bio-Bibliographical Source Book.* Westport, Conn.: Greenwood Press, 1990.

Masiello, Francine. *Between Civilization and Barbarism: Women, Nation, and Literary Culture in Modern Argentina.* Lincoln: University of Nebraska Press, 1992.

McGrady, Donald. *Jorge Isaacs.* New York: Twayne Publishers, 1972.

McHale, Brian. *Postmodernist Fiction.* New York: Methuen, 1987.

McMurray, George R. *Spanish American Writing since 1941.* New York: Ungar, 1987.

Mejía Vallejo, Manuel. *Hojas de papel.* Bogotá: Universidad Nacional, 1985.

Menton, Seymour. *La novela colombiana: Planetas y satélites.* Bogotá: Plaza y Janés, 1977.

———. *Latin America's New Historical Novel.* Austin: University of Texas Press, 1993.

———. *Magic Realism Rediscovered, 1918–1981.* Philadelphia: Art Alliance Press, 1983.

———. "*Respirando el verano,* fuente colombiana de *Cien años de soledad,*" originally published in *Revista Iberoamericana* 41, no. 91 (April–June 1975): 203–217.

Miller, Beth, ed. *Ensayos contemporáneos sobre Jaime Torres Bodet.* Mexico City: Universidad Nacional Autónoma de México, 1976.

———. "Historia y ficción en *Oficio de tinieblas* de Castellanos: un enfoque Gramsciano." In *De la crónica a la nueva narrativa mexicana: Coloquio sobre literatura mexicana,* ed. Merlin H. Forster and Julio Ortega, 407–422. Mexico City: Editorial Oasis, 1986.

Motte, Warren. *Playtexts: Ludics in Contemporary Literature.* Lincoln: University of Nebraska Press, 1995.

Neale-Silva, Eduardo. *Horizonte humano. Vida de José Eustasio Rivera.* Madison: University of Wisconsin Press, 1960.

Neustadt, Robert. *(Con)Fusing Signs and Postmodern Positions: Spanish American Performance, Experimental Writing, and the Critique of Political Confusion.* New York: Garland Publishing, 1999.

Olivera, "El romanticismo de José Eustasio Rivera." *Symposium* 14 (1960): 7–25.

Ong, Walter. *Orality and Literacy: The Technologizing of the Word.* London: Methuen, 1982.

———. "The Writer's Audience Is Always a Fiction," *Publications of Modern Language Association* 90, no. 1 (January 1975): 9–21.

Orgambide, Pedro, and Robert Yahni, eds. *Enciclopedia de la literatura argentina Enciclopedia de la literatura argentina.* Buenos Aires: Editorial Sudamérica, 1970.

Ortega, Julio. *El discurso de la abundancia.* Caracas: Monte Avila, 1992.

———. *El hilo del habla: La narrativa de Alfredo Bryce Echenique.* Guadalajara: Universidad Guadalajara, 1994.

———. *El principio radical de lo nuevo: Postmodernidad, identidad y novela en América Latina.* Mexico City: Fondo de Cultura Económica, 1997.

Ortiz, Lucía. *La novela colombiana hacia finales del siglo veinte.* New York: Peter Lang, 1997.

Pacheco, José Emilio. "Torres Bodet, 'Contemporáneo.'" In *Ensayos contemporáneos sobre Jaime Torres Bodet,* ed. Beth Miller. Mexico City: Universidad Nacional Autónoma de México, 1976.

———, comp. *Diario de Federico Gamboa, 1892–1939.* Mexico City: Siglo Veintiuno Editores, 1977.

Pajares Tosca, Susana. "*Condiciones extremas:* Digital Science from Colombia." In *Latin American Literature and Mass Media,* ed. Edmundo Paz-Soldán and Debra A. Castillo, 2:70–87. New York: Garland Publishing, 2001.

Parkinson Zamora, Lois, and Wendy B. Faris, eds. *Magical Realism: Theory, History, Community.* Durham, N.C.: Duke University Press, 1995.

Paz, Octavio. "Prologo." In *Poesía en movimiento: México 1915–1966,* comp. Octavio Paz, Alí Chumacero, José Emilio Pacheco, and Homero Aridjis. Mexico City: Siglo XXI, 1966.

Paz-Soldán, Edmundo, and Debra Castillo, eds. *Latin American Literature and Mass Media.* New York: Garland Publishing, 2001.

Peavler, Terry J. *El texto en llamas: El arte narrativo de Juan Rulfo.* New York: Peter Lang, 1988.

Peavler, Terry J. and Peter Standish, eds. *Structures of Power: Essays on Twentieth-Century Spanish-American Fiction.* Albany: State University of New York Press, 1996.

Pérez Firmat, Gustavo. *Idle Fictions: The Hispanic Vanguard Novel, 1926–1934.* Durham, N.C.: Duke University Press, 1982.

Picón Salas, Mariano. "A veinte años de *Doña Bárbara.*" Prologue to reprint of *Doña Bárbara,* by Rómulo Gallegos, 1929; reprint, Mexico City: Editorial Orión, 1971.

Pocaterra, José Rafael. *Política feminista.* Caracas: Tipografía Cultura, 1913.

Pope, Randolph, ed. *The Analysis of Literary Texts: Current Trends in Methodology.* Ypsilanti, Mich.: Bilingual Press, 1980.

Rama, Angel. *Los dictadores latinoamericanos.* Mexico City: Fondo de Cultura Económica, 1976.

Richard, Nelly. *La estratificación de los márgenes.* Santiago, Chile: Francisco Zegers, 1989.

Rivera, José Eustasio. *La vorágine.* 1924. Reprint, Buenos Aires: Losada, 1970.

Rodríguez Monegal, Emir. *El Boom de la novela latinoamericana.* Caracas: Editorial Tiempo Nuevo, 1972.

Rojas Herazo, Héctor. *Respirando el verano.* Bogotá: Ediciones Faro, 1962.

Ruffinelli, Jorge. *El primer Mariano Azuela.* Xalapa: Universidad Veracruzana, 1982.

Rulfo, Juan. *Pedro Páramo.* 1955. Reprint, Mexico City: Fondo de Cultura Económica, 1981.

Sáenz, Inés. *Hacia la novela total: Fernando del Paso.* Madrid: Editorial Pliegos, 1994.

Sainz, Gustavo. *La princesa del Palacio de Hierro.* Mexico City: Joaquín Mortiz, 1974.

Salas-Elorza, Jesús. *La narrativa dialógica de Sergio Pitol.* Cranston, R.I.: Ediciones Inti, 1999.

Saldívar, José David. *Border Matters: Remapping American Cultural Studies.* Berkeley: University of California, 1997.

———. *The Dialectics of Our America.* Durham, N.C.: Duke University Press, 1991.

———. *The Rolando Hinojosa Reader: Essays Historical and Critical.* Houston: Arte Público Press, 1984.

Saldívar, Ramón. *Chicano Narrative: The Dialectics of Difference.* Madison: University of Wisconsin Press, 1990.

Sánchez, Rosaura. *Chicano Discourse: Socio-historic Perspectives.* Houston: Arte Público Press, 1983.

———. "Discourses of Gender, Ethnicity, and Class in Chicano Literature." In *Feminisms: An Anthology of Literary Theory and Criticism,* ed. Robyn R. Warhol and Diane Price Herndl, 1009–1022. New Brunswick: Rutgers University Press, 1997.

Sarlo, Beatriz. "El imperio de los sentimientos: Ficciones de circulación periódica en la Argentina (1917–1925)." *Hispamérica* 39 (1984): 3–17.

Schwartz, Kessel. *New History of Spanish American Fiction.* Coral Gables, Fla.: University of Miami Press, 1972.

Shaw, Donald. *Antonio Skármeta and the Post-Boom.* Hanover, N.H.: Ediciones del Norte, 1994.

———. *The Post-Boom in Spanish American Fiction.* Albany: State University of New York Press, 1998.

Sicardi, Francisco. *Libro extraño.* Barcelona: F. Granada, 1894–1902.

Skinner, Lee. "Pandora's Log: Charting the Evolving Literary Project of Rosario Ferré." *Revista de Estudios Hispánicos* 29 (1995): 461–476.

Sklodowska, Elzbieta. *La parodia en la nueva novela hispanoamericana.* Amsterdam: John Benjamins, 1991.

———. *Testimonio hispanoamericano: Historia, teoría, poética.* New York: Peter Lang, 1992.

———. *Todo ojos, todo oídos: Control e insubordinación en la novela hispanoamericana (1895–1935).* Amsterdam: Editions Rodopi, 1997.

Sommer, Doris. *Foundational Fictions: The National Romances of Latin America.* Berkeley: University of California Press, 1991.

————. *Proceed with Caution, When Engaged by Minority Writing in the Americas.* Cambridge: Harvard University Press, 1999.

Sommers, Joseph. *After the Storm.* Albuquerque: University of New Mexico Press, 1968.

Souza, Raymond D. *Guillermo Cabrera Infante: Two Islands, Many Worlds.* Austin: University of Texas Press, 1996.

————. *La historia en la novela hispanoamericana moderna.* Bogotá: Tercer Mundo Editores, 1988.

————. *The Poetic Fiction of José Lezama Lima.* Columbia: University of Missouri Press, 1983.

Stanzel, Franz. *Narrative Situations in the Novel.* Bloomington: Indiana University Press, 1971.

Steele, Cynthia. *Politics, Gender, and the Mexican Novel, 1968–1988.* Austin: University of Texas Press, 1992.

Stoll, David. *Rigoberta Menchú and the Story of All Poor Guatemalans.* Boulder, Colo.: Westview Press, 1999.

Swanson, Philip. *The New Novel in Latin America: Politics and Popular Culture after the Boom.* Manchester, England: Manchester University Press, 1995.

Tittler, Jonathan. *Narrative Irony in the Contemporary Spanish-American Novel.* Ithaca: Cornell University Press, 1984.

Torres Bodet, Jaime. *Narrativa completa.* Mexico City: Editorial Offset, 1985.

Unruh, Vicky. *Latin American Vanguards: The Art of Contentious Encounters.* Berkeley: University of California Press, 1994.

Uribe Piedrahita, César. *Toá.* Bogotá: Instituto Colombiano de Cultura, 1979.

Valerio-Holguín, Fernando. "Primitive Borders: Cultural Identity and Ethnic Cleansing in the Dominican Republic." In *Primitivism and Identity in Latin America,* ed. Erik Camayd-Frixas and José Eduardo González. Tucson: University of Arizona Press, 2000.

Vélez-Ibáñez, Carlos. *Borders Visions: Mexican Cultures of the Southwest United States.* Tucson: University of Arizona Press, 1997.

Verani, Hugo J., ed. *Las vanguardias literarias en hispanoamérica.* Mexico City: Fondo de Cultura Económica, 1986.

————. *Narrativa vanguardista hispanoamericana.* Mexico City: Universidad Nacional Autónoma de México, 1996.

Vincent, Jon. *João Guimarães Rosa.* Boston: Twayne Publishers, 1978.

Warhol, Robyn R., and Diane Price Herndl, eds. *Feminisms: An Anthology of Literary Theory and Criticism.* New Brunswick, N.J.: Rutgers University Press, 1997.

Williams, Raymond Leslie. *The Colombian Novel, 1847–1987.* Austin: University of Texas Press, 1991.

————. *Mario Vargas Llosa.* New York: Ungar, 1986.

————. *The Modern Latin American Novel.* New York: Twayne Publishers, 1998.

————. *The Postmodern Novel in Latin America.* New York: St. Martin's, 1996.

————. *The Writings of Carlos Fuentes.* Austin: University of Texas Press, 1997.

Yáñez, Agustín. *Al filo del agua.* 1947. Reprint, Mexico City: Editorial Porrúa, 1969.

Yúdice, George, Jean Franco, and Juan Flores, eds. *On Edge: The Crisis of Contemporary Latin American Culture.* Minneapolis: University of Minnesota Press, 1992.

Yurkievich, Saúl. *Suma crítica.* Mexico City: Fondo de Cultura, 1997.

Zavala, Lauro. *La precisión de la incertidumbre: Posmodernidad, vida cotidiana y escritura.* Toluca, Mexico City: Universidad Autónoma del Estado de México, 1999.

Index

Pacheco, José Emilio, 84, 85, 125, 132, 133, 134, 149, 159–161, 183, 186
Padilla, Ignacio, 215
País de cuatro pisos, El (González), 169
Pájaro de memoria (Eguez), 188
Palacio, Pablo, 52
Palacios, Antonia, 96, 103
Palacios, Arnoldo, 93, 98, 99, 103
Palacios, Eustaquio, 13
Pales Matos, Luis, 39
Pañamanes, Los (Buitrago), 178
Pantaleón y las visitadoras (Vargas Llosa), 175, 176, 196
Papeles de Recienvenido (Fernández), 48
Paradiso (Lezama Lima), 126, 129–130
Paredes, Américo, 47, 98
Parente Cunha, Helena, 177
Parra, Violeta, 182
Parra Sandoval, Rodrigo, 187, 214
Paseo internacional del perverso, El (Libertella), 187
Paso del Norte, El, 23
Pasos, Joaquín, 41
Pasos perdidos (Carpentier), 100
Patán, Federico, xi, 168, 213
Paz, Octavio, vii, 120, 139, 189
Paz, Senel, 189, 218
Paz Soldán, Edmundo, 205, 215, 217
Pedreira, Antonio S., 39
Pedro Páramo (Rulfo), 94, 105, 106, 114–117, 119, 120, 121, 122, 130, 144
Pellicer, Carlos, 41
Pentágano, El (Di Benedetto), 94
Penteado, Darcy, 181
Pepe Botellas (Alvarez Gardeazábal), 174
Pequeños seres, Los (Garmendia), 101–102
Percusión (Moreno-Durán), 187
Perec, Georges, 183, 216
Peregrinos de Aztlán (Méndez), 170
Pereira da Graça Aranha, José, 7
Pérez Firmat, Gustavo, x, xi, 50, 72

Peri Rossi, Cristina, 167, 177, 179, 187
Perros del paraíso, Los (Posse), 168
Peso de la noche, El (Edward), 131
Petterson, Aline, 213
Picón Salas, Mariano, 58
Piglia, Ricardo, vii, 117, 182, 183, 186, 188, 193, 194, 196, 199–200, 201, 205, 210, 211, 212, 216
Piñón, Nélida, 165, 168, 177
Pitol, Sergio, 185–186, 191
Pizarnik, Alejandra, 167, 177, 179, 191
Plata quemada (Piglia), 211, 212–213
Pocaterra, José Rafael, 14, 19, 27–29, 31, 32, 33
Pocho (Villareal), 93, 101, 102
Política feminista (Pocaterra), 19, 22, 27–29, 32
Poniatowska, Elena, 172, 177, 178, 179, 181, 205–206, 208, 209
Pope, Randolph, xi, 61
Por favor, redobinar (Fuguet), 216
Porfiriato, 9, 12, 13, 23, 26–27, 32
Por la patria (Eltit), 193, 199, 200, 201
Por que me ufano de meu país (Celso), 7
Portrait of a Paladin. See Mío Cid Campeador
Porzekanski, Teresa, 187
Positivism, ix, 9, 10, 17, 19, 157
Posse, Abel, 168
Postboom, ix, 165, 170–176, 177, 178, 182, 183, 190, 191, 193, 210, 233 n. 1
postmodernism, vii, 69, 73, 75, 76, 77, 82, 85, 117, 129, 132, 133, 134, 145, 149, 159, 160, 161, 165, 166, 167, 169, 170, 175, 176, 177, 178, 180, 181, 182–191, 193, 195, 197, 198–199, 201, 202, 205–219, 221 n. 2, 233 n. 2
Post-postmodernism, 205, 215, 216, 218, 219
Poststructuralism, 212
Potdevín, Philip, 215, 216–217